Neal-Schuman Library Technology Companion: 3RD EDITION

A Basic Guide for Library Staff

John J. Burke

Neal-Schuman Publishers, Inc.

New York   London

Don't miss this book's companion blog!

For updated resources and materials,
as well as an opportunity to comment on the book,
visit http://techcompanion.blogspot.com

Published by Neal-Schuman Publishers, Inc.
100 William St., Suite 2004
New York, NY 10038

Printed and bound in the United States of America.

The paper used in this publication meets the minimum requirements of American National Standard for Information Sciences—Permanence of Paper for Printed Library Materials, ANSI Z39.48-1992.

Library of Congress Cataloging-in-Publication Data

Burke, John (John J.)
   Neal-Schuman library technology companion : a basic guide for library staff / John J. Burke. — 3rd ed.
      p. cm.
   Includes bibliographical references and index.
   ISBN 978-1-55570-676-0 (alk. paper)
   1. Libraries--Information technology. 2. Library science—Technological innovations. 3. Libraries and the Internet. I. Title. II. Title: Library technology companion.

Z678.9.B85 2009
025.00285—dc22

                                                                    2009023646

Table of Contents

List of Figures and Tables

FIGURES

TABLES

Preface

Technology infuses every aspect of every day in every library, and thus basic technology skills are a prerequisite for everyone who works in a library. I designed the *Neal-Schuman Library Technology Companion: A Basic Guide for Library Staff*, Third Edition, to give colleagues a sound and sensible way to consider, access, and use library technologies to better meet the needs of our users. This book and its companion blog (http://techcompanion .blogspot.com) are designed to be a one-stop overview of all technologies used in libraries today.

The pages that follow describe the broad scope of systems, software, and specialized devices available to libraries and show how they are integrated into our institutions' unique processes. The book offers basic definitions, suggests applications and uses, considers adoption issues, and troubleshoots potential problems. All busy professionals need to learn how to evaluate these technologies and assess their usefulness, so the guide provides essential know-how in planning, security, purchasing, and more. Perhaps most important, a solid grounding in the topic will make library staff members more comfortable when speaking with colleagues or interacting with patrons.

This third edition of the guide revises the basics and explains the advances introduced in just the past few years. Library 2.0 technologies have become more central to the work of library staff, open source software is more widely used, and MP3s have further revolutionized the sharing and use of audio content. Two new chapters, 0 and 10, add guidance from the field on the technologies most heavily in use and a closer look at the interactive, mashed-up offerings of Web 2.0. Chapter 2 is fully updated with new sources for tracking down technology information. The world of information technology changes at a relentless pace and today's library managers, new librarians, support staff members, and students need a simple way to become informed and stay current.

The *Neal-Schuman Library Technology Companion* contains 19 chapters arranged in five parts.

Part I, "Library Technology Basics," explores the basics.

- Chapter 0, "What Folks in the Trenches Know That You Should Too," adds some context to the study of these information technologies and services by revealing the results of a survey of working library staff members and the technologies they regularly use.
- Chapter 1, "The History of Information Technology in Libraries," delivers a historical overview of the technologies that have affected libraries.
- Chapter 2, "How to Find Information on Library Technologies," presents resources for learning more about the latest developments and issues.
- Chapter 3, "Evaluating, Buying, and Implementing Technology," offers a guide for appraising and purchasing equipment and putting systems into operation.

Part II, "Technology Tools for Libraries," examines the apparatus.

- Chapter 4, "Computers in Libraries: Desktops, Laptops, Tablets, Handheld Devices, and Office Applications," shows how the computer has evolved and what its new uses allow.
- Chapter 5, "Computer Networks in Libraries: The Internet, Modems, WiFi, and E-mail," takes on the wired—and now wireless—world.
- Chapter 6, "Whither the Library Catalog? Library Systems, Discover Layers, and Open Source Options," reveals the vast growth in computer access products.
- Chapter 7, "Storage Devices in Libraries: Paper, Microfilm, DVDs, MP3s, and Flash Drives," explains various techniques to record, retrieve, and access information.
- Chapter 8, "Library Databases and Electronic Resources: Full-text Periodicals, E-books, and E-reference Collections," addresses this important and growing body of materials.

- Chapter 9, "The Internet's Impact on Finding Information: A Is for Amazon, G Is for Google," explores both the technical and societal changes brought on by the Internet.
- Chapter 10, "Web 2.0: Social Networking, Second Life, and Skype," marks the advent of new communication tools and technologies for interacting with our patrons.

Part III, "How Libraries Put Technology to Work," takes the information from the previous chapters and incorporates it into the day-to-day workflow.

- Chapter 11, "Meeting and Supporting Patron Technology Needs: Universal Design and Adaptive/Assistive Technology," helps ensure that your technologies meet and serve the needs of your wide range of users.
- Chapter 12, "Library 2.0 and the Library: Virtual Reference, Blogs, and Usability," emphasizes the importance of creating an Internet presence for your library with unique services for patrons.
- Chapter 13, "How Library Staff Learn and Teach: Screencasts, Distance Learning, and Course Management Systems," demonstrates how technology can aid in staff development and training.

Part IV, "Building and Maintaining the Technology Environment in Libraries," explores how to intelligently employ technology in everyday situations.

- Chapter 14, "Protecting Technology and Technology Users: Spam, Spyware, and Security Strips," presents guidance for protecting the library and its patrons from the dangers of the cyberworld.
- Chapter 15, "When Things Fall Apart: Troubleshooting Tips for Every Technology User," assesses typical problems and suggests ways to handle them as they arise.
- Chapter 16, "Building the Technology Environment: Ergonomics, Infrastructure, and Gaming," will help make any facility comfortable and accessible.

Part V, "Where Library Technology Is Going and How to Get There," concludes the book.

- Chapter 17, "Writing a Technology Plan," addresses the important issues of long-range planning and offers steps to start your planning process.
- Chapter 18, "Our Technological Future: Ranganathan Meets Googlezon," looks ahead to how technology will continue to impact our tradition of service.

A glossary of useful terms is located at the end of the book. Terms found in the glossary appear in boldface within the text.

There is a great deal of information within these pages, but there is even more information to discuss. Visit the companion blog for updated resources and materials, as well as an opportunity to comment on the book. The blog is located at http://techcompanion.blogspot.com. (Not sure what a blog is? See Chapter 9 or the Glossary). You may also reach me with your questions and comments at techcompanion@gmail.com.

Acknowledgments

I would like to thank my wife Lynne and my children Madeline, Anna, Philip, and Andrew; the many students and library staff members I have had the pleasure to teach through formal classes and workshops; and my colleagues at the Gardner-Harvey Library of Miami University Middletown for their guidance, help, and support in making this book possible. I offer special thanks to my research assistant, Spenser Pruett.

I owe a great debt to the countless individuals who asked me technology questions, large and small, over the years. In the process of answering those questions I learned quite a bit about library technologies and what they are capable of (even when they do not work as advertised). I am grateful to Neal-Schuman Publishers and to my editor, Sandy Wood, for their encouragement and for this opportunity to pass my knowledge on to you.

Above all, I offer thanks to God for my family, my life, and the daily strength He gives me.

PART I

Library Technology Basics

Chapter 0

What Folks in the Trenches Know That You Should Too

As Lewis Carroll wrote in *Alice in Wonderland*, this book will "begin at the beginning." In this case, the beginning is to examine a premise that carries throughout this work: library technologies are ever-changing, and you need to have a working knowledge of them to succeed in library work. I rely on my own experience in libraries and my interactions with colleagues (as well as my attention to professional literature and electronic discussions) to help shape what I share in this book. I decided to take this one step further for this edition of the *Neal-Schuman Library Technology Companion*. What if I asked library staff members from all types of libraries to tell me what technologies and **technology** skills they use regularly? The remainder of this chapter describes what happened.

LIBRARY TECHNOLOGY SKILLS SURVEY

In the fall of 2008, I created a Web survey to gain insight into the regular technology tasks of library staff members. The survey consisted of nine questions. It was posted to a variety of **electronic discussion groups** focused on academic libraries, public libraries, library technology experts, library support staff members, school librarians, special librarians, and catalogers. The survey was designed to be available for three weeks, and I hoped to gain at least 200 responses from a diverse group of individuals working in libraries. In the end, my hopes were well exceeded by receiving 1,800 responses. This was a wonderful sample to work with in assessing technology use. The following are the library electronic discussion groups where the survey was posted:

> alao (academic)
> alao-ssig (academic library support staff)
> autocat (multitype cataloging)
> cjc-l (academic)
> collib-l (academic)
> libsup-l (multitype library support staff)
> LIS-PUB-LIBS (public libraries)
> lita-l (multitype library technology)
> lm_net (school)
> ohiolink (academic)
> oplinlist (public)
> oplintech (public library technology)
> publib (public)
> sla-dite (special library technology)

DEMOGRAPHICS OF THE RESPONDENTS

Despite the large response and the diversity of electronic discussion groups selected, the respondents are not a perfect cross-section of library staff from all types of libraries. Fifty-four percent work in academic libraries, 25 percent in public libraries, 11 percent in special libraries, and 10 percent in school libraries. In terms of their education, they were also not a broad-based sample: 80 percent listed an MLS degree, other master's degree, or other graduate work as their highest level of education. While 20 percent of respondents were unable to choose a single primary area of responsibility to describe their work at their library, those who did choose an area were a bit more distributed among library departments and tasks: 16.4 percent in cataloging, 16.3 percent in library administration, 13.7 percent in reference, 10.2 percent in library IT (**information technology**)/ systems, and 8.1 percent in instruction. Nearly half of those who chose "Other" on that question communicated that they performed all or nearly all of the various functions of their libraries. Finally, in terms of their careers in libraries, 36 percent have worked for 10 or fewer years, 35 percent for 21 or more years, and 28 percent between 11 and 20 years.

THE MOST COMMON TECHNOLOGIES AND SKILLS

Despite the demographic mismatches to the larger population of library staff members, I still believe that the respondents' answers provide a clearer vision of the universe of technology skills used in libraries. Respondents were asked to select from a list the technologies or technology skills that they used on a regular basis in their jobs. Table 0-1 shows this list, ranked in order of those chosen by the highest percentage of respondents.

It is interesting to be able to identify four skills from the list as essential skills for nearly all respondents (**e-mail**, **word processing software**, Web searching, and searching library databases) and another four as expected of a vast majority of respondents (using an integrated library system, navigating the Web, teaching people to use technology, and using spreadsheets). This group of eight shows what nearly any library staff member should have in one's skill set to meet job requirements in various settings.

As we move farther down the list, there is still a great diversity of skills still expected of a large percentage of the respondents. Some were not as common as I expected (e.g., **instant messaging**) while others are more prominent that I thought they might be (e.g. scanning). I was heartened to see a strong representation of people who "make technology purchase decisions," since I think this capacity should be on hand at various levels of the organization. The rarest skills appeared to be those connected to more specialized IT activities (perhaps no surprise there).

The "Other" designation on the question found respondents highlighting a wealth of other technologies and skills that they are responsible for. **Wikis** and social networking (which will be covered in Chapter 10) were the most common additional technologies, and ones that I certainly should have had on my list. Cataloging software received a number of mentions, as did **course management software**. Some of the unique or less common

Table 0-1
Technologies or technology skills used on a regular basis

Technology or technology skill	Percentage of respondents
E-mail	97.9
Word processing	96.2
Web searching	94.1
Searching library databases	92.7
Using an integrated library system	86.3
Web navigation	80.7
Teaching others to use technology	79.1
Spreadsheets	78.3
File management/operating system navigation skills	62.3
Troubleshooting technology	61.9
Presentation software	60.1
Scanners and similar devices	57.8
Database software	54.1
Educational copyright knowledge	47.6
Creating online instructional materials/products	43.0
Making technology purchase decisions	40.2
Installing software	38.7
Web design	36.7
Instant messaging	32.6
Computer security knowledge	28.4
Blogging	28.2
Installing technology equipment	24.9
Graphic design	21.3
Assistive/adaptive technology	18.1
Network management	10.9
Other	9.8
Computer programming	8.5

tasks provide interesting pictures of the individuals and their libraries: "Fixing printer problems—because IT takes an hour+ to come over and do anything about it," "E-games: Wii, etc.," "Music and Video editing," "Accounting software," "microfilm readers," "creating macros," "Adobe photoshop," "Facebook, MySpace," "making posters, bulletin boards, bookmarks, craft projects, etc.," "ripping audio," "use of digital cameras and the software for them," "Unofficial software testing—IS knows if we can't break it, it's probably OK for the rest of their customers."

THE MOST COMMON WISHES FOR TECHNOLOGIES AND SELF-DEVELOPMENT

I also asked respondents to answer two additional questions: (1) what technology skill they could you learn to help them do their jobs better, and (2) what technology or technology skill would they most like to see added to their library. Answers to the first question were all over the map, with one respondent stating "Technology is always changing always learning." "Advanced" or "better" were repeatedly applied as adjectives to wished-for skills with a number of technologies. High on several people's future training agendas were Web design, HTML, various Web 2.0 **applications**, creating databases, and using Access. Nearly 200 suggested that they did not have a need for additional technology skills, mostly without explanation, though some shared that their jobs did not require them (or would not allow them) to use more technology, and others held that technology is not the answer to all library-related problems. No argument here. One person captured the difficulty of fitting professional development into a busy schedule: "I could always learn more about everything I do, but there are serious time constraints." Five people recommended that they or their coworkers should be cloned.

On adding technologies to their libraries or technology skills for themselves or their coworkers, respondents' replies ran the gamut. Blogging, instant messaging, and **podcasting** were popular technology choices, along with SMART boards, wireless (access, printing, etc.), and a new integrated library system (ILS). Talents in Web design, Web 2.0 technologies, programming, and graphic design were strongly sought. Rather than adding new technologies or talents, there were calls for more staff on hand to deal with current technologies and for greater comfort and abilities from current staff. As one respondent put it: "Not any in particular—but would like to see more enthusiasm for new technologies."

WHAT CAN WE LEARN FROM THE SURVEY?

Clearly every library position and every library setting is different. Without a doubt, the survey could have been more representative. My hope is that the results give you, as they have given me, a confirmation that a common palette of skills exists with which we all need to grow our abilities. As well, many other tasks and capacities (both on the survey and suggested by the respondents) may well become expected of us as new technologies arrive and our libraries change. The chapters ahead will help you become more aware and develop your knowledge. My recommendation is to turn the page and "go on till you come to the end: then stop."

QUESTIONS FOR REVIEW

1. What are the top ten technologies or technology skills required in your position?
2. Were you surprised by anything in the survey results?
3. What technology skill could you learn to help you do your job better?
4. What technology or technology skill would you most like to see added to your library and your library staff?

SELECTED SOURCES FOR FURTHER INFORMATION

Crawford, Walt. 2008. "Making It Work Perspective: Technos and Tech-musts." *Cites & Insights* 8, no. 4 (April). Available: http://citesandinsights.info/v8i4d.htm.
> Walt examines various lists (his own and those of other bloggers) of technology skills that individual "techie" librarians lack and those that are recommended for every library staff member to have. He examines the interplay of which technology abilities are accepted as needed for all staff and suggests that absolutism is not the best expectation.

Ennis, Lisa A. 2008. "Talking the Talk: Communicating with IT." *Computers in Libraries* 28, no. 8: 14–17.
> A short list of tips for getting along with the IT professionals in your environment.

Gordon, Rachel Singer, and Jessamyn West. 2008. "Tech Tips for Every Librarian." *Computers in Libraries* 28, no. 9: 54–55.
   Thirteen essential computer tasks every frontline library staffer should know how to do.

Miller, Rebecca. 2008. "Future-proof Your Library: LJ's Movers & Shakers Strategize About How to Secure a Vital Future." *Library Journal* 133, no. 13: 30–33. Available: www.libraryjournal.com/article/CA6585850.html.
   This article, though aimed more largely at strategic moves for libraries to make, does emphasize characteristics of library staff that will make the library more successful in the long term.

Thompson, Susan M., ed. 2009. *Core Technology Competencies for Librarians and Library Staff: A LITA Guide.* New York: Neal-Schuman.
   This group of essays addresses in more detail the expectations for a variety of library positions in public and academic libraries. It also addresses ways in which to measure and develop these technology competencies.

Chapter 1

The History of Information Technology in Libraries

Libraries have long played an essential role in containing, preserving, and sharing information. Countless civilizations have, over thousands of years, produced and relied on various types of information, from creation stories to herd counts to tax rolls. These facts, philosophies, and communications were recorded because individuals in these societies saw some purpose in sharing this lore and information with others in the present and in preserving it for future generations. The explosion of information we have seen over the past two decades is merely the latest phase in a long-running battle: how can societies maintain their collections of facts, history, images, **data**, and fiction as the amount of these items increase rapidly? Over thousands of years, libraries were adopted as a mechanism for accomplishing these purposes; were it not for libraries, we would have little or no knowledge of past generations or civilizations.

At each step along the way, libraries would have failed in their efforts without information technology. We tend to imagine technology as involving only computers and electronic devices, but technology encompasses both products and processes that people create. Handling information requires a diverse collection of practical tools and processes. Looking at technology in the library world, processes would include the methods for rebinding books or classifying the items in a collection, and DVD recorders or full-text **periodical databases** are examples of products.

Information technology as a whole, then, includes any items or methods for containing, transmitting, and storing information.

TRENDS IN LIBRARY TECHNOLOGIES

Two main goals have driven library use of technology: better serving the needs of the library's community, and streamlining the workflow of the staff.

The technologies that have impacted and continue to impact the library world fall into three main groups: (1) those created specifically for libraries and library work, (2) those created within the larger world and adapted for use in libraries, and (3) those created in the world and brought into libraries without much alteration.

The first group would encompass developments such as Dewey's classification system, the **card catalog**, and the machine-readable cataloging (MARC) record. The creation of library systems to offer online catalogs and manage circulation and cataloging, the continuing molding of **Internet**-based databases by vendors to fit library needs, and libraries' own alterations of Web site design for internal purposes fits into the second group. We see many examples of the third group in staff use of technology, such as telephones, fax machines, copiers, bar-code readers, and many computer applications.

TEN KEY DEVELOPMENTS IN INFORMATION TECHNOLOGY

Many information technologies have been created over the years. The library itself is a technology developed to handle information storage and retrieval. Here are ten key developments in information technology that have affected libraries and their work over the centuries, in roughly chronological order. Some of these technologies are still in full use today, whereas others have been replaced or had their roles reduced. They represent both processes for retaining or organizing information and manufactured tools or other products. All technology is designed to meet a particular need, and while only a few needs ever disappear completely, humanity is always finding new ways to better address long-standing needs. It is important to remember the former roles of these obsolete technologies as we look at today's technologies and toward the technologies that may replace them in the future.

Development 1: Writing and Paper

The development of written language and alphabets is the starting place for a discussion of information gathering. Writing's roots can be seen in prehistoric cave paintings, an early pictographic method of communicating information by drawing symbols and pictures to represent concepts. Pictographs allow an individual to preserve information (at least in the short term) for his or her own use and also to share with others. If one writes on something that will last (the next key development in technology for libraries), the information can be passed on beyond the life of an individual and perhaps for many generations.

Compare writing to the other method for passing information along through time: memorization. In many cultures, individuals (called *griots* in West Africa) were able to memorize genealogies, stories, and cultural historic events and recount them as needed. A *griot* would train someone, usually a child, to memorize the information and therefore pass it on to succeeding generations. While memorization can be an effective way to contain a set group of information, long-term use presents some difficulties.

First, since only one person or a small number of people remember the information, an accident, plague, or untimely death could completely wipe out the information. In addition, access to the information is limited since only that small group can reveal it. Second, since the information is memorized in a distinct pattern, it can be difficult for the *griot* to recall individual bits of information, such as the date of a battle, or the name of an individual's daughter, without recounting large parts of what they have memorized. Third, despite an exceptional effort, some details are bound to be lost or corrupted through memorization. Even intentional corruption can easily occur since there is no written record to use for comparison. The safety of, access to, and integrity of the information are major problems that a written record can overcome.

The physical item that an individual is writing on has a huge impact on how easy it is to pass the information along. Two elements of passing information should be considered: time and distance. Cave paintings are handy to show to folks who live near you and to share with future generations, but they are awfully difficult to send to a friend in the next valley. This element of transporting information guided the development of writing material from cave walls, to stone tablets, to papyrus scrolls, to goat or cowhide (vellum), to linen- and now tree-based paper. Paper is relatively cheap to produce in quantity, is lightweight, and can last for a fairly long period of time.

Development 2: The Printing Press and Books

With a system of writing and a medium to place it on, the communication of ideas could be accomplished relatively easily and cheaply. Paper writings were bound into books (as vellum had been) and passed along. However, the issue of making multiple copies of a work remained a laborious process.

Enter the Gutenberg revolution of the fifteenth century. The invention of movable type and the printing press first in China and then in Europe by Gutenberg gave people the ability to make their writings available to a larger audience at a much quicker pace. Humanity entered into a time period in which improvements and innovations changed the publishing process and the audience for books. Printing became faster and faster, paper grew cheaper and cheaper, and literacy increased among the populace. These changes set the stage for libraries to develop on a large scale: many items were being printed and people wanted to read them. Libraries had existed in earlier civilizations (notably among the Babylonians, Romans, and Greeks) but had been available only to a small elite. Printing allowed information to reach a wider audience and libraries to serve as intermediaries between the growing amounts of literature and a growing literate population.

Development 3: Classification Systems

Libraries have had to deal with ever-increasing amounts of printed materials since the dawn of the printing press. Once the number of books in a library exceeded the librarian's memory, a method for locating a specific item or finding materials on a topic was needed. One major breakthrough in organizing and using this information was the development of classification systems.

Unlike today, where libraries tend to choose among two or three "universal" systems, in the past classification schemes were tied to a given library or collection, meeting the local needs of that particular entity. Every library came up with its own way to organize materials by broad categories of knowledge. A tremendous change came about in 1876 with the development of the Dewey Decimal System. Melvil Dewey's subject-oriented system for organizing books caught on and was adopted by a large number of libraries. Today, 95 percent of public and school libraries and 25 percent of academic libraries use the system. The Library of Congress Classification System, developed to organize that library's immense holdings, was later adopted by libraries (primarily academic ones) as an alternative standard. Both systems work on a similar principle: arrangement of the collection by the subject matter of the item.

Classification systems helped libraries to tame the growing mass of information. With them, library users could freely browse the collection by topic to find what they needed. The adoption of standardized systems also let libraries work together more smoothly and made it easier for patrons to understand how to use multiple libraries. With this innovation in place, libraries could move to make their service more efficient and their users' experiences more fruitful.

Development 4: The Card Catalog

The creation and standardization of a tool to help people locate the information in a library was an impressive development in information technology. While libraries had been organized by some sort of classification system for years, the invention of the card catalog in 1791 in France (using the backs of playing cards, which at the time were blank) and the tremendous growth of its use by libraries from the 1850s onward gave library users an additional method for finding items beyond browsing the shelves. It enhanced the work of libraries in at least two ways. First, it improved the chances for the library staff to locate materials and therefore to provide service to their patrons. The card catalog allowed the library's collection to be searched from one location without having to browse and scan the shelves. It added convenience as well as the ability to use multiple entry points (author, title, and subject) to access the collection.

Second, the creation of a relatively easy to use tool to find library information allowed the public to participate directly in the research process. The catalog was relatively simple to use: if you wanted to find books by Louisa May Alcott, you looked in the drawers for the As and then paged through the cards until you found her works. Once catalogs became standardized, it was easy for patrons to walk into any library and see what was available on a subject, written by an author, or whether a given title was held. The card catalog was the first example of an end user searching tool: the patron gained the freedom to search and library staff discovered a new instructional endeavor.

Development 5: Library Systems and the MARC Record

With classification systems and card catalogs in operation, libraries were doing a fine job of managing information. There came a point, however, when individuals in the profession saw there could be easier ways to manage large collections of materials and provide access to the catalog for a large number of users. They looked to the power of computers to help make libraries more efficient. Several libraries joined forces with computing professionals in the late 1960s to create the first automated library systems and their descendants, which operated from large mainframe computers and had "dumb" terminals for library staff and users to access the systems. Each item in the catalog was represented in a machine-readable cataloging (MARC) record, which contains bibliographic information along with subject headings, call numbers, and other useful information (see Figures 1-1 and 1-2 for current examples). As we will see in Chapter 6, these systems allowed libraries to keep track of the items they own and are circulating without a large number of cards and paper. The quest for these systems drove

Figure 1-1
Screenshot of an OPAC record for an item

Start Over
(Request item) Export MARC Display Return To Browse Statewide Search Another Search
(Search History) ⌄

AUTHOR ⌄   purcell gary   Search

Record 4 of 4
Record: Prev Next

Author	Purcell, Gary R
Title	**Reference sources in library and information services : a guide to the literature / Gary R. Purcell with Gail Ann Schlachter ; foreword by Charles A. Bunge**
Imprint	Santa Barbara, Calif. : ABC-Clio Information Services, 1984

LOCATION	CALL NO.	STATUS
SW Depository	Z666 .P96 1984	AVAILABLE

Descript.	xxvi, 359 p. ; 24 cm
Note	Includes indexes
Subject	Reference books -- Library science
	Reference books -- Information science
	Library science -- Bibliography
	Information science -- Bibliography
Add author	Schlachter, Gail A
Call #	Z666 .P96 1984

Record 4 of 4
Record: Prev Next

libraries into the computer age, setting the foundation for the world of digital information we see now.

Development 6: Personal Computers

Personal computers (PCs) have made a huge impact on society, including in libraries (see Chapter 4). PCs increased libraries' computing power and allowed greater flexibility in choosing their local office and management software than was possible with mainframes. PCs also provided a platform for libraries to experiment with new media types, such as CD-ROMs, and to start accessing **remote information services** (**periodical** and

Figure 1-2
Screenshot of a MARC record for the same item

```
LEADER 00000cam  22000008a 4500c
001    9970678
005    19850509121151.0
008    830913s1984    cau     b    00110 eng
010    83019700
020    0874363551 :|c$45.00
040    DLC|cDLC|dOCL|dMIA
049    MIAA
090    Z666|b.P96 1984
100 10 Purcell, Gary R
245 10 Reference sources in library and information services :|ba
       guide to the literature /|cGary R. Purcell with Gail Ann
       Schlachter ; foreword by Charles A. Bunge
260 0  Santa Barbara, Calif. :|bABC-Clio Information Services,
       |c1984
300    xxvi, 359 p. ;|c24 cm
500    Includes indexes
650  0 Reference books|xLibrary science
650  0 Reference books|xInformation science
650  0 Library science|xBibliography
650  0 Information science|xBibliography
700 10 Schlachter, Gail A
```

shared cataloging databases and eventually the Internet). In a relatively short period of time, libraries moved from having just one or two PCs in the backroom to offering dozens of machines to the public as "**information appliances.**" Today's library is unimaginable without the personal computer as both a staff resource and as a means for the public to access library resources.

Development 7: Online Searching

An exciting development of the computer age for libraries was the ability of companies to start computerizing periodical indexes and other resources and then provide them to libraries using a telephone line and a modem. Starting in the 1970s, libraries were able to access resources they could not afford to keep in house and to search these resources much more easily than paging through their print predecessors. Companies such as Dialog, BRS, and Lexis-Nexis offered libraries access to periodical indexes and full-text newspapers, magazines, journals and reference sources. Users would choose one or more indexes or periodicals to search and then enter terms to try and find related citations, **abstracts**, or articles.

The advent of **online searching** was the first time that libraries had to contend with having resources available that they did not physically own. Connecting to these online services could be expensive (users were charged a set fee per minute), but many libraries were willing to offer this service to their patrons. Early online searching was done by library staff members, partly because the command language for searching was difficult to learn and partly because of the expensive connection fees. Eventually, the methods of searching grew easier (and pricing plans began to change) and library patrons, known as "end users", could more successfully attempt searching on their own. The move toward our current situation of the virtual, online library was underway.

Development 8: Audiovisuals

As with computers, **audiovisual items** were created within society at large and came to libraries as new packaging for information. Adding **media items** such as DVDs, videocassettes, and compact discs to the library over the years (see Table 1-1) changed the complexion of the collection. They also caused challenges for the staff in terms of their shelving, location, and protection. In the past, libraries may have had only the book version of a popular title; today, a library is likely to need to find space for the book and various versions of the book in media formats. For example, for J. K. Rowling's *Harry Potter and the Deathly Hallows*, a library might have the book, compact disc and audiocassette (abridged or unabridged) audiobook versions of the book, a DVD of the movie made from the book, and a compact disc of the movie soundtrack (not to mention various electronic versions of any of these—digital videos, audio e-books, etc.). The rich diversity of nonbook formats has allowed libraries to better serve their communities, who expect to have access to a wide variety of media. Their growing inclusion in the collection caused libraries to rethink their collection

Table 1-1
Timeline of invention dates for audiovisual items

Audiovisual Medium	Date Invented
LP records	1948
Audio cassettes	late 1950s
VHS videocassettes	1976
Videodiscs	1978
Compact discs	1982
CD-ROMs	1984
DVDs	late 1990s
iPods	2001
iPhones	2007

Source: The dates for CD-ROMs and earlier media were taken from *Current Technologies in the Library: An Informal Overview* by Walt Crawford (Boston: G. K. Hall & Co., 1988).

development and organization practices and to more readily adopt new media.

Development 9: The Internet

The Internet has had a strong presence in libraries and library planning for over 15 years. From the early days of library **gopher sites** and the first Web sites to today's full text periodical indexes and virtual reference, the Internet has become a mainstay of the library world. The Internet continues to stimulate library staff to retool their delivery of services to patrons and to reconsider how they can best present the wealth of free online information alongside library-purchased print and digital resources. Libraries are using the Internet as a delivery mechanism to access resources and provide them to patrons within and away from the library. They offer to help library patrons by answering reference questions via text messaging, instant messaging (IM), e-mail, or **chat** in an attempt to assist no matter the time of day or where they are located. They are working to organize Web sites and library-licensed resources to help patrons find what they need. Libraries can claim many Internet successes yet still face several challenges from this work in progress.

Development 10: A Techno-savvy Populace and a Society That Requires Technology

Developments in libraries are, and should be, driven in part by the expressed needs and expectations of each library's community. We have seen in some of the early developments in this list that society often created something new and libraries decided to include it in their collections. This process has been influenced and driven by our patrons requesting items or by people in our communities taking an interest in new media or services before we actually adopt them. Look for the receptiveness of our communities to new technology to continue to shape libraries.

Technology demands are not always driven by user choice, however. As society grows more dependent on various information technologies, some patrons find themselves caught in the digital divide. They may be required to use computers or access materials on the Internet to complete homework or fill out government forms or pursue commercial activities, and yet these patrons cannot afford access to the required technologies. Libraries are taking on the responsibility of providing this access.

WHAT ARE LIBRARIES USING TODAY?

We find libraries today using a wide variety of technologies. Most have online catalogs and offer public **Internet access**. Most include a number of different formats for storing information: books, periodicals, electronic reference sources, and DVDs. Libraries as a whole are spending increasing amounts of money on electronic resources and the infrastructure to support them, often at the expense of traditional, print-based materials. As well, the more libraries invest in electronic resources, the less flexible they can be in choosing whether to continue with these expenditures. With this impact in mind, it is crucial for us to understand library technologies in order to help make the right decisions for our library. The rest of this book will look at current library technologies in detail and examine what the future may hold.

QUESTIONS FOR REVIEW

1. What are the three groups that library technologies could be placed into?
2. What current technology, in your view, could have as large an impact as the ten key developments in this chapter?
3. Is there an unmentioned key development that you would add into the list of ten?
4. How would you define the term "technology"?
5. Describe the impact that you have seen one of the ten developments have in your own library.

SELECTED SOURCES FOR FURTHER INFORMATION

Aqili, Seyed Vahid, and Alireza Isfandyari Moghaddam. 2008. "Bridging the Digital Divide: The Role of Librarians and Information Professionals in the Third Millennium." *The Electronic Library* **26, no. 2: 226–237.**
  The article provides an overview of the digital divide and the roles that librarians and information professionals can play in bridging it.

Battles, Matthew. 2004. *Library: An Unquiet History.* **New York: W. W. Norton.**
  Battles' book is an intriguing look at the ancient origins of libraries and their development into the modern age.

Crawford, Walt. 1988. *Current Technologies in the Library: An Informal Overview.* **Boston: G.K. Hall & Co.**
  This source gives an excellent history of the technologies available in 1988, from microfilm to computers.

Lerner, Frederick A. 1998. *The Story of Libraries: From the Invention of Writing to the Computer Age.* **New York: Continuum.**
  An excellent history of libraries and librarianship.

Lester, June, and Wallace C. Koehler Jr. 2007. *Fundamentals of Information Studies: Understanding Information and Its Environment,* **2nd ed. New York: Neal-Schuman.**
  The book includes an overview of library and information science, with references to historic developments in the field.

Musmann, Klaus. 1993. *Technological Innovations in Libraries, 1860–1960: An Anecdotal History.* **Westport, CT: Greenwood Press.**
  An interesting history of library technologies developed, adopted, or adapted during a century of tremendous change for libraries.

Wiegand, Wayne A. 1996. *Irrepressible Reformer: A Biography of Melvil Dewey.* **Chicago: American Library Association.**
  Wiegand's work provides a full history of Dewey's life and his impact on librarianship, from his invention of the classification system to his work in the American Library Association (ALA) and his efforts to professionalize library work.

Chapter 2

How to Find Information on Library Technologies

Since technology changes at a rapid pace, it is never enough to simply know about and understand the technology owned by a single library. You need to know where you can learn more about technology and whether you are responsible for planning for new technology or just trying to understand and use what is already in your library. This chapter discusses some places to turn to find answers to technology questions. Knowing where to look for technology facts can be very empowering; it can give you the confidence to know that you can find an answer. As with library reference work, it is more important, and more possible, to know where to look for technology information rather than to know all of the information yourself.

REASONS TO USE TECHNOLOGY INFORMATION SOURCES

There are many reasons in library work to search for information on technologies, for both general and library-specific technologies. The following are the four most common reasons people who work in libraries search for information on technology:

- *For general awareness.* As noted, technology is changing rapidly and we need to keep up with current happenings.

A library organization can feel overwhelmed by the plethora of new choices on the market and new desires on the part of staff or the community. Library personnel need to have some sense of what is on the cutting edge and how it may apply to libraries. My views on the future of technologies in libraries continue to change based on the information I find and the trends I discover. You may not wish to follow every new development in technology, but you will benefit from using a source of information to keep you abreast of major happenings.

- *To compare products and services.* As libraries try to find technology solutions to fulfill the service needs of their communities, they often need to compare a number of similar products. This occurs when a library is not aware of a specific product or service to meet its needs or when a competitive bidding process is required for purchasing technology. Turning to library colleagues, comparisons in journals, or other sources of advice and information can be very helpful. Suggestions of specific technologies or solutions can then be sought and compared to determine the best option.

- *To find a known product or service.* When specific product or service solutions are already identified, a library will need to locate information about them. The information might be descriptions provided by a vendor, critical reviews in formal publications, or the advice and experience of colleagues. Some information a library may seek includes: (1) where a product can be purchased, (2) specific pricing information, (3) the success or failure in the use of the item in libraries, and (4) suggestions for, and comparisons with, alternative products.

- *To configure existing technology.* Once a technology is in place in a library, the questions do not end. Libraries always need more information about installing a product, configuring it to work correctly with other products, and troubleshooting problem situations. There are times when you will want to find out what else you can do with a piece of technology beyond the original purpose you had in mind.

TYPES OF TECHNOLOGY INFORMATION SOURCES

There are many avenues for staying abreast of technological change. The following are the most commonly used methods:

- *Web sites and blogs.* The Internet is a gold mine for technology information. This information may be in the form of vendor Web sites, **blogs** for specific technologies or library systems issues, directories of libraries, product reviews, how-to documents, and technology references.
- *Electronic discussion groups and e-mailings.* Electronic discussion groups, both particular to libraries and to more general technology issues, can serve as incredible daily update tools as well as forums for specific questions. A number of established library groups devoted to technology and services mail out daily tips on software products or Internet searching that can be helpful for refining your abilities. There are also sites that have archived earlier discussion group postings that can be searched for answers to your technology questions.
- *Periodicals.* A number of periodicals cover information technology that is pertinent to libraries. Since many items of information technology are also used beyond libraries, general-interest technology periodicals can be useful resources, as can general periodical indexes and more specific library indexes (such as Library Literature).
- *Continuing education.* While much can be learned from reading periodicals and searching the Internet, at times a professional development workshop or class can be even better. You can prepare yourself to work with a given technology by participating in a focused continuing education workshop. Other opportunities may give you the chance to get an overview of new technology developments. A large number of workshops and conferences are offered every year, and one may well coincide with your current or future needs for technology information. Online Webinars from vendors or library organizations are also a helpful way to gain information without requiring you to travel.
- *Conference exhibits and trade shows.* Gathering technology information would not be complete without visiting the

exhibits at a conference or sampling the wares at a trade show. Attending these events is helpful for seeing what new technologies are available or for quickly comparing a number of similar products. You also have the opportunity to closely examine equipment or software and to ask questions, which is not always possible when using the Internet or while reading a product review.

- *Visiting libraries.* Finally, we cannot forget the value of seeing technology in the field and communicating with nearby folks who are already using it on a daily basis. Visiting a library that has already implemented the technology you are interested in can give you an idea of how the technology will work in your library. Keeping in touch with a network of local colleagues can help you identify libraries to visit. You can contact vendors and ask for a list of local satisfied customers or pose a question to an electronic discussion group to turn up local or regional libraries that you can visit. You may find that you can rely on a local or regional library association or you may just need to create your own informal group of interested parties to help you keep pace.

SELECTED SOURCES FOR FURTHER INFORMATION

The following list of resources is by no means exhaustive. It does provide some excellent starting places to help you make a habit of staying informed. Look beyond your everyday needs and you will be better prepared for future developments in your own library. Sources are listed in each category in rough order of their usefulness (though your mileage may vary).

Web Sites and Blogs

Trends and Technology News

WebJunction (www.webjunction.org)
An online community where "library staff come together to connect, create, and learn." Originally funded by the Bill and Melinda Gates Foundation and the Institute of Museum and Library Services (IMLS), WebJunction is now hosted by OCLC.

A tremendous collection of documents on library technology topics and issues, links to useful Web sites, discussion forums to find colleagues who have faced (and hopefully solved) the issues you are facing, course materials, and a host of other resources of interest to libraries. A project is now underway to create state-oriented versions of WebJunction that will use content from the main site and then contribute content to the central effort.

Cites & Insights (http://Bitesandinsights.info)
A monthly online publication that includes in-depth coverage of technology trends written by author and technology guru Walt Crawford. His observations and analyses of recent publications are a must scan.

Innovative Internet Applications in Libraries
(www.wilton library.org/ innovate.html)
Just as the title suggests, this site links to several examples of interesting ways to "save the time of the reader" using the Internet. The site shares not only a sampling of Web sites, blogs, and other services and programs created by libraries but also suggests current awareness resources and points toward some how-to sites and documents.

Top Tech Trends (www.lita.org/ala/lita/litaresources/toptechtrends/toptechnology.htm)
A biannual discussion of technology and library users by the Library and Information Technology Association's Top Technology Trends Committee. The discussions happen at the American Library Association's Midwinter and Annual Conferences.

Seven Things You Should Know About (www.educause.edu/7ThingsYouShouldKnowAboutSeries/7495)
Created as part of the EDUCAUSE Learning Initiative, these short monthly pieces provide informative introductions to a variety of technologies (from Skype to Wii to flip cameras) along with possible educational uses for them.

SirsiDynix Institute (www.sirsidynixinstitute.com)
This site, sponsored by the SirsiDynix integrated library system company, offers free Webinars (and archived podcasts) on technology topics by leading figures in library and information technology. Topics range from video on the Web to technology

planning to a survey of new consumer technologies. The site also features the blog Stephen's Lighthouse, written by Sirsi-Dynix Vice President for Innovation Stephen Abram, that covers his musings on various library technology topics.

Blogs

ALA TechSource Blog (www.alatechsource.org/Alog)
ALA's site for its technology publications also includes a blog with posts of trends and news in library technology. This team effort of 11 bloggers provides a great overview of library technology happenings combined with helpful coverage of technology events within ALA's divisions.

It's All Good (http://scanblog.blogspot.com)
Personal reflections on "all things present and future that impact libraries and library users" from four staff members at OCLC. Interesting insights and thoughts with a technology focus.

The Shifted Librarian (www.theshiftedlibrarian.com)
Jenny Levine's blog, which focuses on helping librarians "shift" into understanding and using the information technologies that their patrons use. Jenny is the Internet Development Specialist and Strategy Guide for the American Library Association.

Tame the Web (www.tametheweb.com)
Tame the Web is a blog written by Michael Stephens, Assistant Professor in the Graduate School of Library and Information Science at Dominican University in River Forest, Illinois. He shares student projects, interesting discussions, and commentary on the latest happenings in library technology.

ResourceShelf (www.resourceshelf.com)
A daily updated library blog of "resources and news for information professionals." Excellent focus on industry trends and online searching for all library types.

LibrarianInBlack (www.librarianinblack.net)
This blog is written by Sara Houghton-Jan, Digital Futures Manager for the San Jose Public Library. It serves as "a one-stop shop for all Techie Library Staff." A very useful site for information on technological issues and trends in libraries.

Glengage (http://glengage.com)
Glen Horton, the Technology Coordinator for the Southwest Ohio and Neighboring Libraries regional library consortium, is the man to watch for what's happening in and around libraries with technology. He is continually investigating how libraries are applying new technologies and watching for new technological innovations that libraries might want to take on. His annual presentations on "Technology Trends and Libraries" bring the information technology swirl of information into focus, and he posts links to his latest slides on the blog (just search for the presentation title).

Disruptive Library Technology Jester (www.dltj.org)
The tagline for this blog reads "we're librarians, we're disrupted, and we're not going to take it anymore." It is written by Peter Murray, Assistant Director for New Service Development at OhioLINK (Ohio's academic library consortium). Peter uses the blog to explore change in libraries and the technologies they use, both incremental and disruptive.

Open Directory Project: Library and Information Science: Weblogs (www.dmoz.org/Reference/Libraries/Library_and_
Information_Science/Weblogs/)
An extensive listing of additional library-related blogs with a brief description. It is worth a look to discover additional resources not mentioned previously.

Dictionaries and Glossaries

Wikipedia (www.wikipedia.org)
A collaborative online encyclopedia that includes articles on a wide range of subjects. Despite much criticism and discussion of its value as an information source, I find that it has excellent explanations of current technology topics (but don't just trust me—read them critically on your own).

Webopedia (http://webopedia.internet.com)
A searchable dictionary of computer and Internet technology terms. A very extensive source that includes a brief definition for each term along with links to related terms and Web sites that offer additional information. A number of entries also include diagrams or images.

CMP's TechWeb TechEncyclopedia (www.techweb.com/ encyclopedia)
A similar source to the *Webopedia*. Includes lengthy definitions of terms and links to related concepts.

ODLIS: Online Dictionary of Library and Information Science (http://lu.com/odlis)
An up-to-date dictionary of terms relating to library and information science that includes a number of entries relating to technology. It is compiled by Joan M. Reitz.

How-to Documents

MaintainIT Project (www.maintainit.org)
The project is funded by the Bill and Melinda Gates foundation to compile information on how public libraries support public access computers. It produces freely available "cookbooks" on various aspects of public computing and technology planning. There is also a blog that covers recent developments in and discussions of public computing issues. Much here is applicable to various library settings.

Library Success: A Best Practices Wiki
(www.libsuccess.org)
This wiki is a collaborative collection of documents and links covering library-related issues of all kinds, with an emphasis on sharing best practices. The section on "Technology" linked from the list of contents has excellent explanations of many library technologies and suggestions on implementing them in your institution.

Knowledge Hound (www.knowledgehound.com)
A directory of how-to information sites on a variety of subjects. The "Science and Technology" section has a number of subtopic areas that list useful guides for computers, the Internet, software, and more.

WebJunction (www.webjunction.org/basic-troubleshooting/ resources/wjarticles)
WebJunction includes a section on supporting and troubleshooting computers and other equipment that may be helpful.

About.com Computing & Technology (http://about.com/compute)
This section of the About.com site includes collections of articles and links to additional Web sites on various technology topics.

Product Reviews and Vendor Information

CNET (www.cnet.com)
This site includes lots of technology information, product reviews, how-to documents, and advice. It is the place to start when you are planning to buy computers or other technology items.

ZDNet (www.zdnet.com)
A very similar site to CNET, but another excellent source for product reviews and buying guides.

Library Technology Guides (www.librarytechnology.org)
"The Library Technology Guides website aims to provide comprehensive and objective information related to the field of library automation." The site is an excellent source of library-systems-related reports, articles, and trends. It includes a directory of library system vendors.

Library Resource Guide (www.libraryresource.com)
An annually updated directory of library services and suppliers compiled by Information Today.

The Librarian's Yellow Pages (http://librariansyellowpages.com)
A comprehensive listing of library vendors that may be browsed by type of product or service or searched by keyword.

MacInTouch (http://macintouch.com/)
Provides news, tips, and reviews of Apple Macintosh products and software as well as of other Apple products (iTunes, iPhone, etc.).

Planning and Building Libraries (www.slais.ubc.ca/resources/architecture/)
A collection of links to vendors and projects relating to the construction and equipping of libraries.

Individual Vendors
Other vendors can also be found through Google (www.google.com) or other search engines.

Electronic Discussion Groups

Web4Lib (http://lists.webjunction.org/web4lib)
A very active discussion group that focuses on Web-related technologies in libraries but regularly discusses other issues including public computer setup, scanning, and search engine developments, to name but a few regular topics.

LM_NET (www.eduref.org/lm_net/)
While this list focuses on school librarians and school library issues, many of the discussions have a strong technology focus, particularly on electronic resources and educational technology. A highly active group.

LITA-L (http://lists.ala.org/sympa/info/lita-l)
The mailing list for the Library and Information Technology Association (LITA) division of ALA. A good blend of workshop/conference/job announcements along with interesting technology articles and discussion of questions from list members.

SLA-DITE (http://units.sla.org/division/dite/sladite_new.html)
The mailing list of the Information Technology division of the Special Libraries Association (SLA). A general purpose list to ask questions for technology recommendations or to discuss new technology trends and developments.

Individual Groups
There are many other library-related electronic discussion groups, including a large number devoted to specific technologies or products. A good resource for finding others is the Open Directory Project's listing of library and information science chats and forums. Be sure to also click the link for "mailing lists" from this URL: www.dmoz.org/Reference/Libraries/ Library_and_ Information_Science/Chats_and_Forums. You can also try a search in Google Groups (http://groups.google.com) to locate other library discussion groups that may be indexed there.

Tip and Trend E-mail Newsletters

LISNews (http://lisnews.com/)
A blog of library-related news happenings that includes discussions that grow out of the individual postings. You can sign up for e-mail updates of new postings. .

Current Cites (http://lists.webjunction.org/Burrentcites/)
A free monthly e-mail that contains annotations of information technology articles and other items written by a team of librarians and library staff. An easy way to scan the professional literature for technology-related publications.

Free Pint (www.freepint.com)
A free newsletter that covers electronic information sources and searching techniques. It is mailed out every two weeks. While *Free Pint* started with a focus on business research, many of the sources are of general interest to those interested in Internet searching. As well, a number of technologies (e.g., Second Life) are discussed that may be of interest to a more general audience.

Periodicals

Subscription information for the following titles is available on each periodical's Web site.

Library-oriented (Technology Focus)

Computers in Libraries
Information Today
10 issues per year
www.infotoday.com/cilmag
Feature articles on applications of computer technologies in libraries and reviews of technology products. Has a very practical focus. Sample full-text articles are available.

Information Technology and Libraries
Library and Information Technology Association
Quarterly
www.lita.org/ala/mgrps/Civs/lita/ital/italinformation.cfm
Feature articles on applications of information technology in libraries. Subscription included with LITA membership. Table of contents and abstracts are available.

Library Hi-Tech
Emerald Group Publishing
Quarterly
http://info.emeraldinsight.com/products/journals/journals
.htm?id=lht

Feature articles on emerging technologies in libraries. A bit more research-oriented than *Computers in Libraries*, but the publication includes a variety of practical case studies as well. Sample full-text articles are available.

Library Technology Reports
American Library Association
Eight issues per year
www.techsource.ala.org/ltr/
Extensive reviews, studies, and testing of various examples of library technology items, from open source integrated library systems to gaming in libraries. Selected issues are available in full text.

Online
Information Today
Bimonthly
www.infotoday.com/online
Articles, reviews, and product information on databases and other electronic library resources. Also includes coverage of more general library technology issues, such as Webcams. Sample full-text articles are available.

Library-oriented (General Focus)

American Libraries
American Library Association
Monthly (except for combined June-July issue)
www.ala.org/alonline/
Magazine for ALA members that includes excellent "Internet Librarian" and "Technology in Practice" columns along with occasional technology-related feature articles. Subscription is included with ALA membership. News stories and some columns (including "Internet Librarian") are available in full text.

Information Outlook
Special Libraries Association
Monthly
www.sla.org/io
A publication for SLA members that includes the technology column "Info Tech" as well as occasional technology-related articles. Subscription is included with SLA membership. Tables of contents for each issue are available.

Library Journal
Reed Business Information
20 issues annually
www.libraryjournal.com
This periodical includes articles on various library topics, and it is also noted for its reviews of books and media items. In addition to special articles on technology topics, it includes a number of technology-related columns (e.g., "Library 2.0," "Transparent Library," Digital Libraries," and "Gaming") and special reports on e-reference sources. News stories, articles, and columns are available in full text.

School Library Journal
Reed Business Information
Monthly
www.schoollibraryjournal.com
A publication for school librarians that includes regular technology-oriented articles and product reviews. Full-text news stories and articles are available.

Other Sources
In addition to the titles mentioned above, two excellent resources for finding technology information are published in other library-related periodicals. The periodical index *Library Literature & Information Science Full Text* (H. W. Wilson Company; www.hwwilson.com/Catabases/liblit.htm) is the gold standard in its coverage of the library and information science field. The Informed Librarian Online (www.informedlibrarian .com) is a unique resource for scanning the monthly output of some 312 library and information-related periodicals. The free version of the service provides a monthly e-mail update to new issues with links to selected items. A premium subscription service provides full access to the tables of contents for the periodicals and adds access to a selection of full-text articles, a searchable archive of past issues, and a search interface to all linked periodical issues.

General Technology

Far too many periodicals on this subject exist to list here, but a number of good periodicals are out there that may well help with a particular technology information need. They range from computing periodicals such as *Macworld* (www.macworld.com/) or *PC Magazine* (www.pcmag.com/) to broader technology titles such as *Better Buys for Business* (www.betterbuys.com) or *T.H.E. Journal: Technological Horizons in Education* (www.thejournal .com). These periodicals and others can be reached using a general periodical index (whatever you have access to) to find product reviews or information on a wide variety of technologies.

Continuing Education, Conference, and Trade Show Opportunities

There is no comprehensive, national, or international directory of library continuing education or professional development events. Some state organizations provide calendars for individual states or selected regions. Check with your state library or local or regional library organizations for assistance in finding a calendar of local events. The following resources can help you find events offered by national and international library organizations.

Yahoo! Listing of Library and Information Science Organizations (http://Cir.yahoo.com/Reference/Libraries/ Library_and_Information_Science/Organizations)
The Yahoo! **search directory**'s listing of various international, national, state, and local library and information science organizations. Look at the Web sites of these organizations to see what conferences or professional development opportunities they are offering.

American Libraries: Calendar of Library Events (www.ala.org/ala/alonline/Balendar/Balendar.cfm)
A site listing conferences and meetings sponsored by ALA and its divisions (arranged by division or by date), along with the future activities of various organizations.

Calendar of SLA Events (www.sla.org/Calendar)
A calendar of professional development opportunities offered by the Special Libraries Association and its chapters (it also has an advanced search interface).

Find Libraries Near You

While attending a program on a given technology or even visiting a vendor at a conference can be quite useful, there is nothing quite like seeing a technology at work in a library. Aside from just being neighborly and being aware of other libraries in your area, it pays to know who to visit to see new technologies at work. Here are some methods for tracking down local or regional libraries.

The World Wide Web Library Directory
(www.travelinlibrarian.info/libdir/)
An international directory of over 8,800 libraries located in over 130 countries. Libraries may be browsed by country or searched by keyword.

American Library Directory
(www.americanlibrarydirectory.com)
This source is an invaluable resource to locating libraries in the United States and Canada. The print version of the directory may be found in many libraries' reference collections. The online version offers a free registration option that allows users to search the directory and find library addresses.

National Center for Education Statistics: Search for Public Libraries
(http://nces.ed.gov/surveys/libraries/librarysearch)
An advanced search tool for locating public libraries in the United States and its territories.

PUBLICLIBRARIES.COM: State Libraries & Archives
(www.publiclibraries.com/state_library.htm)
This page offers an alphabetical list of links to state library Web sites. Most state libraries maintain directories of libraries in their state that can be searched by location or zip code.

A final suggestion is to post a message to one or more of the electronic discussion groups mentioned previously (or those found in the directory of lists). You could ask if any libraries near your location are already using a given technology.

MODERATION IN ALL THINGS

As information professionals, we are all too aware of the dangers of having too much information descend on us. The preceding pages have given you many sources of information for you to consult, some as long-term subscriptions and others as momentary, need-based consultations. Be sure to not let the number of blogs, listservs, and print and e-subscriptions overwhelm you. Choose a few sources to regularly consult to stay abreast of trends and then leave others for future needs. I heartily commend you to read a 2008 article by Sarah Houghton-Jan, "Being Wired or Being Tired: 10 Ways to Cope With Information Overload," in *Ariadne* 56 (July). It is available at www.ariadne.ac.uk/issue56/houghton-jan.

QUESTIONS FOR REVIEW

1. Name three reasons for consulting technology information sources.
2. Do many periodicals have free full-text articles available on their Web sites? Name two that do offer this service.
3. What methods are you currently using to keep up with technology developments (or other professional happenings) that may affect your job?
4. Find two or three resources in the list above and try monitoring them for a month. During that time, keep track of useful information you learn. This practice will help you decide whether a given resource is really worth watching.

Chapter 3

Evaluating, Buying, and Implementing Technology

Now that we have explored how our technological world came to be, and now that many resources for investigating technologies and keeping track of their further developments are in hand, it is time for a structured look at getting the technology into place. Libraries must determine their technology needs and which technology or technologies can best meet those needs. Once identified, the next steps are to compare, choose, purchase, and implement the technology. By systematically evaluating the technologies or products, buying them, and then putting them to work, libraries can successfully add the right technology at the right price. It will be helpful to have this process in mind as we explore individual technologies in the following chapters.

KNOW WHAT YOU NEED

The first consideration to make when adding technology is whether you have a need for it. We cannot evaluate whether or not a given technology is useful to our situation unless we know what need it is meant to address. Sadly, there are situations in which a new technology is chosen and implemented due to "technolust" (choosing technology due to its glitz rather than actual need) and then never used. Start with a need, and then base your evaluation on how well a given technology meets it.

The process of needs assessment is discussed in more detail in Chapter 17 as part of the technology planning process. Here we can consider how we become aware of technology needs. Common ways include:

1. *Personal or colleague observations.* Staff members may notice that too few public computers are available and that patrons are often milling about the reference area while they wait for a computer. Technical services staff may suggest that an additional printer, or bar code reader, or computer is needed to make the processing of library materials easier. Reference staff may note that access to a digital image database would help students with a recurring graphic design project. You might wonder if a new, faster copier would shorten lines of patrons waiting to make copies.

2. *Patron requests.* Patrons may ask directly for the ability to plug in flash drives. A faculty member might lobby for a specific database to use in his or her teaching. Patrons might ask when your library will offer downloadable audio e-books like the library over in Model City does.

3. *Surveys or suggestion boxes.* This is more of an active method than the previous two, in which observations or requests come up in the normal course of business. Whether aimed at patrons or at the library staff, survey results can turn up interest in new or updated technology options. The survey (print, electronic, or both) might be focused on technology or might be a broader one used to gauge patron satisfaction. As well, more informal electronic or physical suggestion boxes could catch ideas for technology additions to the library or its collection. Libraries are now more focused than ever on assessing patron satisfaction (and they should be concerned with staff satisfaction). Surveys and encouraging suggestions will gain input that libraries need for various areas of operation.

Keep in mind that the elements of perspective and participation impact the need assessment process. In terms of perspective, what staff members guess that patrons really need might not be what patrons really want. A technology that patrons would love to have may not be economically feasible for the library to provide. Perhaps the idea is just the interest of one person and would not be wildly popular. As far as participation, surveys and suggestion boxes might attract the interested few (or just those with something to get off their chests) but not provide a valid view of your target audience, whether it is composed of patrons or staff or both.

If a particular new technology suggestion would involve a large change in the library's services, such as adding a public scanner or starting an electronic reserve collection, then the groups who are most likely to be interested in or affected by the change should be surveyed or have discussions on the idea. This is a way of gaining focused responses and brainstorming that can shape the actual technology you choose and how it is implemented. Surveys or questionnaires aimed at patrons can serve to market the eventual adoption of the technology and may prove that the need is stronger than initially realized. Whenever possible, try to build evidence that supports the need so that funding agencies and library administration can create justifications to support budget requests for the technology.

It is also worth considering that sometimes we need to start with ideas rather than needs. As you develop your habit of watching technology trends, you will run across many nifty technologies that can address a need in your library. You may not have that need yet, though. So you save these ideas until the time is right. Perhaps the methods above will discover a need that turns your idea from mere "technolust" into a valuable solution.

LOCATE AND EVALUATE TECHNOLOGY CHOICES

From our identification of needs we now turn to the search for solutions. There may at times be a number of technologies that could meet the need. Sometimes the technology solution is clear, but the individual manufacturer or version still needs to be decided. Chapter 2 offers a number of methods and sources for seeking information and advice on technologies. These sources will prove helpful to locate the right technology or at least some possible choices. Consider the following nine criteria when comparing equipment, media, and electronic resources.

1. Is the technology suitable? Does it really meet the needs that have been identified? The needs analysis should have identified some problems to be solved. Now we need to determine if a technology or product can provide the solution.
2. Is the technology close to obsolescence? Even if the technology meets the need, is something better coming along? With all technology we face the issue of it becoming obsolete more quickly than we would like. This question generally forces us into a choice between the new and growing technology and the old and widespread technology.
3. How durable is the technology? Can a copier stand up to heavy use? Can a database provider handle large numbers of users accessing their service? Will DVDs hold up to the perils faced by circulating materials? Technology is expensive enough that it should be around long enough to justify its expense.
4. Does the technology fit into the library's environment? Is the item something that fits the mission of the library? Can a piece of equipment fit into the space of the library? Some technologies are neat to have but would not advance the mission or goals of the library. This is a checkpoint for assessing whether it is the role of the library to meet the need.
5. What implications does the technology have for training? Will it be difficult or easy to learn? Will bringing in this technology seriously affect training services? Sometimes the amount of training required can avert you from adding a particular technology right away.
6. What maintenance, upgrading, or updating needs does the technology have? Are these possible to complete within the library, or will they require outside assistance? Consider workflow—the requirements for staff to interact with the technology outside of the information-seeking process. Also consider associated costs beyond purchase.
7. If the technology has problems, are people available locally (within the library or its community) who can provide support? The technology may be easy to deal

with or it may require expertise. If the library has the expertise on hand, fine. If it does not, the library needs to decide whether it is worth acquiring the expertise or if the expense of outside experts is acceptable.

8. How does the price of the technology compare with similar technologies? What will the total cost of this technology be both initially and over time? Its ability to fit the need should outweigh discussions of price, assuming the funding is available. However, there are sometimes acceptable alternatives to expensive technology, or perhaps the need will have to go unfilled for a while longer.

9. Is this technology the most appropriate way to provide this information or service? Is there another format that would work better? Ultimately, the library needs to decide if the technology is really the most suitable choice. This final checkpoint should either eliminate nagging doubts or bring new ones to bear.

THE PURCHASING PROCESS

How purchasing actually flows in a library will differ greatly depending on institutional requirements and processes. Many institutions structure purchasing depending on the amount of money you are spending. For instance, a purchase of $500 or less requires the use of Form X whereas purchases of $5,000 or more require Process Y (and attached Form Z). Any substantial expense, such as migrating to a new library system or choosing among companies to lease a dozen copiers from, will involve a more formal process than buying individual DVD titles. Decisions that have large, long term financial implications, such as purchasing a new library security system, placing security tags on the entire library collection, and then regularly purchasing further tags for new acquisitions, may well be made by the library staff alone, even though the library's funding source will see increased demands in the library's supply budget for years to come.

The **request for proposal** (RFP) process is a common one used for those larger expenses mentioned previously. A request is sent out to vendors who can supply the technological product or products that are desired. The RFP is a document that very carefully describes and spells out the criteria for the item(s) to be purchased. Vendors, if able to meet the criteria, will respond to the library or its funding agency with a proposal outlining how they will provide what is requested. There is often a competitive bidding process involved that gives the contract for purchase to the lowest bidder. At some point within the process, the library is able to evaluate the proposals or bids and decide which one is the best. If by chance the lowest bidder does not meet the criteria, the library can write a justification for selecting a higher bidder and have this decision approved by the funding agency. The RFP process can be very slow and sometimes quite frustrating if no bids exactly fit the criteria. However, it does offer a means to evaluate a vendor and justify a decision. A term I've also heard for this process is "intention to negotiate" (**ITN**), at least within library database or systems circles.

BUYING GUIDES AND TIPS

When ready to purchase, it is vital to keep the following four practices in mind:

1. *Try before you buy.* Always find a way to look at and use a technology before implementing it in your library. It is great to both look at a demonstration version provided by the vendor and to look at the same item in use at another library (if possible). Conferences with vendors' exhibits can be a great source for additional browsing and examination.
2. *Compare models and technologies with a vengeance.* It is far easier to just pick the first thing that works, but closely examining several options assures you will meet your need in the best way.
3. *Know when to stop looking and start buying.* As a counter to the previous tip, be sure that you can control your comparison shopping so that you do not accidentally avoid fulfilling the need that got you started. There comes a point when you have looked far enough and can make a decision.
4. *Do not fall prey to myths about technology.* There are all sorts of myths out there, but here are a few of the most common: (a) wait before buying—that technology will stabilize

eventually, (b) wait before buying—prices for that item will fall before long, (c) wait before buying—that technology is about to become obsolete, and (d) it's cheap and it's here—we'll figure out something to do with it. The first three myths assume that technology changes take place in a defined pattern. However, technology is always changing, and if you follow these myths you will wait forever to find a stable, eternal form of the technology. The last ignores the hidden costs of any technology. The technology may be cheap, but it will probably cost the library more in space, time, and upkeep and will likely need to be replaced.

IMPLEMENTING THE TECHNOLOGY

Finally, the moment you've been waiting for! The mental image of the technology actually being used in your library provides a powerful vision that can keep you going through all of the twists and turns of evaluating and purchasing. Now the time for implementation arrives, and you must be ready for any last-minute obstacles.

Implementation preparations can differ greatly depending on the technology in question and its scope or audience. Replacing a staff printer is a much different process than launching a new time monitoring system for public Internet computers. There are some common considerations, though, that can guide your thoughts toward starting off a new technology. Consider the following issues:

1. *Installation*: Whether the technology requires a true hardware or software installation, there is some process of adding the item into your environment. It might involve planning new loan rules and adding item records for the MP3 players you are going to check out, or testing the new wireless network, or ensuring that the new metasearch software can actually run searches on the catalog and your 178 periodical indexes. Questions that come into play here include who will handle the installation (can someone in-house do it?), what other parts are required (other technology, furniture, etc.), and when the installation

will happen (is there a deadline, and how can this be coordinated to avoid delays at heavy use times?). Brainstorming about the details involved with any installation of technology can help you better coordinate the activity and avoid pitfalls.

2. *Training*: The new technology will not be much of a help to anyone unless sufficient training is provided. Training must be planned with the audience or audiences of the technology in mind and must take into account the different levels of ability these groups will need to have with the technology. You would expect that both patrons and library staff need to know the basic operations of your new self-checkout system, but only staff would need to know how to troubleshoot issues with the scanner or how to adjust on-screen instructions. While it is true that some technological changes (such as replacing common office equipment) may not require a lengthy training session, be sure to check on individuals' comfort with whatever new technology you implement. As well, keep in mind that individuals have different learning styles and that a single hands-on session may not be enough. Provide additional sources of information (handouts, manuals, vendor Web sites, etc.) for later consultation.

3. *Marketing*: You need to let people know that the new technology is in place. Some installations provide their own marketing ("What is that thing next to the reference desk?" or "Hey, my new computer is here!"). Other alterations and additions may not be so obvious. Much could be written here about the importance of marketing library services to patrons to increase their use of the library. If the new technology is something that your patrons will use directly, be sure to communicate with them about it.

4. *Assessment*: Looking ahead a bit further, keep in mind that you will want to evaluate how well the new technology is working in your library. Right from the beginning of its implementation you can begin gathering a record of successful and unsuccessful interactions. Often a list of this sort can help fine-tune the design of user interfaces (for instance, a Web site or database search screen) or

assist in diagnosing technical problems or bugs in the technology or with its installation.

ON TO THE TOOLS

With the close of this chapter, our foundation for discussing library technology is in place. You should now have a sense of what technologies have greatly impacted library work, where to find information on these and newer technologies, and how to approach each situation of buying new technology and putting it to work. It is time to proceed with a survey of technology tools that your libraries are already using (or could be soon).

QUESTIONS FOR REVIEW

1. How can you gather input on potential technology needs for your library?
2. Describe the RFP/ITN process.
3. Practice evaluating the addition of a new technology to your library. How would you answer the nine questions on evaluating technology choices for, say, adding digital audiobooks to your setting?
4. What are the four practices you should follow when buying technology?
5. What issues impact your implementation of new technology in your library?

SELECTED SOURCES FOR FURTHER INFORMATION

Anderson, Joseph. 2007. "WebJunction's Focus on Buying Hardware and Software." Dublin, OH: WebJunction. Available: www.webjunction.org/purchasing-advice/articles/content/437033.

> An overview of the purchasing process with links to various WebJunction tools and other resources. Be sure to look at the full list of documents on the subject for other useful tips at www.webjunction.org/purchasing-advice.

Cohn, John M., Ann L. Kelsey, and Keith Michael Fiels. 2001. "Translating Needs and Priorities into System Specification and a Request for Proposals." In *Planning for Integrated Systems and Technologies: A How-To-Do-It Manual for Librarians* (pp. 77–100). New York: Neal-Schuman.

> Outlines the RFP process and offers advice and forms to use in your preparation of these documents.

Computers in Libraries publishes a series of "Helping You Buy" articles each year in issues of their journal. They offer suggestions on specifications to pay attention to and questions to consider as you choose a product. You can browse a given year's articles at the journal's Web site (www.infotoday .com/cilmag/).

Lipinski, Tomas A. 2008. *The Librarian's Legal Companion for Buying and Licensing Information Resources.* **New York: Neal-Schuman.**

Guidance on understanding and negotiating licensing agreements for software and electronic resources. A crucial issue for networked resources of all kinds.

Stephens, Michael. 2008. "Taming Technolust: Planning in a Hyperlinked World." (Archived podcast of SirsiDynix Institute event, October 22). Available: www.sirsidynixinstitute.com/seminar_page.php?sid=105.

In this one-hour podcast, Michael suggests ten steps for library staff to take to better shape their choices about technology and how it is implemented and used. The presentation builds on an excellent article he wrote in 2004 titled "Technoplans vs. Technolust" for Library Journal (November 1, 2004), which is available at www.libraryjournal.com/article/CA474999 .html. The article cautions against losing focus by following too many intriguing technologies at once.

PART II

Technology Tools for Libraries

Chapter 4

Computers in Libraries: Desktops, Laptops, Tablets, Handheld Devices, and Office Applications

Computers are a ubiquitous feature of society with impacts in every sphere of life. Libraries are no exception. They make computers available to library patrons and staff members alike. Even in our highly technological age, an understanding of computers is not a universal skill, and computers can cause moments of frustration. The goal of this chapter is to provide the information essential to helping you understand the basic pieces of a computer and how computers operate. Many of the remaining chapters in the book address more specific uses of computers (for instance, integrated library systems in Chapter 6 and library Web sites and services in Chapter 12). This chapter will serve as a guide to the computer itself and its accompanying technology as well as provide a list of some common library uses for this technology.

DESKTOP COMPUTER ESSENTIALS

Computers are very complex devices that can seem daunting to operate. A few basic points should help you understand their makeup. We will discuss various types of computers by the end of the chapter, but let us start with the **desktop**. The name is suggestive of a computer that needs to sit on a desk or table.

Desktops are personal computers, just like those you may have at home. A desktop consists of the "box" or **central processing unit** (CPU, the part of the computer that contains the main components of the system), some **input devices** such as a keyboard and a **mouse**, and **peripherals**, including **monitors**, **printers**, or **scanners** (see Figure 4-1).

Every component in a desktop CPU is plugged into the **motherboard**, a piece of circuitry that serves as the foundation for the workings of the computer. There is a **processor**, which powers the calculations the computer must make to run software and process information. **Random access memory (RAM)** also helps the speed and performance of the computer by giving software some space in the memory to work in while it is running. There are also a variety of **cards** on the motherboard, components that serve specific functions for the computer. These include **video cards** that allow items to display on the monitor, **soundcards** that control audio output, and modems or network cards that allow

Figure 4-1
Photograph of a computer workstation

the computer to communicate with other computers through a variety of networks. Some of these cards and their functions are built into the motherboard, while others can fit into slots on the motherboard, being added or changed out as needed.

Space to store information in desktops comes in two varieties: the RAM is memory space that can temporarily hold the computing processes that software spawns, and ROM (read-only memory) contains information that cannot be altered by the user. Storage devices of various kinds are needed for long-term storage and moving software and other files from computer to computer (see Table 4-1). A hard drive typically has the capacity to hold many different software programs and files and serves as an internal storage device. External or removable storage is available in the forms of floppy drives, CD (compact disc) and CDRW drives (compact disk read/write), DVD and DVDRW drives, flash drives, and tape drives.

HOW COMPUTERS ARE MEASURED

Table 4-2 contains terms of measurement that are used to express the capacities of computer equipment. Their definitions should help you understand what this equipment can do and how you can compare similar pieces of equipment.

Table 4-1
Table of computer storage media and their capacities

Drive Type	Media Type	Media Capacity	Primary Use(s)
Floppy	3.5 in. floppy disk	1.44 MB	Small file storage and backup
CD-ROM	CD-ROM disc	700 MB	Application distribution and use
DVD-ROM	DVD-ROM disc	4.7 GB–17 GB	Application distribution and archival storage
Tape	Magnetic tape	Up to several GB	Archival storage and and backups
No drive (USB port)	Flash drives	Up to 64 GB	Mobile memory for file storage or using and distributing applications

Table 4-2
Computer-related measurements

Measurement	Definition
Bit	Simplest level of computer information. A bit can have the value of 0 or 1
Byte	Eight bits, which is enough memory to represent a single alphanumeric character
Kilobyte (K)	One thousand bytes; equivalent to a short note on a single sheet of paper
Megabyte (MB)	One million bytes; equivalent to 200–300 pages of text
Gigabyte (GB)	One billion bytes; common measurement of hard drive and storage space
Megahertz (MHz)	Common measurement of the internal speed of a computer's processor
Bits per second (Bps)	Common measurement of data transmission through modems or computer networks

COMPUTER SOFTWARE

The previously mentioned items are collectively termed computer **hardware**. Hardware includes any physical part of, or addition to, a computer as well as the complete device itself. Now comes **software**, the programs that make the computer do what we want it to do (and, on occasion, things we were not really planning for it to do). A piece of software is also known as an application or, from older days of computing, a program. A variety of types of software are available, from games to educational applications to financial management packages. I will discuss software that is commonly used in libraries later in this chapter and in a number of the following chapters. One particular type of software to begin with is **operating systems**.

OPERATING SYSTEMS

Operating systems provide the environment in which all other software operates in the computer. An operating system (OS) is really just a large piece of software that controls how the computer works. It is important to know which operating system you are working with so that you can choose software correctly. Operating systems have a number of capabilities. In general, they act between the applications we want to use and the computer's processor to make sure that the processor completes needed operations and that we see the results. They allow for **multitasking**, the ability to have multiple applications running at the same time and to switch back and forth between them. For instance, you can be connected to the Internet at the same time you are using a word processor and use both applications in turn as needed. They also provide the ability to change some characteristics of the **interface** we use to interact with our applications. The interface is what you see on the screen and then manipulate using the keyboard and mouse.

The world of operating systems today is primarily divided between Macintosh and Windows computers and their respective operating systems. Windows holds a distinct market advantage, with around 90 percent of machines running a Windows OS. However, there are other players in the game, most prominent among them an open source OS called **Linux**. Apple is now on the version 10.5 of its operating system (known as OS X since version 10.0 was introduced in 2001), although some Macs still run on OS 9 or System 8 or earlier versions. The most current version of Windows is Windows Vista, with earlier versions of Windows XP, Windows 2000, Windows 98, Windows NT, and even Windows 95 still running. Linux, developed and updated by a growing community of users, comes in a variety of versions (or builds). It has made some penetration into the desktop computer market but is still more commonly used on servers. It will be interesting to see how this develops over time.

THE HISTORY OF OPERATING SYSTEMS

One of the initial personal computer operating systems was **DOS** (Disk Operating System). It was characterized by its command line interface in which every task you wanted the computer to complete had to be typed out on the screen at the command prompt or included in a program. Graphics could be displayed within programs, but the enduring image of DOS is text on a screen.

A huge innovation in operating systems came with the advent of the **Macintosh** computer in the early 1980s. The Mac stood in stark contrast to the predominant DOS-running IBM PC of the time. Personal computers at the time were called either Apples, after the Apple Computer company that created the Mac, or IBM-PCs, after the IBM Corporation that produced the first PC. (Even when other manufacturers produced so-called PC clones, they were still called IBM compatibles.) The Mac had a **graphical user interface** (GUI) that consisted of a screen with little graphical images, or **icons**, that could be clicked on to run programs or open up additional screens, or folders, containing more icons. You clicked on the icons using a device called a mouse. The Mac was thought to be more user friendly than the DOS machines and became more and more proficient at displaying and allowing the manipulation of images. This revolutionary development led to the creation of a similar GUI operating system by the Microsoft Corporation called Windows (see Figure 4-2).

THE OPERATION OF COMPUTERS

When you start a computer by pressing its power button and turning it on, it goes through the **boot-up** process. We might think of this process as an annoying delay before we can actually do something on the computer. What happens is that the computer needs to make sure that it has all of its components in order (the RAM, hard drive, and other devices). During boot-up, the computer gets the operating system running and gets you to a point where you can choose an application to use. The operating system runs constantly while you are using the computer.

If you wish to turn your computer off, it is important to first follow the correct procedure to shut down your operating system. This allows the operating system to "get its ducks in a row." It can clear out temporary memory space and cleanly shut down parts of its software. Then you can turn off the power. Some individuals will turn off a computer after completing a task with it, while others will leave the computer running on an ongoing basis. The general recommendation that I have for running a

Figure 4-2
Photograph of the Microsoft Windows desktop interface

computer is to minimize any wasted time that it runs (which somewhat increases your electricity costs) but to also minimize the number of times you turn it on or off (which can wear out the switch on the CPU and stress the operating system). That is to say, turn on your computer when you arrive at work and leave it on until you are ready to go home or until you know that you will not work on it any longer that day.

On occasion a computer may lock up, in that an application or the entire computer stops working. This can be due to a failure or error in a particular application or within the operating system itself. If you can still use the keyboard to type commands or move the mouse, you may be able to close a malfunctioning application and then reopen it to continue your work. This can happen sometimes if you have multiple applications open (e.g., you are using your word processor and your Internet browser and the word processor just stops responding to your commands). If the failure is bad enough that using the keyboard or mouse is impossible (nothing happens on the screen when you type or move the mouse) you will need to reboot the computer to straighten out the problem.

COMPUTER PERIPHERALS

The term *peripheral* refers to a variety of optional computer hardware items that have specific functions. All of these peripherals plug into the CPU, mostly using **USB** ports or connections. USB (Universal Serial Bus) is the dominant method for connecting peripherals, replacing earlier **parallel** and serial connectors.

- *Monitors* are essential for visually interacting with the CPU. They come in two main varieties: **LCD** (liquid crystal display) flat panel and CRT (cathode ray tube). LCD flat panels are much thinner than CRTs, which are rather boxy and take up a good deal of space. Also, images shown on LCD flat panels do not flicker as CRTs do, which can cause eyestrain. LCDs are a bit more expensive, but are now standard options with the decline in CRTs. Libraries tend to be buying LCD flat panels exclusively with the only question being how large of a display they can afford. Screen size is a key part of the puzzle, with physically larger screens giving the user the ability to see more of a document or a Web site at one time (or to view multiple applications at once). Trends are toward buying the largest screen you can afford to give you flexibility to multitask among multiple applications. Larger screens are also useful for multiple purposes, such as Internet viewing, playing DVDs from the computer's DVD drive, or watching digital videos.
- *Printers* are a very common peripheral in libraries and print everything from handouts to budget requests to book labels. They come in three main varieties: laser, ink-jet, and dot-matrix. Laser printers provide the highest quality of printing by thermally transferring toner to paper, much like photocopiers. They are the most expensive (though not prohibitively so) and add additional features such as two-sided printing. Dot-matrix printers represent the

historical beginnings of computer printing and offer relatively cheap printing on form-fed paper. They are typewriter-like devices that use ribbons to print and are quite slow and prone to paper jams. Ink-jets fall somewhere in between the two in terms of cost and quality. They spray ink onto paper to complete the printing process and result in documents that look similar to laser printed documents. They are often chosen as a lower cost method for providing color printing in a library (over color laser printers). Dot-matrix printers are tending to disappear from libraries while laser printers are fairly standard for public and staff use.

- *Document duplication technologies* include scanners and all-in-one devices that scan, fax, copy, and print (see Figure 4-3). Scanners have increased in popularity as equipment costs have decreased and interest in digital images has grown. (More on their uses will be discussed

Figure 4-3
Photograph of an all-in-one scanner/printer/copier

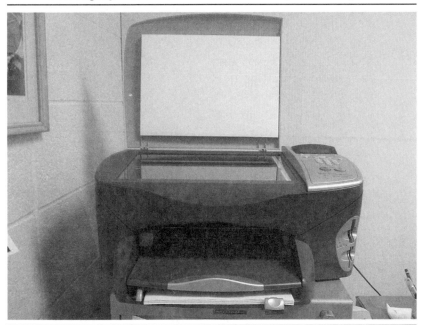

in Chapter 7.) Attaching an all-in-one device to your computer provides the ability to use these functions individually or in tandem to (1) scan and store images or paper documents on your hard drive, (2) print and make copies of electronic documents, and (3) scan and fax documents through the phone line. One downside of these units is that, due to the integration of many different functional components, it may be difficult to correctly diagnose a problem and identify the malfunctioning component. As well, the loss of one function on the unit impairs all of the others until repairs are made.

- *Mice* were introduced to computing with the addition of GUI operating systems. While keyboard commands can be used to navigate a GUI, the mouse is integral to the operation of nearly all computer functions. Cabled mice that plug into USB ports in the CPU are quite common, but wireless mice that transmit signals into a receiver plugged into the CPU are an affordable and durable option. Security concerns may keep them out of public computer use, but staff will benefit from the ease of "mousing around" without the restriction of a cable.
- *Multimedia add-ons* such as speakers, headphones or earbuds, and microphones may be added to a computer as needs dictate. Even small Webcams for Internet videoconferencing can be useful for virtually attending meetings. And digital cameras for recording still images and video should not be forgotten here, although their use may not be applicable to all library settings.
- *Bar code readers and card readers* assist in the completion of circulation and technical services activities. **Bar code technology** (see Figure 4-4) appears as both counter scanners (as used in grocery stores) and as portable wands or pens. Card readers pick up patron data from a magnetic band on the card.

MINIMUM STANDARDS FOR NEW COMPUTERS

Minimum requirements for computers, or anything else, are always in the eye of the beholder. What I find acceptable might

Figure 4-4
Photograph of a bar code reader

seem paltry to one person and seem excessive to another. As well, the machine's eventual purpose will influence your choices; a public computer can probably make do with less hard drive space than a staff computer, for instance. The following criteria may be useful to guide you in your computer assessment and purchasing. These aspects of a computer are the most important ones to consider.

- Processor type: multicore processor (e.g., Quad-core Intel Xeon for Macs or Intel Core 2 Quad for PCs)
- RAM: at least 4GB
- Hard drive capacity: at least 500GB
- USB ports: the more the better (at least 8)
- Drives: a DVDRW drive is essential, and I would not bother adding a 3.5 inch floppy drive
- Monitor: flat panel, 20 inch (or larger, depending on your planned uses)

- Networking: a network card (no need for a 56.6 Kbps modem unless you'll be using a dial-up connection)

If your next computer meets these standards, you can safely be happy with it for about a month or two until the next fast processor or drive or whatever comes out at the same price as you just paid. Realistically, though, since we cannot keep pace with technology, these minimums will keep your computer in good order and able to handle software for at least four years. For most libraries, you will need your machine to last at least that long. Buy the best you can afford at any given moment in time.

COMPUTERS IN OTHER FORMS

While we are discussing computers, it makes sense to mention related devices that you will see in library settings. Though different in form, these devices make use of the same computing processes and principles as desktops do.

Laptops

Laptops have been developed to take the computer's CPU, monitor, keyboard, and mouse along with you in a single unit. Mobility is the key element of this device, which gives you the freedom to use software applications wherever you wish— given access to power or a long-lasting battery. Gone is the need to be tied down to a desktop. The popularity of laptops has pushed them recently to hold a larger share of the overall computer market than desktops.

The laptop fits easily on your lap and consists of a bisected, hardened plastic rectangle. An adjustable, fold-up LCD screen makes up one half of the laptop and also serves to protect the laptop's keyboard. The keyboard half of the unit also contains the laptop's **motherboard**, processor, hard drive, and additional components. A mousepad located below the keyboard offers the user the option of moving the mouse icon at the touch of a finger (you may also plug in a standard mouse if you wish).

Laptops originally suffered from difficulties in miniaturizing computer components. Early efforts were not very powerful and quite slow in operation, and they also weighed a ton, making it hard to be truly mobile. Recent developments have brought laptops much closer to desktops in terms of processor speed, while reducing their weight tremendously. Laptops may contain DVD drives or may have the option of plugging in an external drive. A wide variety of screen sizes are available, roughly from 9-inch through 20-inch screens. Other than their size, they are very similar to desktop machines in their operation and capability. USB ports are a must in whatever quantity you can find them.

Wireless networks, a development we will discuss more in the next chapter, has increased the mobility of laptops and clearly sets them apart from desktops. A laptop equipped with a wireless network card (essential for all laptops) and in proximity to a wireless network can access the Internet or other networked resources without having to rely on wall plugs and cables. This further freedom gives the laptop new potential in library use, particular in settings where library users desire the chance to roam throughout the building with laptops (their own or the library's) or where adding **network cabling** is not possible without ruining the library's aesthetics.

Tablet PCs

Tablet PCs, while still only a small percentage of laptop sales, offer another innovation on the laptop platform. Tablets are very similar to laptops in their composition and computing power but offer a new interface for interacting with software. While they tend to have built-in keyboards and mousepads much like an ordinary laptop, the intended way of interacting with software on a tablet is by tapping or drawing on the screen using a **stylus**. This penlike object, though not attached to the tablet in any way (other than by a tether to keep the user from losing it), is able to transmit commands and other inputs through the tablet's responsive screen. In addition to using the stylus much the same as you would a mouse, the tablet also has software that will allow you to write on the screen in your own handwriting (block or cursive) and either saves your text as an image or translates it into typed text. Tablet PCs can run Windows XP or Vista, or Linux, or can be modified to run **Mac OS** X, though Apple does not sell an official tablet of its own. This innovative interface may make its way into libraries over time.

Mobile Devices

While laptops and tablets can be quite mobile, this category represents an explosion of devices that bring computing power and applications in a small package. There are two main types to be aware of: **smartphones**—cell phones with added capabilities and input options (tiny keyboards), and **netbooks**—very small computers with features similar to those on a laptop (including built-in keyboards) but at a very tiny size. These tiny devices have developed over the past 15 years from cell phones that had address books, calendars, and contact lists, and from PDAs (**personal digital assistants**—a basically dead technology) and PocketPCs with those same functions plus a limited group of software applications. Now they stand as widespread devices with ever-growing functions that library staff should be aware of. The availability of mobile devices points us toward a concept known as **ubiquitous computing**. Computers can be ever-present with us because they are so easy to take along everywhere we go. A great number of applications and files can be accessed in a device that fits easily in a belt clip, pocket, or purse.

Smartphones and netbooks use a variety of operating systems, some of which are specially created for mobile devices and others that are commonly used in desktops and laptops. Smartphones with specialty operating systems, like BlackBerry and PalmOS, are more focused on communications such as voice and e-mail, calendaring, address books, and basic note-taking abilities. Those that run on a standard OS allow for a variety of functions more similar to those seen in computers. Standard OS choices in smartphones include Windows Mobile (a special version of Windows) and Linux (the Openmoko phones are one example). The very popular iPhone from Apple runs Mac OS X, and Google is a new competitor on the market with its Android OS and G1 smartphone. All of these OS choices allow for the development of additional applications, with those in the standard OS models allowing for greater similarity to what you'd see on your desktop. Another big plus with smartphones is that they are not as dependent on wifi as netbooks are since they are designed to communicate from wherever you go (and have bars).

Netbooks tend to use more standard computer OS choices. Some interesting examples of these machines included the following. The OQO Model 02, with a 5-inch screen and thumb keyboard, uses Windows Vista and XP. Asus's Eee PC will run either Linux or Vista, with an 8.9-inch screen and full-sized keyboard (larger screen sizes are available). The Everex Cloudbook runs on Ubuntu, a version of Linux, and is designed with mobility in mind—the placement of the mousepad on the right side of the keyboard allows the user to access files and browse the Web while walking around. Dell and Hewlett-Packard also offer smaller versions of their laptops, the Inspiron Mini 9 and Mini 1000, respectively. Small size and weight are achieved in some of the machines by using flash memory chips rather than a traditional, heavier hard drive. Speed and performance may be reduced quite a bit, but for basic tasks of e-mail, Web surfing, listening to music, and word processing, they work well. Though the machines are wifi dependent for network access, they can be tethered to cell phones to gain greater range in their use. You can also see a reverse version of this with Celio's Redfly, a netbook-sized screen and keyboard device that allows for easier display and interaction with the applications on a Windows Mobile smartphone.

Where do these devices fit into libraries, then? These devices may be used by library staff members to communicate with one another and with patrons or to provide access to cataloging systems and other Web-based resources when working on projects in the stacks or assisting patrons wherever the staff member is located. But beyond these staff uses, there has been an interest in making electronic books (e-books) available through these devices, among others. There is also the issue of patrons being able to access the library and its databases through the device and to run searches. Already several libraries have their public catalogs set up to allow patrons to text call numbers to their cell phones. If libraries expect these mobile users to depend on their services, they will need to ensure that interface designs will match up with the smaller screens of these devices. As any computing platform becomes popular among a significant number of patrons, the library must be prepared for the design and service implications that come with that platform.

LIBRARY USES FOR COMPUTERS

Libraries have found ways to use computers in every facet of their operations. Some uses are primarily available to staff members, while others are used by both staff and the library's public. Even as this book is written, a library somewhere out there is probably adding a new use. At the present time, however, the following are the primary categories of use for computers in libraries.

Collection Organization and Control

Libraries hold the maintenance, organization, and growth of their collections as a major facet of their missions. As such, the areas of a library organization dedicated to these services have been early adopters of computers. In particular, the cataloging, acquisitions, and circulation operations of libraries have used library systems or independent pieces of software to accomplish their tasks. The volume of work in these areas, as well as the fact that they each involve tasks with a fairly repetitive process, has made them clear targets for automation. Adding records for items to an online catalog, ordering materials from vendors, and tracking circulation and fine information are daily technology tasks in most libraries. Some libraries also use mobile devices for running inventories of their collections.

Interlibrary Loan

The practice of borrowing materials from other libraries and lending owned items existed before the computer age. What computers have meant to interlibrary loan is that it can be much easier to locate libraries who own a desired book, video, or periodical article. Also, the management of borrowed and loaned items is much more convenient than with paper files. While much of the transmission of materials still takes place through the postal service, courier services, or fax, computers have added the ability for periodical articles or book chapters to be transmitted via the Internet. The addition of an inexpensive scanner allows for the digitization of documents and their transfer to a receiving library.

Electronic Reference Resources

As we discussed in Chapter 1, the ability to access reference and informational resources from beyond the library building has strongly impacted libraries over the latter quarter of the past century. Libraries are providing periodical and reference databases to their communities both from within the library and from individual users' computers at home or work. The resources themselves are usually not housed in the library but rather on the computers of multiple vendors and consortia. The scope and depth of a library's collection can be quickly multiplied by the addition of these resources, provided they are well chosen.

Internet Access Tool

Providing Internet access to staff and the public is crucial since the Internet has become an important information resource for libraries as well as a medium to connect to electronic resources. Libraries need to provide access in ways that that fit their missions, and for many libraries this means having access to the Internet from a number of public computers as well as from most or all staff computers. Having computers available with the requisite peripherals and speed to handle Internet communication is a must. For a number of people in any community, the local library's access might be the only means available to reach resources on the Internet.

Management/Office Tool

Libraries have elements of their work that are no different from any other business enterprise. As such, libraries need to have software that is commonly found in business and home settings. Word processing applications can be used for the production of handouts, memos, and reports of various kinds. **Spreadsheet software** is useful for keeping track of budgets and schedules. **Database software** is handy for maintaining mailing lists and for creating smaller databases for managing periodicals and other purposes. These software packages are often sold together in combined "office suites" or as a single piece of software that can fulfill all of the functions described previously. Microsoft Office (including Word, Excel, Powerpoint, and Access) is by far the most common office suite, although some open source alternatives are available, such as Open Office (www.openoffice .org). Another possibility is the Web-based set of free applications available from GoogleDocs (http://docs.google.com).

Instructional Tool

Libraries that have a need for creating instructional materials and presentations will make use of a variety of instructional software. Presentation software (e.g., PowerPoint) can be used to create presentations combining text, still images, clip art, sound, and video that can be projected in a classroom. Software such as Captivate, Camtasia, or Articulate can be used to take presentations from PowerPoint, combine them with sound and with video of browsing through a database or other application, and create video tutorials. These tutorials can be linked to the library's Web site for patrons to watch at any time. More possibilities for instructional use of software is covered in Chapter 13.

Miscellaneous Library Tasks

Many library tasks can be performed using the software in the previous three categories, but a number of tasks require additional software that will vary from library to library and person to person. Staff members responsible for creating documents for a library's Web site will need Web design software on their computers. Catalogers may have software packages installed to access, edit, and download bibliographic records for use in an online catalog. Larger libraries may use online calendar software to create schedules for desk coverage or staff meetings. More of this category of software will be explored in later chapters.

QUESTIONS FOR REVIEW

1. Name the components of a computer that reside in the CPU.
2. Describe the difference between RAM and the computer's hard drive.
3. What is a GUI?
4. Describe the key attributes of a laptop, a tablet PC, and a netbook.
5. Take a look at a computer catalog or ad for desktop computers. If you were trying to buy a computer with the minimum specifications given in this chapter, how much would it cost? What additional capabilities would you get, and how much more would you pay, if you bought a computer with better-than-minimum specifications?

SELECTED SOURCES FOR FURTHER INFORMATION

Turn to the resources listed in Chapter 2 (pp. 26–37) to find more information on the topics covered in this chapter. Product information and further computer concept explanations can be located in the Web sites and other resources listed there.

In addition, you can take a look at the PC Technology Guide (www.pctechguide.com) for an introduction and further discussion of PC components and operations. It includes a number of helpful diagrams, user forums, and easy to understand explanations. For those interested in Macintosh information, try About.com Focus on Macs (macs.about.com). It has links to Mac products and FAQs and troubleshooting information.

Auger, Brian. 2004. "Living with Linux." *Library Journal NetConnect* (Spring): 16–18.
   An overview of Linux and its implementation in a library setting.

Kroski, Ellysa. 2008. "On the Move with the Mobile Web: Libraries and Mobile Technologies." *Library Technology Reports* 44, no. 5.
   This entire issue on the mobile Web discusses what library staff need to know about the mobile Web and describes the implementation of mobile technologies and services in libraries.

Needham, Gill. 2008. *M-Libraries: Libraries on the Move to Provide Virtual Access.* New York: Neal-Schuman.

Explores the technological and social contexts for libraries providing services to mobile technology users.

Strauber, Christopher. 2007. "Handheld Computers in Libraries." In *Library 2.0 and Beyond: InnovativeTechnologies and Tomorrow's User* (pp. 49–61), edited by Nancy Courtney. Westport, CT: Libraries Unlimited.

An overview of smartphones, netbooks, and other small devices and their uses in libraries.

Chapter 5

Computer Networks in Libraries: The Internet, Modems, WiFi, and E-mail

So far we have discussed computers and suggested some of the tasks that might be completed with them. Most of these tasks are impossible to complete without a way for these computers to communicate with others in the same library or across the world. Networks, large or small, wired or wireless, are commonly used in libraries to provide access to shared resources. They expand the library's collection through the electronic resources they bring into the building and they ease the work of patrons who use them to reach the library's resources from home. This chapter will explain how networks operate and how computers use them to communicate. It is fascinating to see how the interconnection of libraries and the wider world leads not only to the completion of tasks we can readily imagine but also provides new service opportunities that can reach untouched communities of users.

WHAT DO NETWORKS DO?

Networks exist to share resources between two or more computers. In doing so, they enable the users of those computers to be connected in terms of communicating with one another and sharing files with one another. In a very simple network, two computers might be networked together to share a printer. Both computers have equal access to one resource, in this case a printer, and avoid duplication (the need to buy two printers). In a more complex situation, a network may be used to share a printer or several printers along with sharing a number of software applications among many computers.

A library may have over 100 computers that need to be able to access the same set of applications (an office suite, e-mail software, locally networked databases, etc.). Rather than purchasing and installing the same applications 100 or more times, the library can network the various applications on one machine—a **server**—so that all 100 users can get to it. Networks make it very easy to share files, applications, and devices such as printers and scanners. They also make it easy to quickly update the software on many machines at once by installing applications on a network server.

Just to note, network managers have at their discretion the ability to run some software from the network server and install other software locally on a computer. There are times when it makes sense to allow the users of individual computers to control the configuration of software that is installed locally. As well, locally installed software will be available for use on the computer even if the network is down.

MAINFRAMES AND SERVERS

Chapter 4 discussed computers first because they are found in libraries in the greatest numbers. Computers that are used to host online catalogs or other networked resources are known as servers. In the days before there were personal computers (PCs), large applications such as a library automation system required very large and powerful computers called **mainframes** to run them. Individual users connected to the mainframe through **terminals**, devices that consisted of a monitor and a keyboard that were cabled directly into the mainframe. Terminals did not have separate CPUs or memory of their own. As PCs became available in the early 1980s, libraries were able to start moving away from terminals and mainframes toward more functional PCs and servers. Just to note, the first library I worked in still had terminals through the mid-1990s. Developments in processors and the dropping prices in computer memory (which continue today) allowed many tasks handled by mainframes to move to network servers that are physically not so different from a standard computer. Mainframes, which have extremely fast processing speeds, continue to complete calculations that are essential to research in science, statistics, and mathematics. For more information on these supercomputers, see the Cray Inc. Web site at www.cray.com.

A server, or **network server** or **file server** or **host computer**, is where the software or other resources are installed that people wish to access over the network. The server will tend to have more RAM (random access memory) and a faster processor than an average computer. Just how much RAM or how fast a processor depends on what the server is being used for. If a server is used to connect a dozen computers to a printer, it need not have even as much RAM as I suggested for a standard computer (4GB) and can run an even slower processor. However, if a server is to be accessed by many individuals through the Internet and is running very memory-intensive applications (e.g., sound or video files), it will need a lot more than the minimum amount of RAM and the fastest processor you can afford.

A library server might be used for one or more of the following functions:

- Hosting the library's Web site
- Hosting library's automation system
- Serving as a file server for word processing and other office software and for staff documents and other files
- Serving up other electronic resources or services (blogs, etc.) within the library

A library may have several servers in place to accomplish these tasks, or it may not have any servers at all. Libraries depend on the servers of their vendors to provide resources and services that are not hosted locally. My own library uses space on our campus's **Web server** to run our Web site and uses networked applications from another server for word processing and other applications. We are connected to servers on our main campus for our library catalog as well as to servers at our regional **consortium** and a host of vendors for our periodical databases and other resources. The demands you place on a server depend on the purposes you have in mind for a network.

NETWORK COMPONENTS

There are a number of items beyond a server that a network needs in order to operate:

- **Network operating system** software
- Computers with network interface cards and network software
- Printers or other peripheral devices with network interface cards
- Cabling to tie it all together
- Resources (beyond printers and devices) to share
- Routers and gateways to connect users to other networks

Now let me offer a few words about the key elements of these components.

NETWORK OPERATING SYSTEMS

A network requires network operating system software of some kind. The operating systems we discussed in Chapter 4 all have networking capabilities as part of their makeup. This means that you can run a small network from Windows Vista or Mac OS X without needing to add additional software. There are also specialized network operating systems that are designed to handle networking processes and communications, such as **Novell Netware**, Windows Server, **UNIX**, and Linux. Whichever option is used, the purpose of the network operating system is to make sure that everything connected to the network (computers and printers and whatever else) can communicate and that the use of those connected items can be managed.

NETWORK CARDS AND CABLING

Each computer, printer, or other device on the network needs two items to complete their linkage. A **network interface card** must be connected to the device and a cabling system must be in place. The card enables the device to send and receive data through the network. The cabling provides a physical link between the devices and the server or servers on the network. There are a variety of cable types and system configurations that a network might use. Some common types of cabling are **unshielded twisted pair** (UTP), **coaxial**, and **fiber-optic**.

- UTP is commonly used for networks that exchange data, such as e-mail and Web-based resources. Category 5 is a popular standard for UTP.
- Coaxial is used mostly for networks that transmit large files or video. It is most prominently used for cable television networks but also for data transmission through these same networks.
- Fiber-optic is a lightweight, extremely well-transmitting cable that is excellent for data transmission. It tends to be more expensive than UTP, however, and figures more prominently in telephone networks that in computer networks. Quite a bit of data is transported through these telephone networks.

HOW NETWORKS WORK

There are three main goals of using a network: security, flexibility, and stability. Security ensures that a particular user can use only the applications or the files they should have access to. Flexibility allows users to sit down at any computer connected to the network, log into the network server, and access the same resources they would at another computer. Stability means that the chances of malfunctions or downtime for the network are significantly reduced.

The network software allows for each user to log in with a specific username and password. Different profiles can be set up on the network server so that staff members' login IDs give them access to different resources or different levels of access to the same resources than the IDs that are set up for public computers. For instance, library staff members will have login IDs that let them access the management side (circulation, cataloging, etc.) of a library automation system from computers in the staff area, at the circulation desk, and even from public computers. Patrons, however, may have default login IDs for public computers that let them access only the online catalog. It is fairly common to limit what can be done on a public computer in terms of installing new software or changing system settings.

Another facet of network operating systems is that each computer that will be connected to the network needs to have network operating system software installed. This is relatively straightforward if the network operating system of choice is already the main operating system for the computer. If it is not, then an additional software package will be installed to allow the computer and server to communicate. In either case, the computer and its network software need to be configured for this communication to take place. Just to note here, methods are available to let computers using different network operating systems (or computer operating systems) to communicate. This is all set up with added applications on the computer. This way, you can have machines using OS X, Window XP, and UNIX all talking back and forth and sharing the same files, printers, and other devices.

No network will run uninterrupted eternally, but there are ways to increase its stability and make users more confident about using it. Redundancy needs to be built into the system so that a malfunction in one part does not stop the entire network. There needs to be another path to follow to keep the network running. One strategy for this is to install a backup server to take the place of a primary server that experiences a hardware or software problem. The switchover can be made without the user noticing an interruption in many cases. On the Internet, many heavily used Web sites have **mirror sites**, which consist of a server (or servers) containing the same data or resources as the primary site but located on a separate network. This option keeps the site running for users even though the main site might have gone down due to server, cable, or other connection problems.

LANS, WANS, ROUTERS, AND GATEWAYS

A **LAN (local area network)** is basically what has been described: a server, some computers, and some cabling. It can involve a dozen computers or thousands of them. Likewise, a large number of servers can be involved. Typically, a LAN is a network that is used by a single library or perhaps by a single college campus. The speed limitations of the cabling used for the LAN make it difficult to extend the network beyond a single organization or small geographic area. This is because as more computers are added to the LAN, the cable needs to handle more traffic and the speed of the network will slow.

That is where a **WAN (wide area network)** comes in. If there is a need to extend access to the same resources or applications that are on one LAN to people using a different LAN, as in the case of a company with multiple offices, a WAN can be built with devices that allow communication through existing communications networks, such as the telephone network. **Routers** help exchange information between separate LANs, and **gateways** help translate between LANs that use different communication protocols, decided by their choice of network operating system. WANs can then accommodate a larger number of individual users and can bring together many more resources for shared use.

WIRELESS NETWORKS

Wireless networks have grown tremendously in popularity and number over the past few years. They use radio signal and infrared transmission technologies to allow computers another way to communicate with other computers and network servers. This allows computers to communicate with servers and other users on networks and exchange information without being plugged into the wall. The wireless network can also support the transmission of print jobs from laptops to a networked printer. Wireless is seen as a way to augment cabled networks by giving users freedom of movement and libraries flexibility in arranging stations for networked resources. The latter option can help for libraries who find it difficult to rewire their building for a network. A library may use both wireless and cable networked stations in tandem to give users flexibility. Library users can bring in their own laptops or borrow them from the library and use them to type papers or do research from anywhere within the building.

A **wireless network** originates from a device that is plugged into a wired network. One arrangement for a network would have a wired server connected to a wireless router that is further connected to wireless access points (WAPs). The WAPs have antennae on them that send signals to, and receive them from, wireless devices. They also boost these signals to carry them through the area covered by the wireless network. In turn, every wireless device has a wireless network card attached to it. WAPs will be strategically placed throughout a library to achieve a strong signal in all areas of intended use. With the proper equipment, the entire library can be a zone—often called a "hotspot"—for accessing online resources.

The other side of this equation is being sure to protect your wireless network from individuals who should not have access to it. Wireless signals do not necessarily pay attention to walls or floors or other physical boundaries that separate the library from the wider world. While you cannot keep your signal from going out into the street or into nearby apartment buildings, you can force users to log in in order to access the network or gain wider access to the Internet. This and other methods of network security will be discussed further in Chapter 14.

HOW DOES THE INTERNET RELATE TO ALL OF THIS?

The Internet is the network to beat all networks. It can be seen as a very large WAN. It is the combination of many LANs and WANs spread out worldwide. It uses a special protocol, called Internet protocol, to make it easy for computers using any network operating system to connect to other servers, anywhere. Each server on the Internet has its own **Internet protocol (IP)** number, or address, that allows anyone using the Internet to connect to the server. The Internet also uses a system of **domain names** to give a more memorable look to server addresses (this system allows for names such as www.muohio.com rather than an IP address such as 129.137.146.2).

The Internet is built on very high speed phone lines that are dedicated to transferring electronic data. These lines are typically **OC-3**, T-3, T-1, and **56Kbps lines**. OC-3 lines are able to transmit

155.52 Mbps and form the backbone of the Internet, quickly transmitting e-mail messages, files, and requests to view Web pages from an individual's computer to another computer or server. T-3 lines make up smaller pieces of the Internet backbone and can transmit 44.736 Mbps. T-1 lines can transmit 1.544 Mbps and can be leased by organizations—companies, colleges and universities, libraries, or individuals—that require high speed connections to the Internet. These organizations can plug a T-1 line into their LAN and provide speedy access to dozens of computers. The route an individual or a library take to access the Internet may look like the diagram in Figure 5-1.

What's an Intranet?

An **intranet** is a single LAN (or a combination of LANs) that is not available to the general public over the Internet. It is an internal network that is limited to a particular company or organization. It makes use of Web technology and Internet protocols to give an Internet look and feel to their network. Some larger libraries or educational institutions may have intranets that allow the sharing of staff resources and secure information among

Figure 5-1
Diagram showing how individuals connect to the Internet

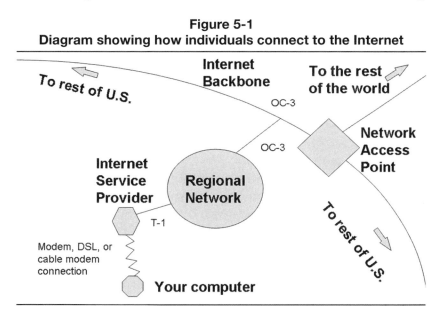

library staff. Other libraries may simply have sections of their Web sites that require staff to log in to see internal documents.

HOW TO CONNECT TO THE INTERNET AS AN INDIVIDUAL OR A SMALL LIBRARY

There are two common options for Internet access available beyond using either leased T-1 lines or dialing in with **56Kbps modems**. For home users, these options are chosen much more frequently than dial-up Internet access using modems. They are often called either high-speed or **broadband** access.

ADSL (Asymmetric Digital Subscriber Line) is a very fast method for connecting to the Internet using existing copper telephone lines. ADSL is commonly referred to or advertised as "**DSL**," which is a family of communications technologies of which ADSL is one example. It requires a special ADSL modem that allows a computer to achieve access speeds between 256Kbps and 9Mbps depending on the individual's distance from the telephone exchange. The service is offered through local or regional telephone companies as well as other **ISPs (Internet Service Providers)**. Speeds vary widely but are often in the 800Kbps to 2Mbps range.

Cable modems use the coaxial cable laid for cable television to provide users with access speeds up to 5Mbps (1Mbps is probably more common). The modems are connected to the home's incoming cable line as well as to the user's computer. Local cable companies, who own the coaxial lines, offer this service as an add-on to your monthly cable bill.

Both of these technologies are somewhat limited for use in that some areas do not have the infrastructure to support either ADSL or cable modems. Rural areas without cable of any kind or limited phone lines may not have either option. For the individual subscriber, the two options are also quite a bit more expensive than dial-up Internet access. However, you do get what you pay for, and for those who choose to go with these options, they provide very fast Internet connections, in some cases equal or superior to a **T-1** line.

Whether a computer user connects to a network through a telephone line or cable, yet another layer of protocols must be traversed for that user to reach the resources at the other end of the connection. The Internet has developed into the number one protocol for that purpose. In the case of users seeking access to library resources, both the library and the user must have Internet access (the lack of which is becoming a rarity). Home computer users must subscribe to an ISP such as their local cable or telephone companies or a national service like America Online (AOL). Large institutions often act as their own ISPs, and small institutions often join consortia to establish Internet accounts. Libraries tend to use one of these institutional plans for Internet service.

HOW DO MODEMS WORK?

Modem technology allows someone with a computer, a modem, and a standard telephone line gain access to the resources on a network. The modem translates the data the computer is sending into a format, or **protocol**, that can be sent through standard telephone lines at speeds up to 56Kbps. Users dial into a modem on the other end, which is connected to a network server, log in, and then are connected to the server and its resources. Modems can be either internal or external devices in the user's computer (they plug in as cards in the back of the CPU). The computer will also have communications software installed that coordinates the translation of requests and information that is transmitted through the modem. Telnet was a very popular version of this software in the past and continues to be used today.

The networks of dial-up ISPs are built on T-1 lines. In the classic arrangement of an ISP with dial-up access, a user dials into a server at the ISP and accesses the Internet using a portion of that line. The access speed that a dial-up user has is limited by the modem or other device they are using. This means that a computer directly cabled into a LAN that is connected to a T-1 line will be accessing the Internet at speeds up to 1.544 Mbps, while a user dialing up from home with a 56Kbps modem will connect to the service and access the Internet at 56Kbps. The ISP is serving as a way onto the Internet for the user, but its own connection speed to the Internet is not completely passed along to each individual user. The T-1 line from the ISP to the Internet allows the ISP to accommodate a large number of simultaneous users.

Today, modems have been replaced by "gateway" technology whenever feasible. Network cards installed inside of the computer perform the job of making the connection to the network that modems once did. The card sends a transmission first to a switching station (usually) and then into the main network cable system. Although telephone lines still serve populations without access to a cable connection, large groups of computer users across the country are now served by network lines that use the high speed **Ethernet** data sending protocol. Using a network card, data transmission speeds of about 10Mbps are fairly standard on a typical work day.

LICENSING AND PATRON AUTHENTICATION

A huge issue in all of this sharing is making sure that the right resources are shared with the right user (or the right number of simultaneous users). The agreements that libraries sign with database providers are designed to ensure that only the patrons of the library are allowed to use the resources. Some licensing agreements also limit the number of individuals who can simultaneously use a database. Libraries tend to offer their resources freely to their communities, and this extends to the many electronic resources they make available on their Web sites: library catalogs, collections of links to Internet sites, library tutorials, and other documentation. When it comes to periodical databases and electronic reference tools, libraries need to draw the line at **remote access** to these services.

There are a variety of ways to conform to licensing agreements and provide patron **authentication**, ensuring that only current patrons of a library are accessing a given resource. These options can be divided into one for users within the library and the other for those outside of the library. The outside or remote access option has patrons log in if they are accessing these resources from home or elsewhere outside of the library. This is pretty flexible in that users can connect to the library's Web site from any computer and click on the resource to have the opportunity to log in. Or, in other systems, users can log in once on entering the library's site to gain access to the entire suite of protected resources. The main downside in either case is that people then have to remember a **login ID** and password and the library has to make sure that it regularly updates its database of valid users. That database may take the form of a proxy server, which passes along a user's authentication to any electronic resources included in the server's settings.

Internal authentication of library users is provided by setting up a range of IP addresses with a database vendor. The addresses have been assigned to all computers in a library or an educational institution. Anyone who tries to access the database from a computer with the correct IP addresses gets in; all other users are kept out. This is easier for users in that they do not need to remember login information to get in. It also works well for libraries with many different computers in-house.

Libraries of all kinds must find ways to make their electronic resources available to their patrons, whether in the library or at home. License agreements are generally written to provide for remote access by users, and then the question becomes a technical and educational one for libraries and their patrons. There are many successful examples of individual libraries and library consortia who made remote access work.

QUESTIONS FOR REVIEW

1. Name four tasks or services that libraries make possible using communications technologies.
2. Explain what a LAN, a WAN, an intranet, and the Internet are.
3. What are the pluses and minuses of a wireless network when compared to a cabled or wired network?
4. How does your library connect to the Internet? What Internet access options are available in the area you live in?
5. What are the required parts of a network?

SELECTED SOURCES FOR FURTHER INFORMATION

Alcorn, Louise, and Maryellen Mott Allen. 2006. *Wireless Networking: A How-To-Do-It Manual for Librarians.* **New York: Neal-Schuman.**
Offers explanations of wireless networking equipment and practical advice on its installation.

Boss, Richard W. "Wireless LANs." Chicago: Public Library Association (November 2008). Available: www.ala.org/ala/mgrps/divs/pla/plapublications/platechnotes/wirelessslans2008.pdf.
   A straightforward fact sheet on wireless networks with good links to additional information.

Courtney, Nancy, ed. 2005. *Technology for the Rest of Us: A Primer on Computer Technologies for the Low-Tech Librarian*. Westport, CT: Libraries Unlimited.
   Includes helpful chapters on computer networks, wireless networks, and network security.

Chapter 6

Whither the Library Catalog? Library Systems, Discovery Layers, and Open Source Options

In the previous two chapters, we have examined the hardware and network infrastructure that libraries need to function in today's technological environment. Our attention must now turn to the types of software that makes the library's internal functions and external services possible. Software (aka applications or programs) was defined in Chapter 4 as items that make computers do what we want them to do. That chapter discussed operating systems, the elemental software for a computer, and much of the basic productivity software that library staff members use. This chapter introduces integrated library systems, equally the most elemental software for library operations.

LIBRARY SYSTEMS

Library systems software was devised to computerize a variety of library operations, including materials check-in, cataloging, circulation, purchasing, and the online catalog (also known in the trade as an **online public access catalog**, or **OPAC**). The process of converting these functions to a computerized medium is referred to as library automation. This conversion movement opened up a software market aimed at libraries, permitting the purchase of individual modules (e.g., a stand-alone circulation system) or of all of the modules combined into a suite, referred to as **integrated library system** (ILS) software. The advantage of opting for an ILS product is that installation commands and routines are standardized throughout all of the modules, and the modules can cross-reference data from other modules. Today, ILS products are often augmented by modules from other vendors that are (hopefully) compatible with the ILS. Library systems are not found in every single library, but they are continuing to grow in use, and now thousands of libraries are using them throughout the world. Very few libraries should continue to exist without a library system of some kind (budget permitting).

A huge impetus for the conversion movement to library systems was the Online Computer Library Center (OCLC). Library systems are highly dependent on **MARC (machine-readable cataloging)** records, each of which contains a number of fields full of information about an item in the catalog. These electronic records are not all created by individual libraries as they need them. Rather, they are largely available from bibliographic utilities, companies that maintain large databases of MARC records and make them available to subscribing libraries. OCLC was the original **bibliographic utility**, encouraging its member libraries to contribute their MARC records into a central database for all to share. OCLC provides a variety of services to libraries, but its central purpose is to maintain a huge computer database of MARC records for print, recorded, and electronic items. These records continue to be created when items are purchased and cataloged by the Library of Congress and the other member libraries of OCLC. Libraries contribute their records to the database and then are able to copy them into their online catalogs. It is a tremendous example of cooperation. Through the WorldCat database (available in a public interface at www.worldcat.org), OCLC's member libraries keep track of millions of published items and share information about them.

WHAT IS A DATABASE?

To understand the magic of an automated library system (and many other library resources), it is good to have a sense of what a **database** is. Databases consist of a collection of **records**, which are made up of a number of **fields**, each of which contains a piece of information. Databases meet a very serious need: to organize information in a way that it can be easily searched and retrieved. Computerized databases exist for all sorts of different functions, from managing mailing lists to helping people find full-text periodical articles.

In a bibliographic database such as OCLC, each record in the catalog contains a standard set of categories of information: author, title, publisher, subject headings, call number, etc. These categories are similar to fields, which can contain any information you would like. A database is built on the premise that you can find the individual records that you need for a given purpose, just as **print catalog** users once used individual cards to find books or other items in a library. Databases can also be searched by certain fields, much as a catalog can be searched by author, title, or subject. Electronic databases are much different than a print catalog because of their greater flexibility in choosing among fields to search, and a **keyword** option is usually available that can search across multiple fields at once.

TOOLS FOR THE TRADE

Library systems may be integrated, nonintegrated, or stand alone. An example of an integrated system would be one that has a module (or software program) to handle an online catalog, and another module to handle circulation, and a third module for managing acquisitions, and a fourth for cataloging new items. All four of the modules would work together and share data between them (e.g., the online catalog shows when an item is checked out using the circulation module). This is also called a **multifunction system**. Most integrated systems are bought as **turnkey** systems, with all of their modules developed by a single **vendor**. A turnkey is a technology that is set up entirely by the vendor, meaning that you only need to "turn the key" (i.e., press the power button) to start it up.

The nonintegrated library system might start out as an integrated one. The library begins with a system from a single vendor, but realizes that there are tasks that this vendor cannot solve with its system, or that other vendors can solve more cheaply or effectively. Rather than stick with the modules a single vendor offers, many libraries have chosen to add tools such as **electronic resource management** systems or **metasearch software** (the ability to search multiple electronic resources at once) produced by other vendors. The systems can work together from a communications standpoint, but they are not designed to be parts of a larger whole. While in the early days of library systems it was unthinkable (or perhaps impossible) to proceed with a hybrid system, today the interoperability of systems makes nonintegrated systems a reality. Some have forecast the end of the single-vendor integrated system as libraries now can turn to a palette of compatible modules from various vendors. Not to be lost in this discussion is the added time needed to plan and test the operations of the nonintegrated pieces.

A **stand-alone system** would be one in which there is perhaps just a single module or a combination of integrated (or nonintegrated modules) that are not networked beyond the confines of the system. This situation may be found in smaller libraries that have automated more slowly, adding, say, circulation management first and then deciding to add an online catalog later. Stand-alone systems as a whole tend to be a creature of smaller libraries, where the system runs on just a small number of computers on a LAN (local area network) or perhaps just a single computer. They typically lack features and functions that larger libraries would require but can be quite developed and are certainly affordable options.

LIBRARY SYSTEM COMPONENTS

A library system contains a number of different **modules**. Each is designed to handle or provide a different task or service. Not every system will have each of the following modules, but the five discussed are the most common ones you will find among integrated library systems.

Online Catalog

The **online catalog** is probably the most well known of the modules since it is where the public interacts with the library system.

It allows patrons to search a library's collections. For this reason, the design of the online catalog's interface (how one interacts with and navigates the catalog) is crucial. Today's interface is typically a Web-based interface (or a GUI—graphical user interface) given the prevalence of this interface in operating systems and on the Web (see Figure 6-1). In earlier days (and not so long ago in some cases) online catalogs were limited to a text menu interface. Some libraries have both of these options available, while newer library systems tend to be GUI only. For some libraries, the online catalog menu also includes links to other kinds of library resources, such as periodical indexes or reference databases. In other cases, the online catalog is just linked from the library's Web site.

Cataloging Module

This module is used to add and modify MARC records for the catalog. Each time a new item is added to the collection, a MARC

Figure 6-1
Screenshot of a Web-based OPAC

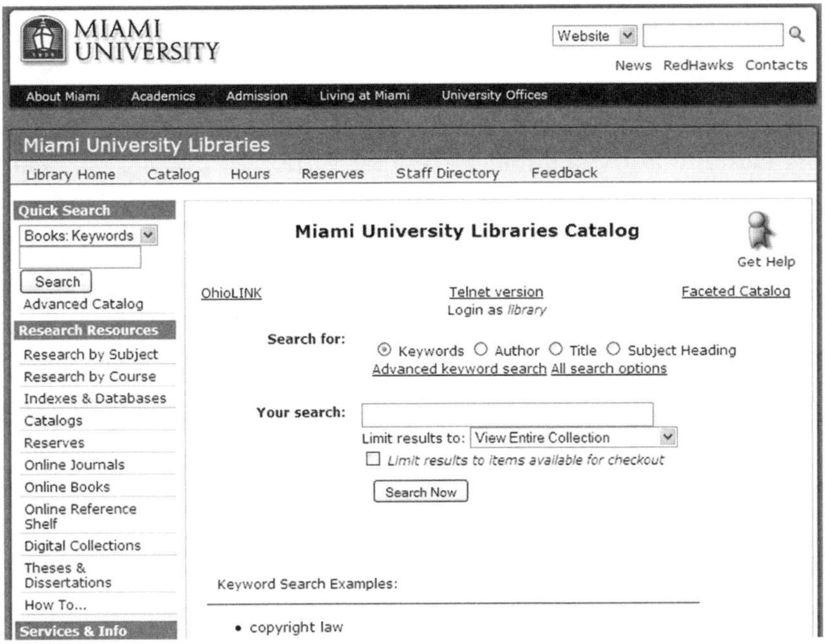

record for it must be included in the catalog. The records can be created from scratch within the cataloging module, or they can be purchased from a MARC vendor (such as OCLC) and then altered to meet local needs. The first option is known as **original cataloging**, where a skilled cataloger examines the item and enters author, title, and publication information into the system and creates meaningful subject headings. The second option is generally known as copy cataloging, where the copied MARC record requires only the addition of a local call number and perhaps other minor modifications.

Acquisitions/Serials Modules

These two modules are actually separate parts of a library automation system, but their functions are rather similar. The acquisitions module is used to electronically order library materials from vendors and then check them into the system as they arrive. The serials module has a check-in function for periodicals that helps the library staff keep track of received and missing issues. The module can also generate claims requests to vendors for these missing issues as well as routing slips to move selected periodicals among library staff members or groups of patrons, such as college faculty members. Both modules can aid library staff in gathering statistics (number of items or periodicals available in a given subject area, for example) and in financial management (generating up-to-date acquisitions budget figures). These tasks are much more difficult under a paper-based system.

As an adjunct service to library systems, libraries have turned to electronic means to select and purchase items for their collections. The process of ordering books and other materials from vendors has automated over time along with other library services. Vendors today are providing sophisticated, Web-based systems for browsing through their catalogs, setting up **collection development profiles**, and placing orders. These systems can be used by single or multiple users at an institution. Faculty members at colleges and universities can even have access to make suggestions for purchases. Some examples of these systems are the GOBI (Global Online Bibliographic Information) system of the Yankee Book Peddler company (www.ybp.com/gobi.html),

Baker and Taylor's Title Source (www.btol.com), Book Whole-salers Inc.'s Title Tales (www.bwibooks.com), and Follett Library Resources TITLEWAVE (www.flr.follett.com/logi). Except for GOBI, all of these services are available for free registration. These systems stand in addition to long-standing (and now electronic) sources such as Books In Print (www.booksinprint .com/bip) and newcomers to the online book information and ordering business such as Amazon.com (amazon.com, which is widely used for library ordering and has a book processing ser-vice available at www.amazon.com/libraries).

Circulation Module

The circulation module (see Figure 6-2) handles the many routine operations of the circulation services department. It can be used to check materials in and out and maintain a record of when items are due. If a patron wishes to place a hold on an item or have an item recalled from another patron, the system can make

Figure 6-2
Screenshot of a circulation module interface

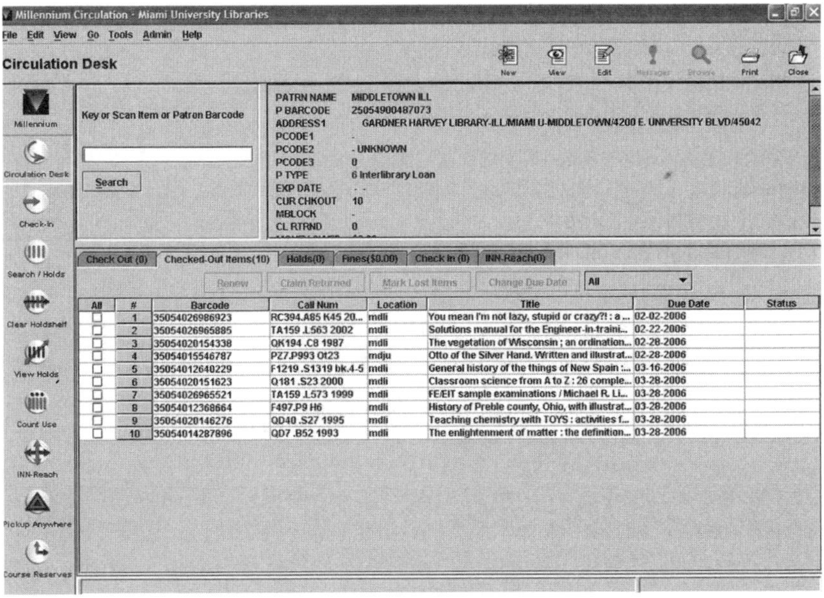

note of the request and send out recall notices. The module tracks overdue fines and damage charges and can generate bills for patrons. It can also generate overdue notices to mail out to patrons. As with the other modules, the circulation module keeps statistics on the number of items circulated and can keep track of circulation by material type and subject area. Circulation modules allow a library staff to replicate their circulation policies in automated form and have the system automatically set due dates, accept holds, etc.

DANCE OF THE MODULES

It is important to understand how these modules interact to make the whole system work. Each module has its own focus, or view, of the overall library system, but an action taken in one module has an impact in other modules. The library system relies on a unique multiple database structure that allows a change in a single item record or patron record to automatically update other records. For instance, when a library patron checks a DVD out, the individual's patron record is updated to indicate that the item is in his or her position and is due on a certain date. At the same time, the item record for the DVD is updated to indicate that the item's status has changed (the DVD is no longer available, but is checked out). This altered status will then show up in the OPAC when another patron searches for the item and locates its record. Similarly, when periodicals are checked in to the system, a notation is made in a check-in record to show that a given issue is now present in the library. This change cascades to a serials holding record, and then is visible as an item record for the periodical in the OPAC. This interactivity eliminates much duplication of effort and makes a library system an extremely powerful tool.

NONINTEGRATED MODULES

In the earlier discussion of hybrid systems, I mentioned two modules that might be added on to an integrated system. Briefly, here are descriptions of four modules that libraries might add on in addition to the ones mentioned previously:

1. Electronic resource management systems are used to help the library keep track of its electronic subscriptions to periodicals and other online resources.
2. Metasearch allows library patrons to search the OPAC, periodical indexes, and other electronic full-text sources from a single search blank (this will be discussed more fully in Chapter 8).
3. OpenURL link resolvers help users identify when their library has the full text of a given periodical article available (more on this in Chapter 8).
4. Digital library products is a generic term for software that helps libraries manage their collections of digital items, whether they are text documents, images, video, audio, or combinations of those.

BENEFITS OF LIBRARY SYSTEMS

Library systems provide a number of improvements to library service:

- The system provides users with a wider variety of ways to search for items at the library than does a print catalog. **Keyword searching** is probably the most obvious addition, but the ability to search by call number or **ISBN** (International Standard Book Number) can be very handy. The more access points you have to a collection of information, the better your chance of finding what you need.
- An online catalog can motivate patrons to use the library more, or at least attract them to the catalog where they may find a larger number of helpful items.
- An online system can help create a technologically savvy image.
- A library system can allow users to access the catalog remotely rather than just within the library.
- Most systems have the ability to link from the catalog to additional electronic resources (periodical indexes, etc.). Whether in a text-based or GUI system, this ability allows for the various electronic resources of the library to be integrated into the catalog.

- Once all of the items in the collection have been added to the system, it is much easier to inventory the collection and provide accurate counts of holdings by subject or type of material.
- Many routine tasks are eliminated or made easier by the addition of a system. One outcome of this benefit is that books and other materials may well end up on the shelf more quickly.

As with anything, there can be drawbacks to a library system. The time-consuming, labor-intensive process of converting from a paper-based system is the primary one. Once the switch is made, the benefits will certainly outweigh any ongoing disadvantages. No library is going to complete the difficult and expensive process to convert to an online system only to find that the benefits will not work for them. Some collections may acceptably be left in a print catalog environment, but these would be tiny, very specialized ones. What I would hope to see is for smaller libraries to join in cooperative efforts to convert to a library system as a library consortium, distributing any temporary disadvantages among the consortium members.

TEN QUESTIONS TO ASK BEFORE PURCHASING A SYSTEM

Life is full of questions to answer, and the process of purchasing a library system is no different. The following is a list of issues to consider before you buy.

1. *How big is the collection?* The answer to this question can have a number of effects. First, if your collection is fairly small, you may not really need an automation system to begin with (or a system may be more trouble to set up than it is worth). Second, the size and complexity of a collection can impact the vendor you choose. Some systems can handle only a small threshold of items, whereas others are unlimited in their capacity. You need to take your future growth into consideration here as well.

2. *How many users will there be?* This question will help you decide whether a stand-alone system on a single computer

(with no other online catalog access) will do or if you expect many simultaneous users. If you do expect to have more than a single user, you can then decide the networking setup you will need and also how many computers you should purchase for in-house use. Be sure to think about how many computers you will need for staff use, including machines at the circulation desk or other service points. For public computers, the total size of your library's community should be considered rather than just the number you expect will be in the library at any given time. The answer to this question will also impact remote access.

3. *Which modules are needed?* Decide which operations of a library system are needed by the library. You may decide that cataloging and circulation are essential but that your existing acquisitions procedures would not transfer well to a particular system's environment. Or you may decide that a fully integrated system is the only logical choice.

4. *How many remote access users should you prepare for?* Remote access is a given for library catalogs. Given that online catalogs are typically Web-based and are not restricted only to logged-in users, there are few barriers to getting into your catalog. The number of simultaneous catalog users can affect the network configuration you use and the power of your server. This is worth discussing with the vendors you are considering.

5. *How long will it take to convert the item records for your collection from cards to MARC records?* This is a process known as a recon. It involves either keying records from scratch based on the information available on cards or copy cataloging records from a bibliographic utility. This is something that the library automation vendor can do for you. However you do it, it is bound to be expensive, time-consuming, and possibly quite frustrating. Just keep telling yourself it is absolutely necessary if you would like to have a working system and do all you can to exert quality control.

6. *Will you weed before converting?* This is a question of process that can have financial implications. You can just

convert your entire collection over to the new system and then weed as needed in the future. However, some libraries decide that it is worth their while to undertake a major weed in advance of a recon so that they save time in conversion. To weed or not to weed becomes part of the planning process for moving to a new system.

7. *What will it take to migrate to a new system?* In this situation you already have a working library system and are moving to a new vendor's system. This is becoming a more and more common situation as most libraries already have systems in place and are either switching systems or upgrading to new systems from their current vendors. Here you need to know how well equipped the vendor is to make this transition for you. Have they ever migrated from your existing system to theirs before? The nice part of this situation is that you already have electronic records for the items in your collection. The potential downside is that some records could be lost in the transition.

8. *Can the user interface of the catalog be modified?* How freely can you alter the appearance of your online catalog screens? Can you change help screens to meet local needs? It would be nice if you had full freedom to rearrange screens at will and easily add additional types of searches to meet your needs. Some systems have major limitations in how modifiable they are. The best you can hope for is some ability to arrange screen items to your specifications and to adjust the help screens.

9. *Is the staff interface acceptable?* We cannot pay all of our attention to the patron interface without thinking of the view that staff will have of the system on a daily basis. Modification may or may not be possible. Still, you need to see if the work staff will use the system for (cataloging items, checking out items, etc.) can be easily accomplished without extra steps. Then you can compare the process in one system to that in another. Also, is help information easily available? Online help has its ups and downs, but its availability can be more convenient than tracking down the requisite volume of the vendor's automation manual.

10. *What are the future plans of your system vendor?* The world of library systems is a fluctuating one. Vendor changes, mergers, and the rapid pace of technological change makes it difficult to assess what the next six months, let alone the next five years, will bring. As you compare vendors, be sure to look at their past track record and at their strategies for the future. Libraries would like to stick with a single vendor for a long stretch, putting off a major change process for as long as possible.

OPEN SOURCE SOFTWARE

Open source software (OSS) has captured the attention of information technology users from across the spectrum. In general, open source offers the promise of easily adaptable software applications that are generally free or low cost initially. The second characteristic in this statement is often misunderstood, but the flexibility of open source software is key to its definition. OSS is software that is created by a collaborative group of individuals and then has its source code distributed to other programmers for them to alter. Individuals can just use the software as it is or change it and then communicate those changes back to a worldwide community of users and programmers. The hope is that the software will be improved faster than a commercial product can be, given that anyone with ability and interest can innovatively improve it and share in the innovations of others.

OSS is often thought of as free software, and this is usually interpreted as free of charge. Two interpretations of "free" are at work here and are often differentiated using the metaphors "free speech" and "free beer." The "free speech" interpretation of OSS means that no one really owns the source code of the software and that everyone should have access to it in order to make improvements. Once those improvements are made, however, a given programmer is able to sell his or her version of the improved software if he or she wishes. The "free beer" interpretation means that the software, its source code, and all later versions should be free for the taking forever. The originators of the open source movement appear to have had "free speech" in mind as their operating plan, while others in the programming community preferred "free beer." Generally, free beer has won out since the source code for most open source applications (all versions outstanding) are freely available in both the intellectual and economic senses. However, the Linux operating system, an early success of open source efforts, hews to the "free speech" side in that while some of its versions are available at no charge, many users install Linux from versions that are sold commercially.

How is open source software used in libraries? Many library staff members use the Firefox Web browser (www.mozilla.com) on their public and staff machines. A number of libraries use Linux on their servers or computers. Quite a large number of library Web sites run on the open source Apache server software (www.apache.org). A variety of projects are either completed or underway to create open source library systems. Other projects include digital image archives, virtual reference software, and electronic reserve packages. The promise of adding needed technology to a library without incurring substantial expenses will keep library staff watching and participating in the open source movement for some time to come.

WHERE DO LIBRARY SYSTEMS STAND TODAY?

Library systems have a long history, and some would say this history has brought us to a period of entrenched vendors and stalled innovation. There is a swell of discontent among library staff with the state of the library catalog and much desire to shake up the current order to better serve library patrons. Three major questions are currently being discussed, with a variety of actual progress made among each.

Will Open-source Systems Make Innovation in ILSs Possible?

As mentioned, open-source software is attractive because it involves a product developed by the community that can be further modified and supported by individuals within that community. Library staff find themselves in a world of library systems vendors in which change is incremental and comes at a high price. Open source library systems have been developed to let innovation run more freely, though the entire process is far from free. Libraries must still maintain the systems and keep staff employed to make adjustments, but the idea is that this is a small price to pay versus the typical route of paying vendors for the initial installation and then annual maintenance fees (plus local maintenance fees and staff time).

Several options exist for open source systems: Koha (www .koha.org), Evergreen (http://open-ils.org), and OPALS (www .opals-na.org), are some established examples, with Koha having the most installations in place. They offer the ability to customize the public catalog side of the operation immensely, adding book cover images, **faceted browsing** (the ability to limit your search by subject heading, date, location, item type, etc., by clicking these choices from a menu on the search results page), and relevance ranking in their searches. Some lack some of the standard modules we might expect in a library system, while others have built fully fledged ILS examples that are up and running. Adoptions are on the rise, and while the initial answer to this question is "yes," only their continued acceptance can put their ability to maintain innovation to the test.

Will a Discovery Layer Interface Make the Catalog More Approachable?

A **discovery layer** is an adaptation of the standard library catalog interface that brings in something of a Google-like simplicity along with a broader reach into information resources. The idea behind it is that library catalogs have become less than approachable to patrons, who would rather use Google to find information. What can be done to reverse this? Well, the discovery layer approach involves moving to a single search blank for users to enter their searches, applying book cover images, faceted browsing, and relevance ranking on the results page, allowing users to tag individual items, and adding in resources beyond those typically found in the catalog (results from periodical databases, Web **search engines**, etc.).

The overall impact is one that can be more appealing to patrons and more inclusive of the vast information resources available through the library (both licensed and free). Both major ILS vendors and open-source options are available to place a more attractive front end on your existing library system (which remains in place). Innovative Interfaces offers Encore (www.iii.com/products/encore.shtml) for its Millennium ILS. AquaBrowser (www.aquabrowser.com) is available for sale to add onto many existing ILSs. OCLC offers WorldCat Local (www.oclc.org/worldcatlocal) as its ILS add-on. On the open source end, you can see VuFind (www.vufind.org), SOLR (the code is at http://lucene.apache.org/solr, and a working example is at http://beta.lib.muohio.edu/drupal), and Scriblio (http://about.scriblio.net). The move is on to change the look of the standard catalog (see Figures 6-3 and 6-4).

Do We Really Need a Catalog?

Even if this look is changed, though, others ask whether this whole catalog idea is one that should endure. The argument runs that catalogs came into being to enable a library's owned items to be organized and searched. There's no question that this invention, starting in the card catalog and working along into the online variety, has helped patrons discover information and locate book and other materials. It is also likely true,

Figure 6-3
Screenshot of the Miami University Faceted Catalog

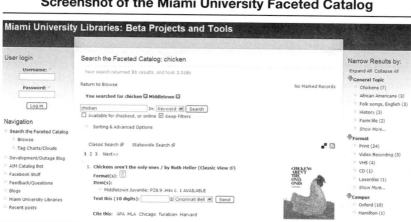

Figure 6-4
Screenshot of the Athens County Public Libraries'
implementation of Koha

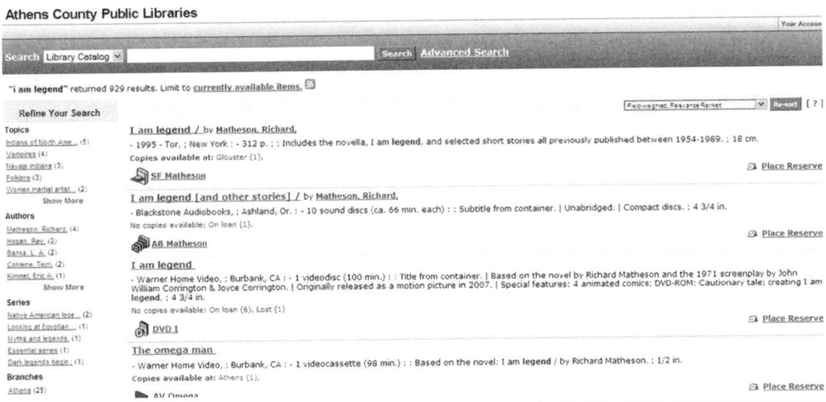

though, that the catalog may be something built more for library staff than for those who use the library. Do our patrons overlook the catalog because it shows only what we (and possibly our consortium partners) own? Do they turn to Google because it shows them a wider swath of information? Do we ignore the larger world of information by concentrating on cataloging only what we own (both physical and electronic) and some selected free e-resources?

Looking back a bit, it seems that there was a move to try to catalog the Web (or parts of it) and bring sites into the system alongside our traditional library resources. Once this failed, due to the immensity of the Web, and our resources grew more and more digital, we now face a catalog that is unable to be complete and unable to compete with Google and other search engines. Maybe the separate catalog should fade away, at least in today's predominant form. Having a more holistic view of information that is not as tied into location or holdings might be a reasonable plan. Somehow or other, though, there must be a way to tie our cataloged information into a metasearch engine along with periodical articles and other digital resources and have one of the new discovery layer options become the new standard interface for libraries.

QUESTIONS FOR REVIEW

1. What brand of library system has your library chosen? Are you happy with its capabilities?
2. Name the common modules in a library system.
3. What is an important characteristic to consider about both the staff or patron interfaces in a library system?
4. What kinds of software do you regularly use in your work?
5. Explain what open source software is.

SELECTED SOURCES FOR FURTHER INFORMATION

Bisson, Casey. 2007. "Open Source Software for Libraries." *Library Technology Reports* 43, no. 3.

> This article introduces the concept of open source software and investigates how these products can be useful in a variety of library applications. Library systems are covered at length.

Blyberg, John. 2007. "Mouse Bites Cat: Taking Back the 21st-century ILS." In *Information Tomorrow: Reflections on Technology and the Future of Public and Academic Libraries* (pp. 31–41), edited by Rachel Singer Gordon. Medford, NJ: Information Today.

> An excellent introduction to the argument for redesigning and reimagining the library system, with key needs clearly articulated. It includes his "ILS Customer Bill of Rights."

Breeding, Marshall. 2008. "Library Technology Guides: Key Resources and Content Related to Library Automation." Available: www.librarytechnology .org.

> A site that includes links to library automation vendors, library OPACs, and lists of articles on library automation trends and topics.

Breeding, Marshall. 2008. "The Viability of Open Source ILS." *ASIS Bulletin* 35, no. 2. Available: www.asis.org/Bulletin/Dec-08/DecJan09_Breeding.html.

> A review of the current implementation of open source ILS options among libraries, with excellent attention paid to the risks and reward of these systems for libraries.

Cibbarelli, Pamela R. 2008. "Helping You Buy ILS." *Computers in Libraries* 28, no. 9 (October): 6–53.

> A review of the features available in most integrated library systems and suggestions on crucial questions for librarians to consider when purchasing a system. Includes a guide to current ILS vendors and their products.

Grant, Carl. 2008. "Gone Open Yet?" *Public Library Quarterly* 27, no. 3: 223–241.

An overview of open source options for libraries. The author encourages librarians to explore and make their own decisions about the usefulness of open source solutions.

The NGC4LIB (Next Generation Catalogs for Libraries) discussion group.
Offers an ongoing conversation on the development of new catalogs. Subscription information and archives are available at http://dewey .library.nd.edu/mailing-lists/ngc4lib.

OCLC Online Computer Library Center. 2008. Available: www.oclc.org.
OCLC's Web site, which can give you a fuller background and description of their services.

OLE (Open Library Environment) Project. 2008. Available: http://oleproject .org.
A project funded by the Andrew Mellon Foundation to investigate methods and approaches to redesigning library systems. The plan is to devise an open-source, community-built library system that will allow libraries to integrate new technologies.

Waller, Nicole. 2003. "Model RFP for Integrated Library System Products." *Library Technology Reports* **39, no. 4.**
Outlines the elements that are required to create an RFP (request for proposal) and provides sample RFPs. Discusses good questions to ask vendors and other considerations for libraries pursuing library systems.

Chapter 7

Storage Devices in Libraries: Paper, Microfilm, DVDs, MP3s, and Flash Drives

As noted in Chapter 1, there came a point in history when people needed to find a way to share and safeguard information. The quest began with oral history and memorization and has continued ever since with new ways to record information. As this chapter will illustrate, people are still finding new ways to contain information and pass it along. They are also creating new types of media, just as words on paper have been followed by sound recordings, film, **hypertext documents**, and so on. We need to understand and be able to use these types of items because libraries, as repositories of information, are bound to see a wide variety of formats. Aside from accessing them and making them available to our patrons, we need to be able to preserve them (or the information in them) for the future.

PAPER

Despite the long list of formats that follow, paper is still the predominant means for sharing written information and still images. Thousands of books are published each year. An ever-growing number of periodicals are available for subscription, though, to be fair, I can see more periodicals moving to electronic-only distribution. Libraries are still buying, shelving, and circulating paper products. Unlike many of the media that follow, the technology of printing on paper has not changed drastically over the past century. The materials for printing have grown cheaper, which has had some bad effects on preservation, but nothing incredibly innovative has happened when we compare this format to the others. Paper is currently a constant for libraries, and it is too early to suggest that its demise is near. Rather than seeing the success of other media for conveying information as a repudiation of paper, we should look at this expansion as a growing diversity of materials, tangible and intangible, that the library needs to provide to its users.

MICROFORMATS

Microformats are fairly traditional formats for libraries, having existed in some form since the turn of the twentieth century. They consist of rolls or single sheets of photographic film with miniaturized images of pages of text or diagrams, etc. The rolls are known as **microfilm**, and the sheets are **microfiche**. Microfilm can accommodate between 1,000 and 1,500 pages per 100 foot roll of 32mm film, which is the standard size used in libraries. Microfiche can hold between 60 and 98 pages per sheet in its standard format. There are versions called ultrafiche that can hold larger numbers of pages. Libraries use microfiche primarily for routine storage of periodicals and special collections of documents (government documents have often been distributed on microfiche in the past). Preservation of periodicals was an early driving force for the creation of microformats, and space preservation has helped prolong it as a medium. Art and medical libraries used microformats for images, and print catalogs were transferred to microfiche in some libraries in the 1980s. Both types of microformats require special reading equipment to view them. There are separate readers available for each format, but many microfilm reader/ printer units can also be used to view and print microfiche.

COMPACT DISC TECHNOLOGY

Compact disc (CD) technology, invented in the early 1980s, has been used for two purposes: recording high quality sound (compact discs) and providing a stable source for recording data such as text and still images, with the additional advantage of being searchable (**compact disc: read only memory**, or **CD-ROMs**). Both types are widely available, and each one has overtaken records and dominate audiocassettes for recorded music and floppy disks for distributing software. Libraries include both types in their collections. CDs are borrowed by music lovers and CD-ROMs may be available with children's software and various other applications. CD-ROMs, the primary format for the "multimedia" craze of the early 1990s, have been available in libraries as containers for digital reference sources (encyclopedias and other tools). They are also included with books as carriers of supplemental material.

The technology consists of round, 4.75-inch discs that are pitted by lasers to retain data. CDs can hold a maximum of 74 minutes of very high quality recorded sound. CD-ROMs can contain up to 600MB (**megabytes**) of computer data and are considered to be very stable. Unfortunately, CD-ROMs are not very good carriers for video because **CD-ROM drives** cannot play video quickly enough to sustain a fluid display. CD players and CD-ROM drives are quite common in society and are also found in libraries (desktop computers routinely have drives that can play CD-ROMs). CDRW (compact disc read/write) drives and blank discs are also widely available for computer users to record their own music or data in the CD format. Again, most desktop computers will routinely have drives that can perform CDRW functions.

DVD TECHNOLOGY

DVD (which stands for nothing, but you will hear "digital versatile disc" or "digital video disc") technology has been around since the late 1990s. It is very similar to CD technology in the following ways: it is the same size as a CD, it uses a laser-pitting process to place information on the discs, and it comes in multiple formats. When we look at those formats, though, we can see the differences between DVDs and CDs. Audio DVDs can hold 50 hours of sound, **DVD-ROMs** (DVD: read only memory) can hold between 4.7 and 17 GB (**gigabyte**) of data, and DVD-Video can hold between 2 and 8 hours of high quality audio and video. DVDs can be single- or double-sided. DVD is a tremendous improvement over CD technology in terms of quantities of data, sound, and video, but it is also a revolution in terms of the speed at which they can be played, which is up to nine times the speed of CDs. The speed issue, combined with its random access to content and its sturdier composition, is what allowed DVD to emerge as the preeminent video storage format over videocassettes.

DVDs do require a separate drive or player to be used. DVD players are commonly available for use with televisions or stereo systems (or a combination) to play the audio and video formats. **DVD-ROM drives** are more commonly included with desktop computers, with a nice feature: they will also play CD-ROMs. DVD provides a tremendous media format that has great potential in many areas. Libraries need to accommodate both DVDs in their audiovisual collections and as a storage medium that can be accessed on staff and public computers. DVDs are the video format of choice for many libraries given that most patrons have DVD players at home. Libraries that provide viewing stations must have DVD players as well. New computers will typically have DVDRW drives installed that allow recording to DVDs. We will need to look ahead to greater use of DVDs for software distribution, multimedia application use, and archival storage.

One current issue with DVD is the appearance of higher quality versions that cannot be played in standard DVD players. HD (high definition) DVD and Blu-ray are becoming more widely available, and they put libraries and their patrons on the spot to purchase updated players. I expect these formats will grow in use quickly and will hopefully see this growth coincide with more inexpensive HD and Blu-ray compatible players.

COMPUTER MEMORY OPTIONS

So many of the methods for storing information covered in this chapter are formats that we find on the library shelves (books, videocassettes, CDs, etc.). With so many electronic library resources today existing on library servers, vendor's Web sites, or elsewhere on the Internet, we need to discuss **magnetic**

media as a storage method. Where do all of the files that make up a full-text periodical index physically sit? Where do you put thousands of hours of digital videos? Generally, they are placed on server hard drives, which can accommodate multiple terabytes (a terabyte = 1,000GB) of data. This is the same situation for almost every document on the Internet. Files are sitting on hard drives and can either be downloaded (transferred directly) to a receiving computer's hard drive or can be backed up to other portable forms of magnetic media.

Magnetic media storage devices work by using electrical impulses to inscribe information in a certain pattern on magnetic material. The material is encased in a container of some kind that can then be accessed by the same device to retrieve the information. We briefly discussed storage device and media options back in Chapter 4. Hard drives, flash drives, floppy disks, and **magnetic tape** all offer storage possibilities for particular purposes.

Hard drives tend to be used to store operating systems, installed software applications, and working or archived files that will be used on a given computer. Current hard drives can contain several hundred GB of data. They can crash or lose files but tend to be pretty safe for data because they stay in one place and are not removed or touched in any way. They are also very convenient to use in that it is easy to save files you are working on to them and then retrieve those files at a quick speed.

Floppy disks, which are not as floppy as they used to be, can be used for moving smaller files around, for running small backups, and for distributing smaller software applications. The once standard 5.25-inch floppy, which was relatively flexible and "flopped" when you shook it, has been replaced by a 3.5-inch model that is hard plastic. There is not much room on a floppy (only 1.44MB) when you compare it to other media formats. Even though we are in an age of files getting bigger and bigger, this is still a fair amount of room for you to store word processing documents or other files that you need to move around with you. Bigger files that exceed the 1.44MB limit can be placed on floppies through the use of compression software of various kinds. Most backup programs will allow you to use multiple sequential floppies to backup files, but there are certainly better options available among the magnetic media. Flash drives, given their small size and dramatically higher memory capacity, will overcome floppies as a source for mobile storage. Finally, floppies are prone to damage (temperature extremes, magnets, etc.) as they are extremely portable and sensitive. I tend to recommend against them and encourage people toward flash drives.

Flash drives (also known as pen drives or key drives) are extremely small hard drives that can be used to move files, software, and even whole operating systems from computer to computer. They fit into a category known as **removable storage**. If an individual is routinely working with large files such as image files, video, or PowerPoint presentations and needs to work on a number of different computers (or even at home and at work), removable storage makes a lot of sense. As well, if you would like to back up a huge number of documents or other data files, removable storage is an easy way to do so. **Zip** and Jaz disks (which look similar to floppy disks but can store between 100MB to 2GB) were a transitional form of removal storage but have now been replaced by flash drives.

More than just moving these files, the flash drive can be a platform for running an OS or application at one machine and then moving on to run the same software at additional machines. These devices work by simply being plugged into a USB port on a computer. They then show up as a separate drive letter on the machine (much as a hard drive or DVD drive will). The drives vary in shape and size a bit, but they are generally just three or four inches long and narrow enough to fit into the USB port slot. With a maximum capacity of 64GB, they are a powerful option for mobile storage. A smaller capacity flash drive of 1GB is a great deal cheaper and smaller than the equivalent number of floppy disks.

Magnetic tape is primarily used as an archival storage medium. Here the magnetic material is not contained in a disk-like item but as a reel that can fast-forward or rewind to locate data, similar to that of an audiocassette. Magnetic tape can store a tremendous amount of data in a compact form, up to several GB of information. The downside of magnetic tape is that information on the tape is inscribed sequentially, meaning that individual files are harder to locate. Individual applications cannot be run from magnetic tapes; rather, program files must be loaded on a hard drive in order to use the application. This medium is excellent for storing data for future use or for completing large backups.

VIDEOCASSETTES

Videotape and the **videocassettes** found in libraries are another example of magnetic media, this time focused on storing video footage. They have existed since the late 1970s. It has only recently been seriously challenged by DVDs as the most popular medium used to store video (although DVDs appear to be winning this battle). Videocassettes contain a reeled, linear tape that provides good quality for video images and their accompanying sounds. They have been widely available in society for some time now and continue to grow in number. Videocassette recorders (VCRs) and players are widely available to enable the contents of videocassettes to be viewed on televisions. They also make it extremely easy to record broadcast television video on videocassette for future use. When coupled with the ability to record video using video cameras, the flexible attributes of this medium have kept it popular for some time. As methods for digitally recording broadcast content and digital video cameras continue to proliferate, this flexibility is no longer the sole domain of videocassettes.

VIDEODISCS (LASERDISCS)

Videodiscs, also known as laserdiscs, were created in the late 1970s to contain high quality audio and video. They resemble extremely large CDs or DVDs and also use laser encoding to hold their data. They also require a special player. They can contain up to two hours of high quality audio and video (one hour per side of the disc) or up to 108,000 high quality photographs and images. They have been used to distribute motion pictures, collections of images, and teaching tools. Videodiscs have appealed to educators because, unlike videocassettes, they can be used interactively for learning purposes. That is to say, you can jump around the material on a videodisc much the same way you can on a CD-ROM or a floppy disk, choosing files or segments in the order you need them. Videocassettes are linear and require you to fast-forward or rewind the tape to get to the section you desire. Their quality is much higher than that of videocassettes, but the amount of available space on them has affected their popularity. Libraries may still have some of these hanging around, but they are certainly not a growing medium.

DIGITAL CAMERAS AND DIGITAL VIDEO CAMERAS

Let's continue the magnetic medium theme but make a brief shift from recorded content to two key tools for recording: digital cameras and digital video cameras. As the discussion of DVDs and earlier video formats shows, the format of choice for captured images and video is digital. The tools are widely available as focused devices with video and/or still image functions, and those functions may also be part of other multipurpose devices (e.g., many cell phones include digital still and digital video cameras). Digital content is mobile; you can move it from the device that captured it to a computer to view it, and then to a DVD to share it, and then to a Web site to make it able to be viewed and downloaded online. Digital content is malleable; if you create it, you can use software to edit it and polish your final product. Digital content is mashable; you can take digital footage and combine it with other digital content (images, video, audio, etc.) to create entirely new content to share. While libraries tend to primarily lend and provide access to "finished" digital content, some may also lend equipment, and it is useful for all of us to understand a bit more about how this content is captured.

Digital cameras are available at a wide range of price points and capabilities. Key elements to consider in choosing a digital camera are the following: (1) resolution (the number of megapixels available, which is a standard characteristic mentioned for digital cameras), (2) video capabilities, (3) optical or digital zoom capacities, (4) memory options, and (5) battery capacities. Briefly, a higher megapixel camera—7 megapixels is a good minimum number to stick with for a quality-but-still-affordable camera—will give you higher resolution images for printing or for resizing for various digital or print purposes. Cameras vary on how much video you can capture with them. Some restrict you by amounts of time, such as one minute, while others will let you record until you run out of memory, but this is a nice extra feature to have. If you decide that you are going to capture extensive amounts of video, you will certainly want to move in the direction of a digital video camera instead.

The zoom issue gets at the type of lens that the camera has. A lens that sticks out from the camera will allow for optical zooming, which is generally preferred over digital zooming (digital zooming can lessen the quality of the resulting image). Here again, it depends on how much zooming you are going to do, and many cameras offer both digital and optical zoom options. Memory-wise, no camera will have much built in memory capacity, so you need to consider which type of removable memory the camera might use. Some common types include CompactFlash, SD (secure digital), or Memory Stick memory cards, with capacities ranging up to 100GB, though sizes below 16GB are much more common. Images can be moved directly from the camera to a computer using a USB or firewire cable or by removing the card and plugging a card reader into the computer. Finally, cameras may use camera-specific rechargeable battery units or they may accept universal rechargeable batteries (often AA size). The second option tends to be more convenient and cheaper since you can have multiple charged batteries on hand to switch out as needed (extra battery units may be more expensive to buy in the long run).

Digital video cameras or digital camcorders operate with some similar characteristics to those of digital cameras. You'll want to have decent zoom potential (10x is the amount I've seen recommended most widely). The cameras save video footage, which takes up a lot of memory, to a variety of removal storage formats. The most common ones are miniDV cassettes or mini DVDs, but some cameras use memory cards for short amounts of video. Some digital video cameras will take still photos as well as video, but they tend to be on the more expensive end. Rechargeable battery units are more standard here, and so long-lasting battery capacities are something to watch for. Cameras can be connected to television or LCD displays to play videos, or you can use firewire or USB cables to transfer video to a computer for storage or editing. A final crucial item to consider with video cameras is the element of sound. Built in microphones are common, but you might also want to add an external microphone for closer placement to the action you're filming or the ability to add a higher quality microphone.

DIGITAL VIDEO COLLECTIONS

Digital video collections are an attractive option for libraries that wish to provide DVD content to remote users or to share it among members of a library consortium. These collections may be created with locally available content, created by members of the library's community. They can also be formed by gaining vendor permission to digitize purchased physical copies of the vendor's titles (hosting the digital video on local servers). Some media distributors offer streaming video services, with library patrons accessing programs from the company's servers. There are also efforts in place in academic libraries to digitize DVDs and videos from their collections that are needed for course reserve (the digitized materials may be retained for future reserve use). Any digitized or originally digital video can be made available as streaming video, where the viewer can watch the video through their Internet connection but does not download a copy, or in downloadable form, if the rights to do so are made available by the video's creator. These options give libraries the opportunity to be flexible in how they make video materials available beyond the standard checking out of packaged video items.

DIGITAL VIDEO RECORDERS

Let me not forget another digital storage mechanism for video: digital video recorders (DVRs). These devices are very popular as ways to store large amounts of video on a hard drive. They are perhaps best known for consumer use in recording large volumes of preset television programs. A set-top device can be added to a television for direct recording to digital. One great benefit of this method is that programs can be watched in uninterrupted enjoyment with commercials removed. Though this element of DVRs has not been put to use in libraries as far as I have learned, another purpose may be in use. Closed circuit television systems used for library security may well record their footage on DVRs rather than VCRs (resulting in easy recording of hours of video without having to change out cassettes). We'll see if other applications develop over time.

AUDIOCASSETTES

Audiocassettes are an older technology, dating from the late 1950s, that have survived by complementing other audio technologies. They coexisted with vinyl records for many years and now do so with CDs. They are also a magnetic medium, consisting of magnetic tape that advances between two reels in a plastic case. Cassettes are relatively inexpensive to produce and can be formatted to carry between 60 and 270 minutes of sound. They are easily damaged and have a relatively short lifespan, so they cannot be used as an archival medium. Their success as a medium meant that many individuals in society had access to the playback equipment they require. This may no longer be the case. Cassettes may still be on hand in libraries, although their linear arrangement makes it more difficult to find an audio track on them than with a CD. Cassettes and cassette players are also small (portable) and cheap compared to other options. Their final moments, especially given the popularity and flexibility of the next medium, cannot be far off.

MP3 FILES AND PLAYERS

Audio files have been available on computers for quite a long time, and they have become widely available on the Web (both legally and illegally). The music industry had been wary for some time of selling individual music tracks online, fearing rampant sharing and copying. While this has occurred at points in the past and continues to occur, the development of stricter controls on file sharing (called **digital rights management**, DRM) and a seemingly inevitable shift away from "container" music sales (album, cassette, CD) toward single track use caused music companies to begin selling (or licensing their recordings for sale by others) online. While audio files can be contained in a variety of file types (.cda for audio CDs, .wma is a Windows media format, etc.), **MP3** (a format that can be played on many different applications and in various makes of players) is the term used to speak about this phenomenon.

Libraries are not directly involved in the collection of individual MP3 files for their audio collections as yet (at least not in large numbers). However, the growth of available downloadable audio and the use of MP3 players could impact our future collections. The **iPod** MP3 player (available in a range of price points) and many other varieties of MP3 players are owned by millions of people. This audience has been approached by libraries so far with the innovation of MP3 versions of books on tape. Services such as Recorded Books and Overdrive offer large collections of popular fiction and nonfiction titles as digital audio books. The titles may be downloaded and played on a computer, burned to a CD, or transferred to an MP3 player.

Some libraries have purchased MP3 players to check out to their patrons with a selection of audio titles placed on them. Others are making use of products from companies such as Playaway: pre-recorded, deck-of-cards sized players with a single digital audiobook on them. These small units are easy to check out to patrons and remove the danger of lost individual CDs from an audiobook set. Others are equipping their public computers for easy CD burning or file transfer to MP3 devices. It will be interesting to watch these developments and see what other information forms are made attractive for an MP3 audience. The various types of storage media that have been discussed are shown in Figure 7-1.

SCANNING TECHNOLOGY

Just a note about something that is not a media format but rather a method for placing information into various mediums. Computer scanners have been improving tremendously over the past several years and the scanners have grown less and less expensive. A computer needs only a scanner and scanning software to transfer physical items, such as periodical articles,

Figure 7-1
Photograph of various types of storage media

photographs, and other items, into digital form. **Optical character recognition** (OCR) software, coupled with scanners, can also be used to turn typewritten or printed copies of text into word processing documents that can be manipulated. Scanners differ in terms of their resolution (600 dots per inch [dpi] is a good minimum) and their color (24–30 **bits** color is acceptable). Higher end scanners would be preferable for image scanning.

Libraries have been using scanners to produce digital versions of archival documents in order to display and archive them. They have also proved popular for adding images or documents into library Web sites as part of the Web design process. Another common task is the creation of electronic reserve collections for academic libraries, wherein periodical articles and other publications are scanned into electronic file formats and made accessible over the Web to students. The growing involvement of libraries in using scanners to create digital versions of information will have an impact on the eventual archiving of these materials. This interest is often aimed at preserving rare originals and making them available to the public.

YOU *CAN* TAKE IT WITH YOU

Library patrons expect to be able to take library items home with them, and now there are many methods to do so. As libraries' collections continue to grow in their additions of new media types, the ability to copy, print, e-mail, download, and scan items should be provided. Copying and printing are longstanding services in libraries and can almost be overlooked in a discussion of new technologies. E-mail is an option that many electronic resources include for users to enter an e-mail address to send an article or reference book entry to themselves or others. The ability to save full-text articles to flash drives or other media is also helpful. As mentioned previously, scanning is less common in libraries but would meet the needs of users who would prefer a document in a digital format.

Copying and printing, though they have been in libraries for many years, are affordable technologies, and costs are generally passed along to patrons. Scanning is relatively cheap from an equipment standpoint but could be fee-based to offset hardware and training costs. The key here is to consider what users prefer in your environment and then try to make it happen. It is easy for libraries to get stuck in a mode of not allowing particular services (or not pushing for a vendor to include a service such as e-mailing articles) only later realizing that there is not much of a barrier to making the service happen.

ARCHIVAL ISSUES

Libraries have an interest in storing information, both in its original format if possible and in another one if needed. There are a variety of considerations to make when considering how to store information for the future. A good spot to begin is with an idea of how long the formats covered above will last. Table 7-1 lists the time period you can expect these formats to last if they

Table 7-1
Table of archival longevity of different media

Storage Medium	Lifespan
Microfilm and microfiche	200 to 500 years
Books and paper	100 to 500 years
CDs, DVDs, Videodiscs	10 to 100 years
Magnetic media (videotape, audiocassettes, floppy disks, flash drives, hard drives, magnetic tapes)	10 to 100 years

are kept under optimum conditions (see the Jones article for more details). These conditions require that documents or items are untouched by human hands and remain in a room kept at 50 degrees Fahrenheit and 25 percent relative humidity.

No one expects that most materials will ever be kept at the optimum level of conditions. It is interesting, though, that the newer media formats are not predicted to last for anywhere near as long as the more traditional formats. What do the numbers in Table 7-1 mean? Well, they should give libraries hope that some of the formats they have heavily invested in (paper and microformats) will be around for a while. As well, they make clear the fact that in order to keep some media long term, a change of container or even a change of formats will be needed at some point down the road. The conversion of images in a book (via a scanner) onto a Web page for display and then onto a CD-ROM for archiving purposes or other use is already being done and will continue. The following issues need to be considered about archiving:

1. The hardware and software requirements for viewing or hearing a given format need to be considered before you choose it to archive items. It would be a shame to choose a format if its hardware or software became unavailable over time. This is almost unavoidable, however, and so archival collections often include not only the media but its hardware and software that will be needed in the future.

2. As mentioned, some thought needs to be given to the best format to keep or whether a new format should be chosen for a given item. Should you keep the eight-track tape of the Doobie Brothers or switch to a CD? Or should you copy it over to a DVD? Or create individual MP3 files for the tracks? Many media allow for easy transfer to a new format for preservation purposes (e.g., copying the contents of floppy disks to a CD-ROM using a CDRW drive). Others are more time consuming and/or have copyright implications, such as scanning a book page by page.

3. Can a highly controlled storage environment for archiving items be provided by a library? This factor can affect what you save and how long you can expect items to remain in good condition.

4. Consider maintaining multiple copies of items that should be archived. Place one in storage and circulate or use the other.

5. Will materials in electronic format remain in high enough use to even bother changing their storage format as time goes on? This is a question for all materials: are they truly of interest to future generations and therefore worth saving? If they are, you need to be thinking of the best ways to save them. This is already an issue for electronic formats, which are much less stable than paper.

6. Will your nonelectronic formats continue to be used so heavily that they will not last very long? Sometimes this can be solved by purchasing multiple copies, but this is not a financially sound plan for all items. How far do you let a useful item go in regular use before it is too damaged to preserve in another format?

7. And what about electronic formats? Will we be able to save our e-mails, Web page versions, Word documents, and digital images for the enjoyment and edification of future generations? Plans need to be made to backup, archive, and pass along files as individuals leave positions. Too often hard drives are simply reimaged and the historical record is left blank.

Libraries need to seriously consider their archiving options and think about how important preservation is to their overall missions. With careful planning and continuing developments in archival technology, these decisions should grow easier over time.

DYING TECHNOLOGIES?

Just for fun, let me mention some technologies that are basically dead. New titles are rarely if ever distributed in these formats and they have been superseded by current technologies. Just looking at this list of technologies should be a sobering moment for those of us for whom these technologies were a lasting (or at least momentary) standard: vinyl records (LPs and 45s), filmstrips, 16mm film, eight-track tapes, floppy disks, zip disks, audiocassettes, and videocassettes. Who will join the list next? My money is on CDs with the explosion of MP3s. Paper? Definitely not yet (and maybe never). Table 7-2 shows current types of media and the storage formats used to contain them.

QUESTIONS FOR REVIEW

1. What are the benefits and downsides of using microformats to store information?
2. How are CDs and DVDs different? What is the technological feature or issue that makes them substantially different in use?

Table 7-2
Current storage formats used for different types of media

Media	Storage Media
Text and still images	Books, periodicals, microformats, computer file storage
Computer files	CD-ROM, DVD-ROM, hard drives, floppy disks, flash drives
Video	Videotape, DVD, videodiscs, computer files
Audio	Audiocassettes, CDs, DVD, MP3 and other computer files

3. How do flash drives and hard drives differ?
4. Name two implications of choosing archival storage formats for information.
5. Does your library offer scanning, copying, printing, downloading, and e-mailing as options for patrons to take articles and other items home with them?
6. Do you remember using any of the dead or dying technologies? Do you still use any of these technologies?

SELECTED SOURCES FOR FURTHER INFORMATION

"CoOL: Conservation OnLine: Resources for Conservation Professionals." 2008. Available: http://palimpsest.stanford.edu.
> An excellent and ever-growing collection of information on the preservation of materials in all formats.

Crawford, Walt. 2003. "Losing the Legacy of Drives and Ports." *Online* 27, no. 4 (July/August): 59–60.
> The author speaks of the end of floppy disks and parallel ports and the model this provides for switching to new media and keeping older peripherals working on new computers.

Donohue, Nanette. 2008. "Nurturing Your Media." *Library Journal* 133, no. 19: 32–35.
> The article covers the growth of audiovisual formats available to libraries and how to add and weed them.

Driscoll, Lori. 2006. "File Storage (and More) in a Flash." *Journal of Access Services* 4, no. 3/4: 173–177.
> Covers the uses of USB flash drives in library settings.

Jones, Virginia A. 1999. "How Long Will It Last? The Life Expectancy of Information Media." *OfficeSystems* 99 (December): 42–47.
> Great background information on the lasting power of the different types of media.

McClain, Buzz. 2008. "Digital Downloads on the Rise." *Library Journal* 133, no. 10: 1–2.
> Discusses the growing use of downloadable video in libraries and what impact the emergence of blu-ray DVD discs will have on libraries providing them for checkout.

Peters, Thomas A. "Digital Audiobook Services Through Libraries." *Library Technology Reports* 43, no. 1 (2007): 5–40.
> A survey of the digital audiobook options available to libraries.

Wilkins, Jesse. 2005. "Migrating to Better Media." *AIM E-Doc Magazine* 19, no. 1 (January/February): 17–18.
> Discusses the process of moving archival data among storage media.

Chapter 8

Library Databases and Electronic Resources: Full-text Periodicals, E-books, and E-reference Collections

Library periodical databases and other electronic resources are heavily used as information sources by library staff and patrons. They are some of the ends accessed by the means covered in Chapter 5: the Internet and local **networks** and the network cards, modems, and software needed to connect a computer to them. Electronic resources, present in libraries for over 35 years, have continued to grow in functionality, variety, and complexity as well as number. These sources have influenced libraries' acquisition of more and more computers to accommodate patron access. This chapter details the types of electronic resources used by libraries and the impact of their use.

AVAILABILITY OF ELECTRONIC RESOURCES

The resources described in this chapter are primarily available via the Web, though this was not always the case. Historically, electronic resources were available only through a direct modem **dial-up connection**. A library would use a computer with a **modem** to connect to a single database or to an online service that offered several different databases (e.g., Dialog or

BRS). In time, versions of the databases became available on CD-ROM, which helped libraries avoid costly dial-up connection fees when they installed the CD-ROM locally.

CD-ROMs

While dial-up users paid an annual fee plus a charge for each minute connected, CD-ROM users would pay a single annual fee that could end up being cheaper than staying connected for many hours over a year. The CD-ROMs could be placed on stand-alone computers or be networked for multiple stations or even multiple libraries. Networking a CD-ROM brought in its own expenses, as libraries would have to pay additional fees to give multiple users access to the resource. Libraries could make a CD-ROM available to a set group of computers (e.g., six networked computers within the library) or to a certain number of concurrent users across a larger network (e.g., the computers on an entire college campus).

CD-ROM-based reference resources have generally left libraries as CD-ROM networked products moved to Web-based versions. With the availability of the Internet as an access mechanism, pay-by-the-minute fees have been transformed into annual subscription costs priced on user headcounts, which are based on enrollment in academic and school libraries or registered borrowers in public libraries. Libraries now pay to connect an entire library and its computers and/or to handle a certain number of simultaneous users in the library's community who connect via the Web. Users no longer need to be connected to a local network to gain access to the resource; as long as they are affiliated with the library or its parent organization, they can use the huge network of the Internet for access. Changes in communications technology have increased the flexibility of using these resources for staff and patrons alike.

Periodical Indexes

Periodical indexes like the *Reader's Guide to Periodical Literature* were among the first electronic reference sources. It is quick and easy to search for article citations in a database by specific fields or by keywords. Add in abstracts and links to full-text articles and these sources become even more convenient for and valuable to library users. Such "one-stop shopping" for articles is possible from within the library or at home. Some excellent examples of general and subject-specific periodical databases are those provided by the ProQuest, Gale, and EBSCOhost families of databases.

The current situation represents a drastic change from the periodical research process of 20 years ago. Then it was a time-consuming process that involved flipping through annual volume after annual volume of a periodical index. When I was in college, I would thumb through printed indexes such as *Reader's Guide* or *Social Sciences Index* to find articles that would work for my topic. Those indexes were arranged in alphabetical order by subject heading, and there were times when it was hard to choose the right heading to use. Once I found citations for articles I had to determine whether or not the library I used owned the periodicals they appeared in. A printed volume alphabetically listed all of the periodicals and gave their locations in the library. I would head to the periodicals area of the collection or up into the stacks depending on which periodical I was after and track down the correct issue. In some libraries you had to fill out a request slip for each periodical so that the staff could bring the issue to you (patrons were not allowed to browse the issues by themselves). Then I would head over to the photocopying area and start the slow process of copying each article. The situation today is heaven by comparison.

The major difference has been the widespread addition of full-text periodical articles to the databases. Publishers and database vendors have worked out agreements to make many thousands of periodicals available in **full text**. For instance, through our university and our regional consortium, patrons at my library can access over 30,000 full-text periodicals. We can speak of "electronic journals" in libraries as a number of different items:

- There are electronic versions of printed periodicals that are made available on the Web by their publishers on a subscription basis (*Science Magazine* at www.sciencemag.org is one example of this). Libraries gain access to the digital version by subscribing to the print periodical and then linking to the Web version in their catalog record for the periodical.

- Individual full-text articles from journals and magazines can be found in electronic periodical indexes.
- Some journals are published in only digital format on the Web and may be free or available via subscription (see the Directory of Open Access Journals at www.doaj.org for a directory of free scientific and scholarly e-journals).
- A number of different publishers' journals may be collected in a single collection by a library or by a regional consortium. The articles in the collection may be browsed or searched as a group or can be linked from periodical databases that the library or consortium offers. An example of this can be seen at the OhioLINK Electronic Journal Center (journals.ohiolink.edu) (Figure 8-1).

Libraries are dependent on these electronic periodical sources, and their use will only grow as more titles become available. Publishers appear to be more and more willing to make their previously print-only content available online.

Electronic Books

The phenomenon of electronic books (**e-books**) brings a new way of experiencing books to the world. Digital versions of

Figure 8-1
Screenshot of OhioLINK Electronic Journal Center

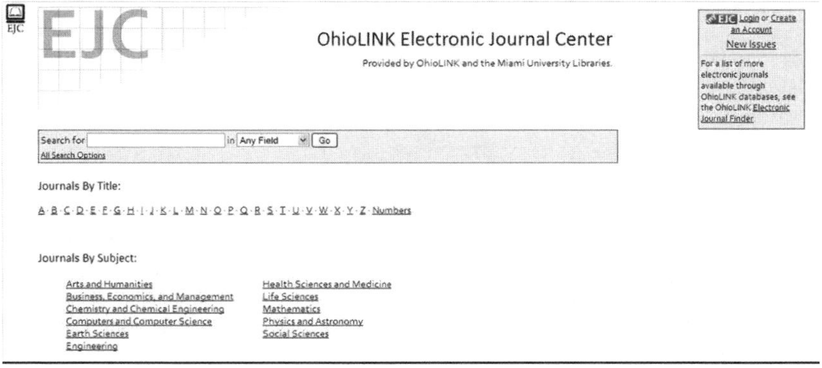

books are created in both text and audio editions and made available for purchase by libraries and individuals as Web-based resources or downloadable files for reading or listening to at home or elsewhere. While there has been a move to digitize books that are no longer under copyright protection and post them on the Web for years (see Project Gutenberg [www.gutenberg.org], Figure 8-2), commercial e-books consist of a mixture of newer and older titles. Some companies who distribute them require that you use their specialized software to view them, while other vendors may allow them to work on a variety of e-book readers and other devices. Typically, the software allows you to place bookmarks in an e-book and change text size, among other features. All e-book publishers protect their titles through a process known as digital rights management (DRM), in which various technologies are used to limit copying and printing (thus staying in line with copyright protections on the title). Vendors such as netLibrary and Overdrive allow you to download text and audio e-books from their collections to various mobile devices (e.g., cell phones and MP3 players) or your computer. Another alternative for audio e-books is Findaway World's Playaway digital audio players, with which individuals or libraries purchase a player device that comes preloaded with an individual book title.

Figure 8-2
Screenshot of Project Gutenberg Web site

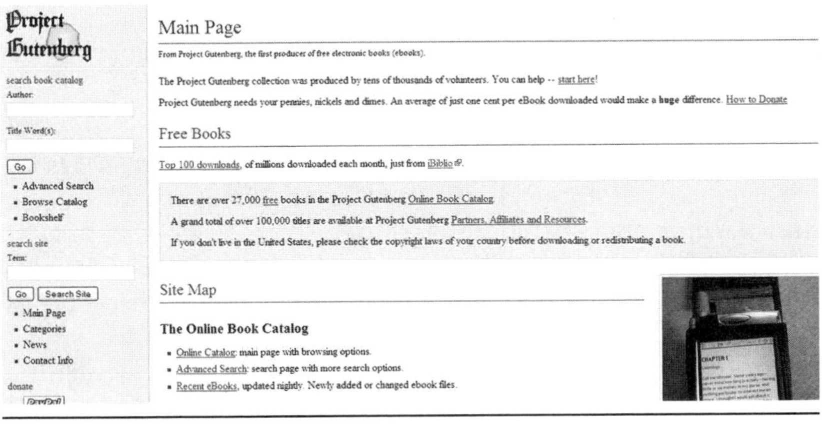

It is hard to tell what this trend means for the traditional book collections of libraries. At this point, most individuals still prefer reading the printed word over the screen word, and this has likely worked against the widespread acceptance of e-books. An ever-growing volume of titles, new developments in reader devices (like the Sony Reader (http://en.wikipedia.org/wiki/Sony_Reader) and the Amazon Kindle (http://en.wikipedia.org/wiki/Kindle), and the introduction of audio e-books have kept this experiment from ending. We are starting to see situations in which libraries only own e-book versions of some publishers' titles. Safari Books Online (www.safaribooksonline.com) is an example of a service libraries can use to access multiple technology book publishers' works online, freeing them from buying print copies to titles that are quickly outdated. The day will come when some popular titles are published only electronically, and libraries will need to find ways to provide and circulate them.

Electronic Reference Collections

Just as the availability of full-text articles makes research easier, online access to reference sources is a boon to the library's community. Sources include almanacs, dictionaries, directories, encyclopedias, literary criticism collections, and many other selected sources. Most often, they are existing reference sources that are now available electronically. **Electronic reference sources** today are a bit of a hybrid of periodical databases and e-books. Some were designed as searchable resources specifically for the online environment, and others have moved from print to electronic format while maintaining the ability to browse them page by page in addition to keyword searching.

Libraries will sometimes switch over to an electronic version rather than buying a new edition of a print source. Other libraries will maintain both print and electronic copies of a source. Improved searching is a huge advantage, as is having access to regularly updated versions of the sources. These sources can also be exciting for their multimedia aspects, bringing in sound (e.g., the ability to listen to Martin Luther King speak rather than just reading his words) and video (e.g., watching the human immune system attack a virus in a computer model) to help users appreciate and understand the material. Not to be missed from this discussion is the fact that these **electronic resources** are more widely available than their print predecessors, bringing the full-text, image-bearing source to computers throughout a library and into the user's home.

ELECTRONIC ACCESS ISSUES

We will consider a number of advantages and disadvantages of electronic resources further in the following sections. Before that, though, a number of issues relating to their access must be addressed.

Multiple User Identification

Libraries can provide simultaneous access to electronic resources for multiple users. There are a variety of issues to concern ourselves with when we consider the access we wish our community to have to a resource. **Multiple user access** tends to be the norm for most resources. We need to consider where we would like to provide access from (just the library? classroom use? home use?), who we would like to provide access to (everybody? faculty only? library card holders?), and how we are going to make sure that only our designated patrons can get into the resource (known as authentication).

Authentication is crucial for remote access because the licensing agreements we sign when we subscribe will specify our responsibility for ensuring that only authenticated users are using the resource. It can be accomplished by having remote users log into the library's proxy server (providing a user number—library card number, student ID, etc.—and a PIN number or password) before passing users on to the resource itself. This can also be done from within the library by identifying to the vendor of the resource that computers with a certain range of IP addresses are acceptable users.

Technological Requirements

The other access issue beyond meeting authentication requirements is the technology issue: what technology components do a library or an individual need to access the resource? This can include the speed of an Internet connection, the minimum characteristics for a computer, the version numbers of the Internet **browser software**, and the speed of a computer's CD-ROM drive. We need to be aware of the minimum requirements for a resource both for equipping our in-house computers and for deciding whether enough of our patron base can use the resource remotely. The information must be provided to users so that they are aware. As well, a library needs to make enough computers available to accommodate users. For staff-oriented resources, budgeting to upgrade staff computers is needed.

Cost

Cost is noted as a potential minus of electronic resources. In some cases, electronic resources can be bargains for a library when compared to purchasing the print resource or resources the electronic source includes. This can stand out in the case of full-text periodical resources where you might cancel a print subscription as well as the microfilm for a title, realizing substantial savings. On the other hand, some electronic resources will require that you maintain your print subscription to the same source for a certain amount of time, thus forcing you to pay twice for the same item. Careful consideration needs to be made whether an electronic resource will be a feasible expense. Beyond the subscription cost, libraries need to consider the staff time involved in updating software or loading updates to the database itself. In the case of databases that are maintained on a library's own server, the maintenance of the database files and their updates can differ in the time required from resource to resource.

In the case of separate subscriptions to full-text periodicals or electronic journals, libraries face a situation not much different from the one they see with print serial collections. Costs for serials rise dramatically each year, and libraries may find themselves unable to continue with certain electronic subscriptions. The most striking situation has been among scholarly publications and some large publishers such as Elsevier. A number of academic library consortia have had to threaten (and some to fulfill their threat) to cancel their subscriptions from a given publisher to head off substantial price increases from year to year. There is also an "open access" movement afoot in academic circles to make research articles available online at no charge to the scholarly community, bypassing the expensive subscription prices that libraries and others must pay for scientific publications. A loose coalition of scholarly associations, libraries, and publishers is working to make this a workable situation for everyone involved.

Canceling Print Sources

When we have, either by design or happenstance, duplicated one of our print sources with electronic ones (reference books or periodicals), it will probably occur to someone that we should cancel the print version. This happens quite frequently with periodical databases or with **source aggregators** like Lexis-Nexis, which includes a variety of full-text periodicals and reference sources in its databases. This can certainly save us money. The potential downside is that if a particular source is ever removed from the electronic resource, we may end up with a gap in our collection. In libraries where the current version of a source is used to the exclusion of any earlier ones, the impact of this loss may be small. However, in other situations, missing a year (or two) of a heavily utilized periodical title can be disastrous and confusing to patrons ("Why don't you have 2004 issues for this title?"). We need to remember that our subscription to an electronic resource does not guarantee that it will remain the same over the course of the subscription. And, to be fair, many resources improve their electronic versions over time.

Organizing and Integrating

Libraries have long been focused on bringing disparate resources together and organizing them so that they can be found and used. The question libraries face now is how can electronic and print sources be together so that they can be used effectively without one type or another getting lost. On the staff side, library staff must understand where and when to use print resources and where and when to use electronic ones. The issues on the public side of electronic resources are much the same. When we arrange electronic resources on our library Web sites, how can we be sure to lead our patrons to print sources when they are the best ones to use? **Online pathfinders** for a given topic that list electronic and print sources side by side can help. For example, see Figure 8-3, the Miami University Libraries' Research by Subject pages (www.lib.muohio.edu/subjects), or the Ohio State University Libraries' Gateway to Information (http://library.osu.edu/sites/thegateway). Another alternative for libraries is LibGuides (www.springshare.com/libguides), a subscription-based service that provides for easy creation of subject-related guides. Library staff must also be educated to lead patrons to the best source, not just the easiest one to find on the shelf or the Web site.

A related integration issue is that of connecting potentially several sources or collections of full-text periodicals and the

Figure 8-3
Screenshot of Miami University Libraries' Research by Subject page

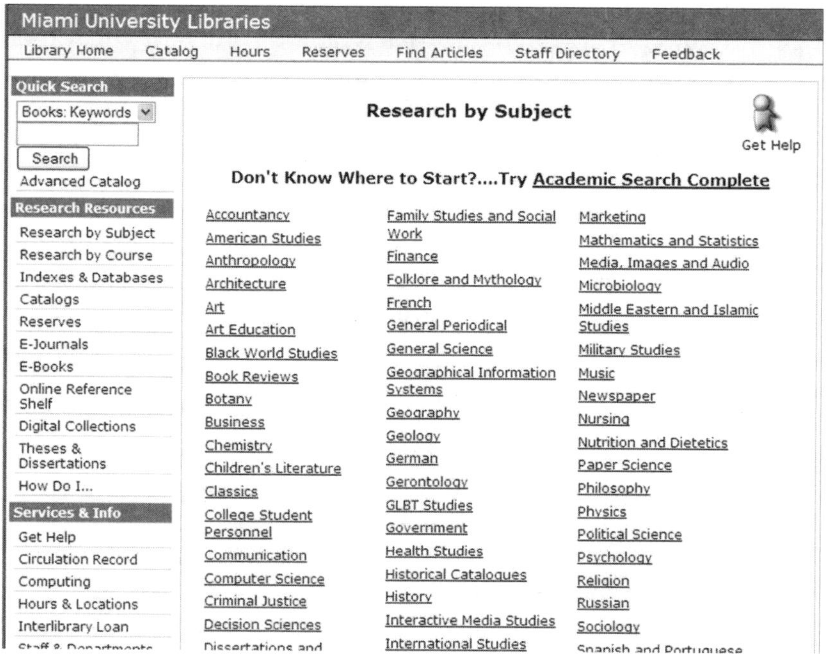

library's print or microfilm periodicals with periodical indexes. Library users can expect that most periodical databases will have their own selections of full-text coverage. A method for connecting each individual database's full text so that a search in Periodical Index A will show links to full-text articles from Periodical Index B, Electronic Journal Collection X, and Periodical Index A, is called **OpenURL** (briefly mentioned in Chapter 6). OpenURL is a protocol for making connections between the indexing databases and the full-text sources through an OpenURL server that includes a database showing periodical title coverages and interlinkages. An excellent example of this in action is OhioLINK's OLinks service (olinks.ohiolink.edu).

Searching

"Why can't we just search all of these tools at once?" This question has jumped out at many a library staff member and library user confronted with a sometimes overwhelming number of electronic resources. Given that the electronic resources described previously (irrespective of type) are all available electronically and are all able to be searched by keyword, it is possible to pursue metasearch: searching multiple sources from a single search blank. Metasearch is also known as federated searching. The existence of Internet search engines that allowed for metasearch, such as Clusty (www.clusty.com) and Dogpile (www.dogpile.com), was also a motivating factor for developing metasearch in library resources. Between systems created in-house by library systems staff and commercial products, metasearch has been implemented in hundreds of libraries.

The concept is fairly straightforward: a library can have an option available on its Web site for users to simultaneously search the OPAC, a number of periodical databases, a locally held collection of electronic documents, and the Internet at large. Several arrangements are used to make metasearching work, and all can work well depending on the library's environment. The "chef's choice" allows users a quick method to enter a search that runs in a group of resources predefined by the library. "Library buffet" allows users to choose the specific resources (from an alphabetical list) that they would like to search, creating their own specialized search strategy. Finally, the "TV dinner" metasearch approach provides users the choice of several sets of resources, usually grouped by subject matter (e.g., nursing, geography) or type of resource (e.g., newspaper databases, library catalogs). A given library may offer one or more of these options.

Results from metasearches may be separated into results sets from each resource searched or can be combined in a single list based on the relevance of the results. For instance, in the first case you might see the first 12 articles from Periodical Database A, then the first 12 articles from Periodical Database B, and then the first 12 items in the library catalog. Links will be available from each resource to continue your search further in that resource. The result is a nice visual sampling of how well each resource can accommodate your topic and can help you choose the best source or sources to pursue the search. The second case shows the power of metasearch even more in that (with good software) the most fitting set of articles, books, Web sites, and e-reference source materials are presented for your topic. You are then able to scan down the list of results without worrying about where the items have come from.

The disadvantage of metasearching is that it is bound to produce a large number of results, which could prove confusing to users. Libraries cannot count on even the best metasearching software controlling the relevance of results for very broad searches such as "war" or "America." It is certainly true that users are probably better off learning about specific tools so that they can selectively choose the best resources. However, this is very much a librarian way of thinking; we cannot expect our users to have or take the time to learn what we know. There are research needs for which a one-stop search option would save the time of the user. An alphabetical list of 50 or 200 databases can be difficult to dive into. Tying together many, if not all, of the resources in our collections presents users with a fuller picture of what a library has available for them.

Options for metasearch include both commercial and open source options. Library Find (http://libraryfind.org) is an open source, freely downloadable software option made available by the Oregon State University Libraries (produced with funding from the Oregon State Library). Ex Libris Metalib (www.exlibris group.com/category/MetaLibOverview) is an example of an add-on module to a library system that can search catalog and periodical indexes at once. Two long-time metasearch products— WebFeat (www.webfeat.org) and Serial Solutions' 360 Search (www.serialssolutions.com/ss_360_search.html)—have recently joined forces and are planning on a combined product in the near future. One last, free option is to build your own metasearch service using the Google **Custom Search Engine** (CSE) service (www.google.com/coop/cse). The service allows you to plug in Web site URLs to build the CSE and then search all of the sites from a single search blank. It's not beautiful, but it's free and extremely easy to create.

Training and Education

Training is crucial to the successful use of electronic resources in a library. If patrons do not understand how (or when) to use the resources, and if staff join them in this ignorance, the library will have wasted a lot of money and will not served its patrons. Any implementation of electronic information sources needs to be accompanied by intensive staff training. Part of this training needs to be aimed at how staff members can help educate patrons who have questions about the new resources or are encountering them for the first time. This should be done in addition to any formal public instruction program the library may have. One effective means for providing quick training that is easy to review (and great for visual learners) is **screencasting**. One great set of these brief video tutorials may be found at the ANTS (Animated Tutorial Sharing Project) collection on Screencast.com (www.screencast.com/users/ANTS). Remember that resources can be used effectively and live up to their potential only if those who use them know what they are doing.

ADVANTAGES AND DISADVANTAGES OF ELECTRONIC LIBRARY RESOURCES

We have already looked in this chapter at some positive reasons for utilizing electronic information sources. Following are advantages and disadvantages of these resources and their use, not all of which apply to each category of resource. These lists will provide the reader with background information that will help in the next section's discussion of some overall issues raised by these resources.

Advantages

1. Electronic resources can be easier to search because they offer more varied search options than do print-based resources. They are also more efficient to use because no paperwork is involved (jotting down or printing citations, etc.).
2. Related to #1, electronic resources are located on the Web and use similar interfaces to other search engines that users may already be familiar with. People are used to turning to the Web as a central location for information-seeking activities, so why not place library resources in easy proximity?
3. Electronic resources provide services that are not duplicated in other formats, such as the integration of full-text articles within periodical indexes.
4. The resources are more accessible than print resources; they can be used by multiple users at the same time and can be made available remotely to the library's community.
5. Using electronic resources can save space in libraries; using full-text online periodicals rather than microfilm or bound periodicals or electronic reference sources in place of reference books.
6. These resources are cheaper to access in the long-run and are easier to update since current data can be added to a central site that is available to all users of the resource.

Disadvantages

1. Electronic resources can be prohibitively expensive for some libraries. They certainly require libraries to carefully examine what they are getting before they subscribe.

2. The resources can stop working at inopportune times, due to either local networking failures or difficulties at the central site.
3. They can be difficult to browse through; keyword searching brings up only exactly matching items as opposed to flipping through a periodical index or reference book.
4. Electronic resources may not be exact replicas of existing print versions or may lose information sources over time, especially in the case of full-text periodical resources, which may lose the rights to provide certain periodicals.

In general, electronic library resources force a library to ask some hard questions about its provision of services. When we move from print to online, we need to know what we will do when the resource is not available (what is our backup plan?). We need to consider how providing full-text resources will change what is printed in the library and how many reams of paper we will start using in a month (or a day). The good thing is that electronic library resources can expand the choices our patrons have. The difficult element is that as we add these resources we grow more and more dependent on resources we have little control over and barely any ownership. The reality is that electronic resources are an inevitable addition for any library, and the best bet is to pursue cooperative licensing arrangements with other regional libraries. This is the present and future of libraries.

QUESTIONS FOR REVIEW

1. Describe the different ways that a library might have access to full-text periodical articles.
2. What are two advantages and two disadvantages of electronic resources?
3. What is a key difference in today's use of electronic resources when compared to the early days of these resources?
4. Explain metasearching. Does your library offer this service?

5. Do you feel adequately trained in the use of electronic resources in your library? Who in your library or elsewhere could help you learn more? (Remember the resources in Chapter 2.)

SELECTED SOURCES FOR FURTHER INFORMATION

"CUFTS Resource Comparison." 2008. Burnaby, BC: Simon Fraser University Library. Available: http://cufts.lib.sfu.ca/tools.shtml.
This resource provides libraries with the ability to compare two to four periodical databases with one another for overall coverage and full-text access to periodical titles.

Freund, LeiLani, John R. Nemmers, and Marilyn N. Ochoa. 2007. "Metasearching: An Annotated Bibliography." *Internet Reference Services Quarterly* 12, no. 3/4: 411–430.
A survey of the literature published on metasearching from both philosophical and practical perspectives.

Gregory, Vicki L. 2006. *Selecting and Managing Electronic Resources: A How-To-Do-It Manual for Librarians.* New York: Neal-Schuman.
A practical guide to the many issues involved in choosing and implementing electronic resources in the library. Offers good tips on organizing and accessing digital content.

Herther, Nancy K. 2008. "The Ebook Reader Is Not the Future of Ebooks." *Searcher* 16, no. 8: 26–40.
This article provides a very helpful history of the e-book reader and brings the most current readers into focus.

Chapter 9

The Internet's Impact on Finding Information: A Is for Amazon, G Is for Google

The Internet is an exciting venue for information seeking and sharing. It is important for library staff to not only understand the Internet technology that connects them and their patrons to library-licensed resources but to also understand the complexity of online information and how to find it. Library staff members have moved away from our dark days of reacting to online information with distrust. Critical thinking and information evaluation skills are a must for us and our patrons. Not to be overlooked is the current phase of libraries competing for attention with Internet information providers (commercial retailers, search engines, etc.) who have created compelling and popular methods for connecting people with information. This chapter will explore the Internet from a user and a library perspective, discuss searching the Internet for information, and address how libraries should consider taking their time-tested information sources back to the drawing board.

THE INTERNET

The Internet is a global computer network that has revolutionized communications and information exchange. Originally developed for military research use in 1969, the Internet has grown into an entity used by just about everybody. As the Internet has grown in commercial and social applications, it is essential for libraries to provide access to it and to use it themselves for information gathering and provision.

The Internet started as a way to share information among researchers working on military research projects. The researchers needed a secure means to share information over long distances. The U.S. military also wanted the network to operate even if some of the connected computers were, say, destroyed in a nuclear attack. The result was a worldwide collection of host computers using high speed telephone lines to share information. The military research focus slowly gave way to more general use by academic researchers. As the number of educational and then business users grew, the Internet suddenly erupted as a public utility in the early 1990s. Individuals with no ties to education, business, or the military were able to get online and tremendously increased the number of Internet users. The U.S. government turned over its operation of the host computers that routed Internet communications, the Internet "backbone," to private telecommunications companies. The Internet continued to grow.

We now find the Internet as a huge collection of computers and information that is experienced daily by hundreds of millions of people. It is a mixture of relevant and irrelevant services and information, depending on the individual. It is available to a growing percentage of the population, yet is unavailable to society's poorest members except through public institutions like libraries. There is serious money at work in the Internet, as companies and organizations establish a presence for their services and search for e-commerce opportunities. It is also a haven for less financially rewarding, but no less valuable, activities such as recreational chatting, sharing support for those in crisis, and exchanging professional advice. There is a freedom to the Internet—the freedom to communicate, to search out information, and to share news. As one might expect, sometimes conflicts occur when this sharing happens, as in the case of recording companies and musicians suing those individuals who place illegal audio files of songs online. What is the Internet? It is in many ways a reflection and an extension of the rest of the world, and as such is valuable to libraries and individuals seeking information about that world.

WHAT CAN YOU DO ON THE INTERNET?

The answer to this question grows longer each year as new software and services become available. There are, however, three main things we can do on the Internet: communicate, locate information, and share files.

An important computing concept that propels these uses of the Internet is a process known as **client/server**, in which a piece of software on your computer (the client) can be used to communicate with one or more databases (the servers) to retrieve information. When you use the Internet, you are running a client application on your computer (an e-mail program, a Web browser, chat software, etc.) to connect to the servers online.

Communication

There are a variety of ways to communicate on the Internet. It is an exciting prospect: the ability to exchange thoughts, requests, and answers with people located all over the planet. Electronic mail is the most common method of online communication and the one with roots back to the Internet's beginning (see Figure 9-1). It allows users to type and send messages back and forth. Messages can be sent to a single individual or to a group of Internet users via an electronic discussion group. Some common e-mail clients are Microsoft Outlook and Eudora. People also use **Webmail** options (e.g. Gmail, Yahoo! Mail, Hotmail, and AOL) where no local software is required other than a Web browser.

Chat and **instant messaging** (IM) are more interactive means of communication in which users type brief messages to one another in real time. Chat tends to be a Web-based technology in which users gather electronically at a set location and communicate on a given topic or whatever is on their minds. IM is conducted on a one-to-one basis through freely available IM clients communicating through a central server. Similar modes of communication (in content though not technology) include **Usenet** newsgroups and Web **bulletin boards**. These

Figure 9-1
Sample e-mail message

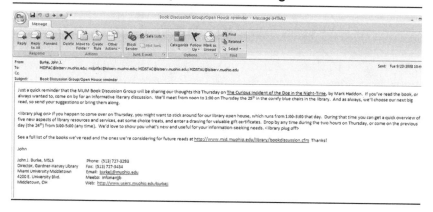

tools tend to resemble e-mail in that they allow interested parties to exchange static messages. Their difference from IM and chat is that the messages remain available to the general public on Web sites.

Not be left out of this discussion are **blogs** and **wikis**. Blogs (or web logs) are online diaries or journals in which an individual or a group can post entries about topics of interest (see Figure 9-2). Entries (or posts) are arranged in reverse chronological order, with the most recent posts appearing first. Readers of the blog can often make comments on the posts to continue the discussion. Wikis are Web sites that can be edited, updated, and improved by anyone. They are used for group work on documents or shared projects and also for larger communities who congregate online to share information through the wikis. These are very interesting developments in information sharing that are having a strong impact on how news spreads and people work together online.

Locating Information

Information sharing is done actively through the communication methods mentioned previously. Passive display of information online is primarily through the World Wide Web. Internet users can use browser software to visit the millions of documents

Figure 9-2
Screenshot of blog

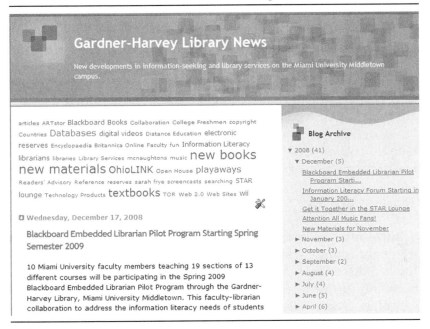

available on Web sites. Internet Explorer, Firefox, and Opera are three common varieties of browser software. Each site has a **URL** (uniform resource locator; for example, www.neal-schuman .com) that a user can enter into the browser to connect to the site. The sites are created using **hypertext markup language** (HTML), a versatile and relatively easy tool that helps create pages of information on the Web. Anyone can place information on the Web, and a great mixture of organizational and personal information is available. Though the Web can be characterized as passive, it does exhibit more than staid, text documents: images of all kinds, audio and video clips, interactive tutorials and games, and more. Add-on software programs, such as media players for sound and video, VoIP (**voice-over Internet protocol**) applications, and others, are often available for free download.

It should be noted that locating Internet information is typified more by searching than browsing. The interlinking of Web information through **hyperlinks** does allow some movement from site to site, but more often than not users will examine sites that they find through search tools. Dating back to the early 1990s (and before) there have been search devices that allowed a user to enter keywords to turn up Internet sites. These tools are often broken into two categories: **search engines**, which allow for keyword searches of large (many billions of pages) segments of the Internet, and **search directories**, which are human-gathered and organized collections of sites that may be searched or browsed. A good example of the former is Google (www.google.com) and one of the latter is the Open Directory Project (www.dmoz.org).

Sharing Files

While e-mail and the Web get the most attention from Internet users, the ability to share files is a crucial aspect of the Internet. Individuals can send word processing documents or image files back and forth for collaborative purposes. Software companies can place demo versions of their products on a Web site and allow people to download them to their computers to try them out. Despite the dangers posed by computer **viruses** potentially contained in files, many software solutions and safe collections of files are available. While a lot of information on the Internet is available in online discussions or on Web pages, it is easy to overlook the mountains of facts contained in files of various formats.

WHY DO LIBRARIES USE THE INTERNET?

Libraries have come to rely on the Internet just as other organizations have. Despite some apprehension on the part of librarians who were not comfortable with computer technology or who wondered if the Internet would replace libraries, the Internet is well suited to aid and reinforce many of their activities and services. There are five basic ways that libraries use the Internet:

1. *Libraries use the Internet to market themselves and to provide their services.* The primary way that libraries do this is through a library Web site (more on this in Chapter 12).

Libraries place information about their services, contact information, and organized lists of resource links on their sites. Since the Web is used so heavily as a marketing tool by the rest of the world, it is sensible for libraries to also take advantage. In addition, libraries are providing actual services over the Internet. Reference service is offered to patrons using e-mail and Web-based forms, and requests to purchase materials or for librarians to conduct instruction sessions can be received the same way.

2. *Library staff members use the Internet to communicate with one another, with colleagues, and with patrons.* Staff can consult with colleagues in other libraries about equipment needs, service policies, and reference strategies, among other needs. E-mail gives staff another way to make contact and pass information along to fellow staff members. Staff also receive e-mails from members of their communities. IM is growing in use as a staff communication tool and as a way to provide reference assistance to patrons. I am not quite ready to accept that "e-mail is for old people," but IM does give libraries a way to reach patrons where they are.

3. *Library staff and users search the Internet for information.* Staff can turn to the Internet as, depending on the question, a first, last, or middle source in their search strategies for reference questions. Library users are already using the Internet as a source for locating information, often in preference to libraries. Libraries need to help guide users to the best information sources for their need. We also need to accept that sometimes the Internet is the best source and make sure that we can guide people in its use.

4. *Libraries use the Internet as a platform for providing access to resources.* A Web site is the most logical way for libraries to offer access to their resources since both subscription and free electronic resources are typically accessible only on the Web. Library Web sites give patrons what libraries hope is a usefully organized listing of electronic resources. As Chapter 8 detailed, some libraries will incorporate print resources (and their call numbers) into Web sites

along with the electronic sources to further integrate their reference collections.

5. *Library staff members use the Internet to research service methods and product information.* Many resources on the Internet can be helpful for finding information in these areas. As mentioned, libraries can turn to colleagues for advice on methods and practices. There are discussion groups for every type of library and specialty within libraries. The sources listed in Chapter 2 are evidence for the case of product information. As well, most library vendors have Web sites to use for surveying their products and contacting them.

INTERNET ISSUES IN LIBRARIES

Nothing in this world is without its problems. The Internet has brought a lot of good into the work of libraries and the research of our patrons, but some issues cannot be overlooked. The first issue has been alluded to: some patrons are dependent on the Internet for information, often to the point of ignoring libraries. This problem has two aspects: first, our patrons, especially those who already ignore the library, need to be educated on the merits of particular library resources for meeting their needs; second, we as library staff cannot fall into the trap of beating down the Internet in order to raise ourselves up. The Internet needs to be treated by everyone as just another information resource, better in meeting some research needs and worse in others.

An interesting part of this issue is the appearance of sites and services on the Internet that offer to answer people's informational questions. Some of these are free sites that link users up with volunteers or experts in various fields who will answer questions related to their expertise (e.g., AllExperts, www.allexperts.com). Others charge a fee or let information providers bid on answering questions (e.g., Yahoo! Answers, http://answers.yahoo.com). It has been interesting to watch these services come and go (e.g. Google Answers), and it will likely continue to be interesting to see if they provide a valuable service to those who use them.

The next issue also involves patrons having too much of a focus on the Internet when they are in our libraries. This time it involves viewing materials within the library (particularly pornography) that is offensive to others. Some might add to this behavior the tendency of patrons to use Internet computers to IM, use personal e-mail, or play games. Both activities can be offensive to both staff and other patrons: the first to staff and patrons who do not wish to view the objectionable material, and the second (which is frustrating for staff) to patrons who must wait to use a computer. Technological solutions for both cases have involved software that attempts to eliminate access to potentially offensive Web sites and/or programs that block access to some services like chat and e-mail.

Some libraries have chosen—and others have resisted—installing filtering software, applications that attempt to restrict access to offensive sites. The software does not necessarily work as it should and can block sites without any offensive content. However, without some steps taken, ranging from user education to filtering, children and others in libraries are able to find or are forced to see images they would rather avoid. The American Library Association opposes mandatory filtering (see www.ala .org/ala/issuesadvocacy/intfreedom/filtering) on First Amendment grounds. There is no easy answer to this situation and neither unadulterated access nor filtering is without its casualties. It is an issue that libraries will continue to face for some time.

LESSONS FROM THE INTERNET FOR LIBRARIES

As discussed, the Internet is widely used by society and library staff alike. While it sometimes appears that people are merely running from site to site on the Internet as though following fads, there is something compelling about certain sites that builds repeat business. Whether or not people would identify themselves in this way, they are exhibiting a certain amount of brand loyalty to individual sites (and those who copy their approaches). What can libraries learn from this combination of societal trends, interactivity, Web design, and new approaches to building community? Is any of this applicable to the library environment? Consider the following three cases.

Amazon.com

Amazon.com has built a successful business selling books, videos, DVDs, and other products through its Web site (see Figure 9-3). This site provides a useful resource for library staff in locating items, confirming their publication information, and ordering them for library collections. Beyond this impact on libraries, though, are elements of the Amazon.com site that make it a first turn for people rather than their local library catalog. First, though, let me remove the issues that individuals may wish to buy books rather than borrow them and that Amazon's catalog is bound to have many more items than that of an individual library. Four interesting aspects that may cause people to turn to Amazon first are the following:

1. Amazon displays selected pages from many books inside of its catalog so that users can sample the item before purchasing it.
2. The full-text of a growing number of items can be searched along with citation information for all other items from the search blank on every Amazon page.
3. Customers can read and write reviews of Amazon items, assisting them in choosing books and expressing their own opinions.

Figure 9-3
Screenshot of Amazon.com

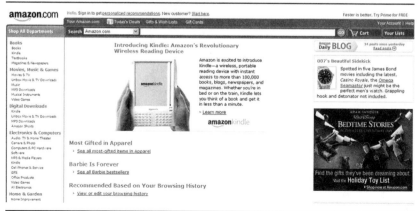

4. Amazon suggests additional items that might be related to the item in question—the famous "Customers who viewed this item also viewed," along with suggested subject headings for the item and related terms. This allows users to find items that did not appear in their original search.

Google

Google has emerged as the predominant Internet search engine and has held its lead over a variety of competitors (see Figure 9-4). In an industry where for many years the race to the biggest database of pages to search drove the competition (and created a new king every six months to a year), Google has held its own on size but added other dimensions. The simple, single-lined search blank of Google is a wonderful example of a simple design. There is nothing unclear about their opening page, no decisions to make: just type your search, and get results. The results screen is very straightforward as well: a list of sites that match, ranked by relevance, presented with a selection of the matching text on the page and its URL. Just scan down to choose a link that might meet your need. The "similar pages" link at the end of every link in the results gives users the opportunity to see if a useful site might lead them to others in the Google database.

In addition, the profusion of specialized searching functions within Google keeps users returning. From Google Maps (maps and directions) and Froogle (a price comparison search) to

Figure 9-4
Screenshot of Google

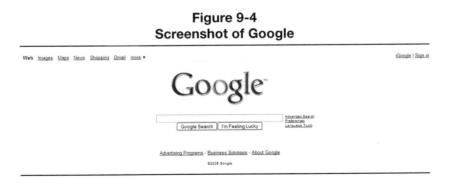

Images, News, and Scholar (an index of online scholarly articles), Google conveys the impression to users that not much escapes its knowledge. With the advent of the Google Books scanning project and provision of many of these titles on the Web, not much may.

Folksonomies and Social Bookmarking

A variety of tools are available on the Internet now that allow users to collect and share lists of items, like Web site links, such as Delicious (http://delicious.com; Figure 9-5) and Furl (www.furl .net) and images, such as Flickr (www.flickr.com). Communities of users can form around common interests, leading to a great deal of (at least online) social interaction and sharing of information. In addition to making these items visible to other users of the services and being able to see how many other users linked the same item, a user can classify each link, creating a **folksonomy**. A folksonomy is a "socially constructed classification system" (Smith, 2004). The idea is that instead of using a set classification system, like the Library of Congress Subject Headings (LCSH), for example, the user decides how to describe the item. These sites yield the following interesting aspects:

Figure 9-5
Screenshot of Delicious

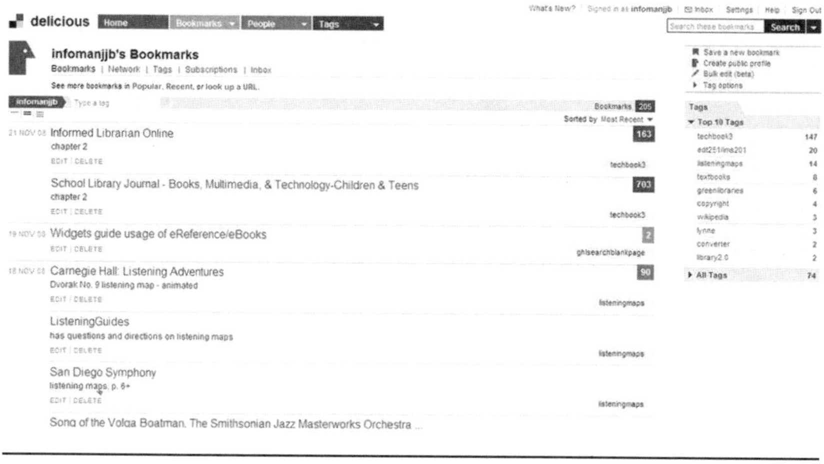

1. Creating lists of interesting sources and sharing them with others
2. The ability for one user to see what others have linked to, gauging the popularity of specific items and following a trail of related items
3. Assigning self-chosen descriptive terms to items, creating a workable vocabulary for organizing your own items and contributing to a community's choices for terms
4. The ability to see the relative popularity of given terms and topics in the larger collection of items

Library catalogs and Web sites do not do the things listed in the previous cases. Could they? Should they? What about other library resources? Should individual periodical articles have "Patrons who viewed this article also viewed . . ." links on their citation screens? Seriously, though, the following list suggests what we can learn from these examples and how our library resources may well evolve.

1. People are social by nature, and libraries could do much to allow for interaction and sharing of interests within our resources. Could we let patrons write reviews of items in the catalog? What about sharing lists of books, DVDs, and articles that they liked? There are privacy concerns here, by all means, but there could be a path that would be acceptable to consenting patrons.
2. The ability to let users choose terms that people actually use to describe items in addition to using standard classification systems would be a very interesting development. Libraries may not be ready to let the inmates run the asylum, but we need to face the fact that people do not think in LCSH. This is part of the success of Google and of folksonomies.
3. Can we be cut down on the options on our pages and help users make a beeline to searching our collections? Google's example might suggest that we can, and the discussion of metasearching in Chapter 8 suggests that the technology is there to integrate sources. The question here is whether library staff members are dismissing the "Googlization" approach because it makes them

uncomfortable or whether we truly see patrons short-changed by it.

4. Are there ways to make connections between individual information sources that are not dependent on LCSH or even highly relevant keywords? Libraries need to see the success of interlinking in the social bookmarking tools or Amazon as a model for us to institute in our services.

QUESTIONS FOR REVIEW

1. What are three main activities individuals can pursue using the Internet?
2. Name some common library uses for the Internet.
3. Does your library have filtering software installed? Why or why not?
4. What is your reaction to the idea of adding approaches from folksonomies, Google, and Amazon to library resources?
5. Explain the difference between search engines and search directories.

SELECTED SOURCES FOR FURTHER INFORMATION

The Blogging Libraries Wiki. 2008. Available: www.blogwithoutalibrary
.net/links/index.php?title=Welcome_to_the_Blogging_Libraries_Wiki.
   A wiki with links to many different library blogs, organized by the type of
   library they are from.
Dempsey, Lorcan. 2005. "The User Interface That Isn't." Lorcan Dempsey's
Weblog: On Libraries, Services, and Networks. Available: http://orweblog
.oclc.org/archives/000667.html.
   This post discusses the possibilities of making our library interfaces more
   like those of Amazon and Google and suggests benefits for doing so.
Lombardo, Nancy T., Allyson Mower, and Mary M. McFarland. "Putting Wikis
to Work in Libraries." Medical Reference Services Quarterly 27, no. 2: 129–145.
   An article that illustrates the many possible uses of a wiki in a library set-
   ting. Serves as a good explanation of the types of activities that a wiki
   can be utilized for in any setting.
Miller, William, and Rita M. Pellen. 2006. Libraries and Google. Bingham-
ton, NY: The Haworth Press.
   A collection of 18 essays on Google and its interrelationship with libraries.
   Essays consider the question of whether Google is a good model for

libraries to emulate, how to use Google to teach information literacy, and privacy concerns with Google.

Ramos, Miguel, and Paul S. Piper. 2006. "Letting the Grass Grow: Grass-roots Information on Blogs and Wikis." *Reference Services Review* **34, no. 4: 570–574.**

The article illustrates a variety of ways that blogs and wikis are used in the world and then discusses how library staff may make use of the information in them.

Sauers, Michael. 2009. *Searching 2.0.* **New York: Neal-Schuman.**

This book reviews current search tools and strategies for Web searching. Provides a helpful introduction to a variety of tools.

SearchEngineWatch. 2008. Available: http://searchenginewatch.com.

A site with reviews of Web search tools and investigations of how they operate.

Smith, Gene. 2004. "Folksonomy: Social Classification." *Atomiq.* **Available: http://atomiq.org/archives/2004/08/folksonomy_social_classification.html.**

A definition and explanation of the folksonomy concept.

Chapter 10

Web 2.0: Social Networking, Second Life, and Skype

In Chapter 9 we discussed the general outlines of technologies and services available on the Internet. Left out of that discussion until now are some additional technologies that are crucial to how the Web operates today and how library staff members can reach out and interact with our patrons. They all, it could be argued, represent means of communication between individuals and groups of people. These tools are new forums for interaction, collaboration, and creativity. Larger than that, though, they also allow for new ways to share content online and re-create content to more user-specific needs. All of these concepts are grouped into the term Web 2.0—the next evolutionary step (perhaps) of the Web itself. This chapter will take a tour of these technologies and how our patrons may already be using them. Now it is for library staff members to decide how to best implement them (if at all) to convey our services.

SOCIAL NETWORKING TOOLS

Social networks are a natural formation of bonds among individuals based on geography, careers, or interests. Social networking software has arisen as a way for people to bond online and chat, exchange pictures, and stay connected through a medium they are already using daily. People join the networks, post as much or as little personal information as they would like, connect with people they already know in daily life, and add on new "virtual" friends drawn from shared interests or locate and reconnect with old friends who are geographically distant. You can send out "friend" requests to invite someone to be your friend. Two examples of social networks are Facebook (www.facebook.com; Figure 10-1) and MySpace (www.myspace.com).

Many libraries, along with other organizations, have attempted to create a presence in social networks. The huge popularity of the networks has made this a natural draw. In some cases this has been effective, but in others there have been few interested parties who wish to "friend" the library. An alternative arrangement has been for library staff members to personally join the network, creating real relationships they can build in both the virtual and three-dimensional worlds. Apart from the

Figure 10-1
Screenshot of Facebook

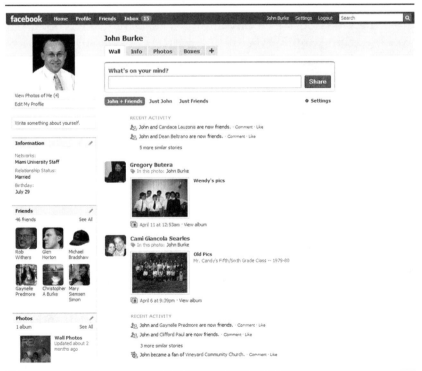

overall goal of going where our patrons are, there is the ability to regularly and easily update your entire group of friends (e.g., with announcements about new programs or databases at the library) and also to add **widgets** or applications that people can use in the social networking software to search library resources. Some examples of these applications from academic and public libraries may be found in a post from Gerry McKiernan's Friends: Social Networking Sites for Engaged Library Services blog about them at http://onlinesocialnetworks.blogspot.com/2008/03/favorite-library-related-facebook-apps.html.

MASHUPS

A **mashup** is a combination of multiple data sources to serve a combined purpose. One example is to take a Web service like Google Maps (maps.google.com) and connect its geographic information to something else. For instance, an individual created a Google Maps map of the United Kingdom and then shows markers on it for daily updated stories featured on BBC News (http://dev.benedictoneill.com/bbc). You can mouse over the story markers on the map for a summary of the story or click on the summary for a detailed account directly from the BBC News site. This combination is a powerful representation of news and events in terms of their location. It provides a completely different look at a news day than you would get from looking at the BBC News site or the headlines of the daily paper.

Several library applications use a similar approach. For instance, here are two you can create using either Google Maps by itself or a site called Community Walk (www.community walk.com) that brings in community-related information into a Google Map (e.g., restaurants, bowling alleys, libraries). One is a map of your library's location, perhaps relative to other community places or showing multiple branches (or in my library's case, our location in relation to the other campuses of the university). You can zoom the map in to show a certain area, and then place pointers to highlight locations on the map. With Community Walk (see Figure 10-2), it is easy to connect the individual locations so that a person wanting directions to location A from location C can easily choose this from a menu and

Figure 10-2
**Screenshot of Community Walk map showing locations that
requested interlibrary loans from a library**

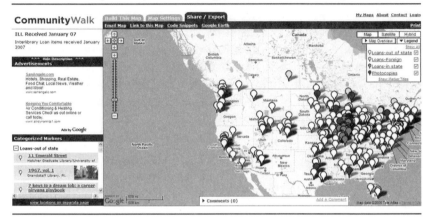

have the information quickly. The second is a neat application of geography to service activities. A library can show the reach of its interlibrary loan services by plotting where it sends its books to other libraries on a map or where it receives books and articles from. It's a much more interesting way to imagine this information than seeing an alphabetized list of states and countries and yet it carries detailed information on the institution making or receiving the loan by clicking on the pointer.

LibraryThing.com is an example of a mashup writ fairly large. It is a community of readers who are able to create personal libraries of books they own or have read. The ability of these readers to discuss books with one another and to tag the items they add puts the service well into the Web 2.0 category. The mashup side of Library Thing is one of its strengths: users can draw in specific information about each book from the Library of Congress or Amazon (two large repositories for bibliographic information) and also locate covers of books to help display their collections. LibraryThing combines the personal selections of one individual with the commentary and subject **tagging** of many other individuals and the bibliographic data of other providers. The overall impact is a powerful representation of a work from its physical description to specific commentary on it from the user who added it to its place in the larger pantheon of works added by LibraryThing members.

LibraryThing (see Figure 10-3) is extremely attractive to the computer literate bibliophile, but has relevance for library staff members as well. While anyone can create a free catalog of their items on the site, libraries may be interested in bringing elements of LibraryThing into their own catalogs (e.g., the tags on a given item and its image may be added to the library's catalog for a fee paid to LibraryThing). The representation of book information in the site has been inspirational to those planning new interfaces. Could we all just catalog our items in LibraryThing? Well, maybe. It does provide a model of a finding tool that has great user involvement.

Yet another mashup is a **custom search engine (CSE)**. This concoction is pretty straightforward: what if you could search just the sites you wanted to without having to wade through a lot of other stuff that shows up in your results from Google or another search engine? What if you could choose the best 10 or 37 or 1,296 sites on a given topic and have a powerful search engine look through those sites for the keywords you enter? Well, now you can. Here, you are mashing up the contents of these multiple sites and making them searchable through another site: a search engine. One example for doing this is the CSE service available through Google Co-op (www.google.com/coop/cse). A Google

Figure 10-3
LibraryThing collection page, showing covers

CSE can include an unlimited number of URLs that are searched by the Google search engine. Another option is Rollyo (www.rollyo.com), which allows you to combine 25 different sites and uses Yahoo! as its search engine. Some sample CSEs may be found at www.searchengineshowdown.com/cse.

The mashups described are all pretty straightforward, in that you can go to a service and choose the data you want to mix. If you are of a more creative programming bent, though, you can get really fancy and work more directly with the code that gives you access to the data of a given source. Many information sites offer their **APIs** (Application Programming Interfaces) to the general public on the signing of a end user licensing agreement. This gives the user access to needed codes from the site that make it easier to construct a mashup to exacting specifications. (A selection of sites that offer APIs is available at www.programmableweb.com/apis.) For an introduction to the process of using APIs to create mashups, I suggest working with Yahoo! Pipes (http://pipes.yahoo.com/pipes), which enables you to combine data sources without knowing much programming at all or needing to gain access to APIs on your own.

SECOND LIFE

Second Life (www.secondlife.com) has become the most recognizable multipurpose virtual world online. Major corporations and universities have spent serious money establishing "islands" within it to market themselves and to serve participants. The Gartner Group, an IT (information technology) think tank, predicts that 80% of active Internet users will participate in a virtual world by 2011 (see www.gartner.com/it/page.jsp?id=503861 for more details). Library staff members and library educators have been eagerly exploring the potential of this environment as a way to connect with the members of their three-dimensional communities.

What is it like to interact in a virtual world? First of all, you need to choose an avatar, an online representation of yourself that can be modeled on your actual appearance or look however you would like it to (be creative!). With an avatar at your command, you can then venture around the ever larger Second Life

Figure 10-4
A Second Life avatar contemplates his surroundings

surroundings, meeting other avatars, visiting various locations, shopping, learning, or what have you (see Figure 10-4). It is intriguing to see the work done so far by members of the library community to educate one another about using Second Life and to connect as information resources to other members of the Second Life community. Take a look at the blog posts and other resources at http://sllibrarians.ning.com/ for more information.

SKYPE

VoIP anyone? Voice-over Internet protocol—the ability to have audio communications over the Internet using your computer—has been around for a while. The quality has improved greatly over the years and is being implemented for ordinary phone communications in a variety of communities and corporate settings. Skype (www.skype.com) is of interest as a provider of VoIP because it allows unlimited free calls between two Skype users. And this is not limited to audio communications, either. Video calls may also be made at no charge. This may just give library staff members a way to reach niche users, people who might be surprised to see Skype information on a library's "contact us" page. But it might also lead to expanding the library's ability to serve distant users (and even to assist those users with a video exchange) without charges on either end. This certainly bears considering as we try to bring expanded services to a wider range of individuals.

WIKIPEDIA

Ah, Wikipedia. The new bane of librarians everywhere? Not in my book, but your evaluation may vary. Wikipedia (www .wikipedia.org; see Figure 10-5) is an intriguing collection of information continuously being created, modified, and updated by, well, just about anyone in the world. It takes the process of creating an encyclopedia to a whole new collaborative level. The idea is that rather than trusting an article on a topic to one or two experts, why not bring in the group mind to add currency, a broader perspective, and a greater range of details to that same information? It is, in some sense, information creation laid bare.

Figure 10-5
Screenshot of Wikipedia

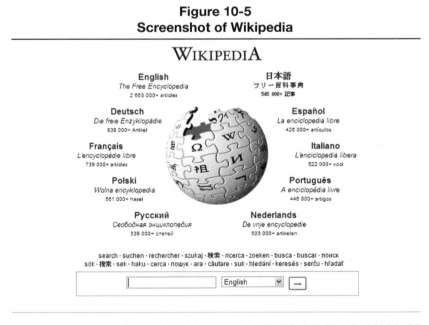

All of the discussions among contributors are saved and their edits and revisions of the original document are immortalized.

It is certainly not a perfect information source, for though high standards of objectivity and good referencing of sources is expected, there are abuses. Wikipedia does bring out excellent information on a variety of topics and certainly covers a wider array of topics than most general reference sources. Information consumers must evaluate the material they find carefully, but isn't that true for all information sources? In the end, Wikipedia brings forward a great deal of useful information—along with questionable information—and opens new debates that can only better inform information users.

TWITTER

Twitter (www.twitter.com) is an interesting extension of the idea of blogging, turning the sometimes lengthy standard of blog posts into something much shorter. Often referred to as "microblogging," Twitter provides an opportunity for anyone to sign up for a free account and then start posting brief replies to the question "what are you doing?" Now, it is probably true that not that many people truly care about everything you are doing from moment to moment in your life (no offense), but the ability to communicate quickly and easily with others to share brief thoughts is attractive to both the poster and their audience. Those who follow a given Twitterer receive updated posts from that individual, called "tweets," on their cell phones, through IM, through e-mail updates, or via RSS (really simple syndication). If a library could connect with an audience interested in hearing brief updates from the library, it might work quite well as an updating service. See http://oedb.org/blogs/ilibrarian/2007/a-guide-to-twitter-in-libraries for links to descriptions of Twitter and its uses in libraries. To my mind, Twitter connects with two trends in society that appear to have great appeal: texting—the short exchange of text messages on cell phones, and the desire to cut information exchange to the essentials in all media. If libraries can find crucial tidbits to pass along, they will find an audience among their patrons.

YOUTUBE

YouTube (see Figure 10-6) exemplifies the Web 2.0 concept of user-driven content sharing. Many thousands of individuals use this site to share the video that they have recorded or otherwise captured. Many thousands of hours of recent news and entertainment programming, movie clips, personal productions, and even educational materials are available to be searched and commented on. Library staff members can utilize YouTube as both an information resource for their patrons and as a platform to add videos marketing the library or teaching the use of databases. We live in such a visual culture, and YouTube is a way to reveal what's going on out there and then participate in the process ourselves.

If we can find ways to connect with our users in and through these Web 2.0 technologies, we are embodying the premise of Library 2.0 service. Library 2.0 takes the principles and technologies of Web 2.0 and applies them to changing library service toward a more interactive, participatory, and responsive model. This will be explored more fully in Chapter 12 in terms of placing technologies and services on library Web sites.

Figure 10-6
Screenshot of YouTube

QUESTIONS FOR REVIEW

1. Can you find an example of a mashup beyond those offered in this chapter?
2. Do you notice library patrons in your library using social networking tools? Does your library have a presence in any social networks?
3. What is your experience in using Wikipedia? Do you recommend it (or recommend against it) to library users?
4. What is VoIP?
5. What might be a benefit of using Second Life to connect with your library patrons?

SELECTED SOURCES FOR FURTHER INFORMATION

Badke, William. 2008. "What to Do with Wikipedia." *Online* 32, no. 2 (March/April). Available: www.infotoday.com/online/mar08/Badke.shtml.
> An article that makes a positive case for using Wikipedia as an information resource and as an arena for students to confront and evaluate materials of varying quality.

Bradley, Phil. 2007. *How to Use Web 2.0 in Your Library*. London: Facet Publishing.
> An excellent introduction to the Web 2.0 concepts and services mentioned in this chapter, with further details on mashups, social networking, blogging, and more.

Farkas, Meredith G. 2007. *Social Software in Libraries: Building Collaboration, Communication, and Community Online*. Medford, NJ: Information Today.
> A solid introduction to social networking, blogs, wikis, and other collaborative tools and experiences that library patrons are using and that libraries should be familiar with.

Stephens, Michael. 2007. "Messaging in a 2.0 World: Twitter & SMS." *Library Technology Reports* 43, no. 5 (September/October): 62–66.
> A good overview of Twitter and text messaging and how libraries can interact with their patrons using them. Offers concrete examples and suggestions on how to get started.

Trueman, Rhonda B., Tom Peters, and Lori Bell. 2007. "Get a Second Life! Libraries in Virtual Worlds." In *Information Tomorrow: Reflections on Technology and the Future of Academic and Public Libraries* (pp. 159–172), edited by Rachel Singer Gordon. Medford, NJ: Information Today.
> This chapter introduces the concept of virtual worlds and explains Second Life. It offers practical implementation suggestions and explores future possibilities for these environments.

PART III

How Libraries Put Technology to Work

Chapter 11

Meeting and Supporting Patron Technology Needs: Universal Design and Adaptive/Assistive Technology

Libraries are all about people, both the people who use its services and the people who work there. People cannot be forgotten in any discussion of technology, and the intention of this book is that the concerns and needs of patrons and staff will not be overlooked. Later chapters will address topics such as usable Web design, **ergonomics**, identity safety, and **troubleshooting** patron difficulties. In this chapter, the focus turns to creating a conducive technology environment for the individuals who use (or who will hopefully use) a library. Some key areas of concern for libraries relate to patrons with disabilities and patrons who use the library as their primary access point for technology. Library staff members need to know what technology barriers patrons may face and how staff members can be open to overcoming them.

UNIVERSAL DESIGN

A very useful concept for library staff members to use when assessing their libraries is **universal design**. This concept, which began in architecture and now reaches into learning and other areas, is centered on the idea of making products and services usable by people with a wide range of skills and abilities. In a library setting, this thought should cause us to ask whether or not our services and collections are truly available to everyone we serve. This does not just relate to patrons with disabilities but also to individuals who may not be proficient English speakers or individuals who may lack knowledge in using computers or other library resources.

With respect to technology, the focus of this book, we need to examine our computers and other computer equipment, our Web sites, and the ways that we use and expect our patrons to use technologies to find, access, and create information. Are these uses of technology sufficiently transparent to a broad group of our patrons or potential patrons? How could they become more transparent? An interesting element in this comes down to language: how can we express library concepts in terms that users can be expected to understand?

There are no quick and easy answers here, but by adopting this approach libraries can continue to improve what they offer and how it is offered. Bear in mind that transparency is not something to be achieved only through passive Web sites or point-of-use signage. The role that library staff members assume as teachers and trainers and intermediaries is ever more crucial and needs to expand in a more universal direction.

THE DIGITAL DIVIDE

We live in a society that is ever more dependent on technology and that requires its citizens to use that technology. Chapter 1 introduced the disturbing split we see in society of a populace that demands technology use and tools from its institutions, including libraries, and of a substantial portion of our citizenry who lack access to technology and skills for using it. This is not to say that half the country loves technology and has it and the other half hates it and does not have it. Rather, we are a society of "haves," who *have* technology available and *have* to use it whether we like it or not, and "have nots," who cannot use technology even if they would like to. And this is not a matter of using technology for games or hobbies, it is a matter of participation in services and access to resources from governments and the business sector.

What is the technology that forms this divide? It is computer ownership or access and particularly Internet access. A Pew Internet and American Life study shows the following broad results: 23 percent of American adults do not own a computer or go online at all, and 20 percent of American adults have never used the Internet or e-mail. The divisions grow stronger when we consider various generational, ethnic, or other groupings and their percentages of Internet access: adults over 65 (26 percent); people who have not earned a high school diploma (29 percent); Hispanics, aged 3 and older (37 percent); and Americans with disabilities (38 percent) (Fox, 2005). Significant numbers of people from these groups are not able to participate as fully as they should.

If people are getting online (as two-thirds of Americans do), where are they gaining access? Another Pew Internet study shows that of all U.S. Internet users, nearly one-quarter go online from a place other than home or work. Of the various other locations out there, including schools and Internet cafes, libraries have been chosen by 26 percent of "third place" users. When we consider American Internet users from households with annual incomes under $30,000, of people who have connected from a "third place," 30 percent have done so from libraries (Harwood and Rainie, 2004). The library is filling a need in assisting users who need additional Internet access or who do not have another opportunity to get online. This is certainly being done in public libraries, along with school and academic libraries as well. And by all means, these numbers merely capture the situation in the United States, ignoring the much lower access percentages in most of the rest of the world. There are technology initiatives underway that attempt to address the global digital divide (e.g., One Laptop Per Child; http://laptop.org).

What are libraries to do in response to this situation? Libraries must rise to the challenge and accommodate the needs of patrons who depend on them for technology access and assistance. This need calls for resources that libraries do not always have in abundance, and for policy changes that may take time to work out to the satisfaction of patrons and staff alike. Libraries must make the case to their funding agencies that they are not just the "people's university" of old but also the "people's technology lifeline." And this means more than just offering Internet access: it may mean offering word processing for job applications or assistance in navigating the Web sites of government agencies. No matter their size or equipment, libraries stand as beacons and sources of hope to those who need technology.

ADAPTIVE AND ASSISTIVE TECHNOLOGY

It is a good practice to make sure that technology is not only useful for the library's community but that it can be used by all members of that community. The following sections are aimed at making sure that part of our community not be overlooked during this process. Members of the library community who have disabilities may require an additional level of both **adaptive technology** and **assistive technology** to enable their use of the library. The following pages will explore some of the items a library may wish to add to ensure that these needs are met. Keep in mind, this section addresses only the technology needed to aid patrons with disabilities. A library needs a comprehensive plan in order to truly serve this valuable part of our community.

TECHNOLOGY TO LEVEL THE FIELD

Assistive and adaptive technology makes the library and its resources work for users with disabilities. The terms "assistive" and "adaptive" are applied to aids that either assist the user in accessing a library resource or adapt that resource in such a way that it becomes usable. Many of these technologies are aimed at adapting computer-based resources (e.g., screen magnification software and trackball controllers), but several technologies are available for helping with more traditional library sources (e.g., teletypewriters and recorded books). A careful assessment of the needs of those with disabilities in the community can help a library staff decide which of the following technologies are required. This assessment and the added technologies can help the library meet the requirements of the Americans with Disabilities Act (ADA). More importantly, it can ensure that the library is meeting its mission by providing all of its users with the information they need.

TECHNOLOGY FOR PUBLIC COMPUTERS

A standard library computer such as the one described in Chapter 3 is not immediately usable by patrons with some disabilities like blindness or limited motor ability. Fortunately, many technological products make computers easier to use for those with disabilities. Consider the following list a survey of products. A library may wish to focus its efforts to meet certain accessibility needs that the staff have identified in the community. On the other hand, libraries can also choose a selection of adaptive technologies to cover many bases.

- *Screen magnifying software* is extremely helpful to patrons with low vision. These applications allow users to control the level of magnification of the screen to fit their specific requirements. These programs offer several options for controlling the area of the screen that is to be magnified at any one time. For example, users can magnify the entire screen at once and scroll through the entire enlarged Web page or document using the mouse. Users may also select to magnify a defined area of the screen and they can maneuver a boxlike frame around the screen to magnify that section. Many other settings are available.
- **Screen reading software** extends the accessibility of any material one can display on a library computer to those with no or extremely low vision. The software will read aloud whatever text appears on a library computer screen, whether it is the library catalog or another resource. Users can choose to use different voices, can adjust the speed of the reader, and can train the reader to skip certain unreadable characters or improve its pronunciation of other words. Of course, anytime a sound-producing device or software appears in a library there is a need for headphones to accompany the software.

- *Touchpad or trackball controllers* are aimed at use by patrons who are unable to use a standard mouse. Both **trackballs** and **touchpads** exert less pressure on an individual's hand, wrist, and arm. For those patrons with developmental disabilities or carpal tunnel injuries these devices make computer use more comfortable or even possible in some cases. Rotating a trackball with the palm of one's hand removes the need to grip a controller with the user's whole hand. Touchpads allow users to control a mouse by moving their index fingers along a pad that corresponds with the layout of the monitor screen.
- An *on-screen keyboard* allows entry by patrons who cannot enter text using a keyboard. While most library resources do not require much text entry, there is still the issue of typing out search statements for the catalog, databases, and the Internet. Even typing in URLs can be difficult or impossible for a user who cannot use the keyboard. This software makes a small keyboard appear on the screen that a user can click on in order for letters to appear in a Web browser or other application. This may be an excellent option for libraries who have patrons with this need. It will probably be better in the library environment than some of the dictation software that can be used with word processing software.

TECHNOLOGIES FOR OTHER SERVICES AND MATERIALS

The technologies described are extremely helpful in making computers and the many electronic resources that libraries offer accessible to people with disabilities. Additional technologies can make noncomputer resources and library services easier to use.

- For patrons who have difficulty hearing, a **teletypewriter (TTY)** connection can offer a means for communicating with library staff members. A TTY device is connected to a telephone at a patron's home and to a telephone at the library. (Libraries will often set up a separate line for this service.) The device allows the patron and staff member to type messages back and forth. This can be extremely helpful for obtaining library information, asking and answering reference questions, and making other requests of library staff. Some libraries have found that virtual reference through Web-based chat or IM can be an effective replacement for standard TTY devices.

- DVD/video viewing station equipment should include the option of closed-captioning so that users with hearing difficulties can still make use of videos. Most televisions or television/DVD/VCR combinations include this as an option. The other side of this question is whether or not the video or DVD itself contains closed-captioning. This should be confirmed before the item is purchased for the collection.

- Book and periodical magnifiers can make traditional library materials more usable for patrons with low vision. These units have a tray on which one can place a print publication. Over the tray is a magnifier unit that displays the publication on a screen. As with the computer screen magnifier, a variety of setting adjustments are available. Another version of this technology is CCTV (closed-circuit television) in which the magnifier device is hooked up to a television of any size for ease in viewing.

- For patrons with extremely low or no vision, recorded books in various storage formats should be made available. Wonderful work is being done by dedicated talking book libraries throughout the world. This particular medium is an easy one to add to any library's collection. Many titles are available as audio e-books in addition to earlier formats (e.g., CDs).

- The Kurzweil Reader in its many varieties has had a tremendous impact on making printed materials available to individuals with no vision. This device scans and audibly reads the information printed on a page.

- Braille translators and printers may also be of use to those patrons who prefer having Braille copies of printed materials. These devices require a computer set up with translating software and with an accompanying printer that prints on paper with Braille characters. The equipment can be quite expensive, but not many libraries will need such a device.

WEB AND INTERFACE DESIGN CONSIDERATIONS

When approaching the design of a Web site or a database interface it is almost impossible to make everyone awaiting the outcome happy. Aside from aesthetic differences, it is difficult enough to choose which features to include and how to make the site or interface easily navigable. What is important in this consideration is remembering that there are individuals using our Web site or databases who are not worried about the nifty images we may spread across our pages or the time we spend considering color schemes. These are individuals with extremely low vision or no vision, who are accessing these electronic resources using screen reader software.

An issue to consider in this situation is that a number of items (such as images) are completely ignored by this reading software. Typically, people who use screen-reading software are also using a simplified, nongraphical Web browser. Web designers need to take a look at how their pages display in browsers such as **Lynx**. Images will not display, but in the HTML coding used to make Web pages there are **image tags** (like a caption) that will appear. Designers need to make sure that important images that communicate information of some type also communicate that information through the image tags. This is but one consideration that interface designers must make. In the Selected Sources for Further Information section of the chapter there are some Web sites that can give further advice on crafting workable sites and interfaces and making sure that standards are met. Section 508 of the Rehabilitation Act (nicely explained at www.section508 .gov) provides standards on Web design that are now required of all U.S. federal agencies. Other community and public institutions such as libraries are tending to follow these site design standards as well. The World Wide Web Consortium (W3C), a Web standards organization, has a page on its Web Accessibility Initiative that can help with accessibility questions (www.w3 .org/WAI).

SUGGESTED LIST OF ADAPTIVE TECHNOLOGY FOR A LIBRARY COMPUTER

1. The Smart Cat from Cirque Software, which is a touch-pad controller (www.cirque.com)
2. ZoomText Magnifier/Reader 9.0, which provides screen magnification and screen reading capabilities (www.aisquared.com)
3. **On-Screen Keyboard** from R. J. Cooper and Associates (www.rjcooper.com)
4. JAWS from Freedom Scientific, which is a screen reading Web browser (www.freedomscientific.com)

QUESTIONS FOR REVIEW

1. What is universal design?
2. Define assistive technology and adaptive technology and give an example of each.
3. Does your library include any assistive or adaptive technology?
4. Do you know of patrons who fall on either side of the digital divide? What do you think your library's role is in assisting those who need access to the Internet and other technologies?

SELECTED SOURCES FOR FURTHER INFORMATION

"ADA Accessibility Guidelines for Buildings and Facilities (ADAAG)." 2007. Washington, DC: United States Access Board. Available: www.access-board.gov/adaag/about.
  This site displays the United States government regulations for ensuring access to people with disabilities. These guidelines and diagrams may be useful when setting up an adaptive computer.

Center for Applied Special Technology. 2008. Available: www.cast.org.
  Includes a variety of information on assistive technology and methods. Includes links to Web page analysis tools that check to see how well a page conforms to W3C guidelines.

EASI (Equal Access to Software and Information). 2008. Available: http://easi.cc.
  Links to a variety of resources on adaptive technology. An excellent resource for questions on making computers and computer applications available to those with disabilities.

Felix, Lisa. 2008. "Design for Everyone." *Library Journal* **133, no. 16: 38–40.**
Includes a great definition of universal design and an explanation of related concepts. Includes an annotated bibliography on universal design and barrier-free design.

Fox, Susannah. 2005. "Digital Divisions." Washington, DC: Pew Internet and American Life Project. Available: www.pewinternet.org/PPF/r/165/ report_display.asp.
Examines the differences in access to the Internet among American users, from those who dial-up and broadband connections to those with no Internet connection at all.

Harwood, Paul, and Lee Rainie. 2004. "People Who Use the Internet Away from Home and Work." Washington, DC: Pew Internet and American Life Project. Available: www.pewinternet.org/PPF/r/115/report_display.asp.
Examines the trends associated with the growing number of users who access the Internet outside of the home or work.

Hensley, Jerry. 2005. "Adaptive Technologies." In *Technology for the Rest of Us: A Primer on Computer Technologies for the Low-Tech Librarian,* **edited by Nancy Courtney. Westport, CT: Libraries Unlimited.**
Covers accessibility needs in libraries and a variety of technologies and practices that can be used to meet them.

"Librarians' Connections." 2008. "Disability Resources on the Internet." Available: www.disabilityresources.org/DRMlibs.html.
A directory of Web sites on disability issues. Includes a section on making library electronic resources accessible to those with disabilities.

Lubin, Jim. 2008. "disABILITY Information and Resources." Available: www.eskimo.com/~jlubin/disabled.
A comprehensive listing of information and products relating to a wide variety of disabilities.

Neumann, Heidi. 2003. "What Teacher-Librarians Should Know About Universal Design." *Teacher Librarian* **31, no. 2: 17–20.**
The article explains the various contexts (architecture, information access, and learning) in which school librarians should consider universal design.

Chapter 12

Library 2.0 and the Library: Virtual Reference, Blogs, and Usability

The Web presence of a library has become crucial to its success, due to the need for a gathering point for links to its electronic resources and to the centrality of the Internet as a place for people to locate information. Library Web sites provide the library with a space to share its services and to tell its story to the community it serves. A lack of attention to the site is a missed opportunity for marketing and has a negative impact on patrons finding the information they need. In addition to the Web site itself, libraries must be focused on building and offering interactive services through the site. What I hope to accomplish in this chapter is to suggest some Library 2.0 tools (such as those discussed in Chapter 10) that can give a library new ways to engage, connect, and communicate with the community of users that it serves. I also think some of the questions asked in this chapter can move a library to reevaluate its internal operations and processes to gain an even stronger service orientation. One thing libraries cannot lose in our information-technology-dominated age is the ability to use technology to accomplish new services.

WHAT DO LIBRARY WEB SITES OFFER?

Library Web sites vary as much as their libraries' buildings do. While there is no "perfect" library Web site model that can be copied from location to location and library to library, there are some common services and features that most sites include (see Figure 12-1). Many of these options are likely to be on or linked from the opening page of the site, but may also be grouped on subsequent pages.

- *Interaction with the library catalog.* Users who are growing familiar with Web-based banking, shopping, and other services have an interest in completing similar library functions online. For instance, the ability to go online and log in to one's library account to renew items or request holds is a great service to patrons. Most library system vendors make these options available to patrons through the catalog interface. Depending on your system and your library's policies, patrons may also be able to sit at home and request materials to be held for them at your circulation desk, whether the item is located at another branch or within your collection. A link to "renew your materials" or "check your library record" is a common item on library sites. Again, depending on the development of your library system, you may also be able to provide more of

Figure 12-1
Screenshot of Georgia State University Library Web site

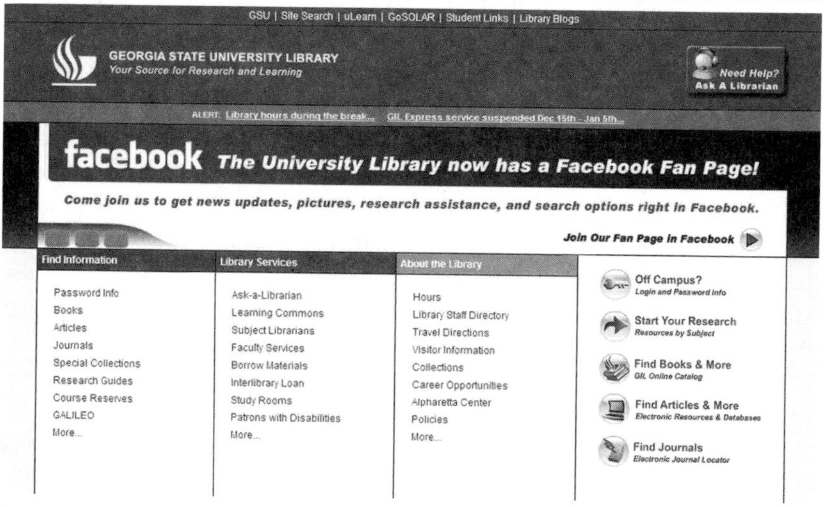

the discovery layer interface to library resources that was covered in Chapter 6.

- *A gateway to electronic resources.* Libraries need to organize the various periodical indexes, electronic reference collections, and other databases they subscribe to so that patrons can locate them. Multiple entry points are fairly typical for resource organizing systems: (1) alphabetical lists, (2) resources organized by subject, and (3) resources organized by type (periodical indexes, encyclopedias, etc.). The key is to give users the best chance to find the resource(s) that will benefit them the most. Metasearching, which was discussed in Chapter 8, is a common link on the opening page of the site in that it helps users try a search before choosing specific resources.
- *Accessing library databases remotely.* Instructions on how to use the library's proxy server or other authentication steps are a natural fit to the library Web site. If users are encountering the Web site from outside of the library they will likely need assistance in accessing licensed resources.
- *Library "how-to" guides or tutorials.* The Web provides great opportunities to place documents or interactive tutorials that can help users make use of the library. Both in-house and remote patrons can benefit from reading, listening, and/or watching explanations of how to choose and use electronic resources, or how to renew a book, etc. There are many examples of useful guides and tutorials on library sites.
- *Virtual reference.* Virtual reference can be conducted in a variety of ways. Its intent is to allow remote patrons to connect with library staff members and have their questions answered. Some methods, such as e-mail or IM, are relatively inexpensive, whereas commercial virtual reference vendor options, which often include Web-based chat, may be fairly expensive (see Figure 12-2). There are several choices to make, mostly revolving around how interactive the library intends this service to be (e-mail is a delayed, asynchronous technology) and when during the day the service will be offered. Regardless of the choice, virtual reference does provide another way to

Figure 12-2
Screenshot of St. Joseph County Public Library IM
reference service page

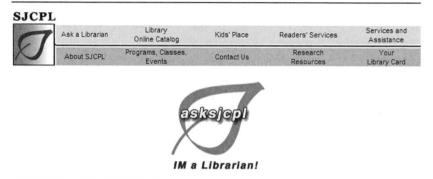

IM a Librarian!

Ask a question via a live chat session Monday through Saturday during library hours of operation. We have user names for AIM, Yahoo! and MSN Messenger. A librarian will gladly help you find the information you seek, be it in print or online.

For AIM: asksjcpl. AIM Online Status Indicator

For Yahoo!: asksjcpl. Yahoo Online Status Indicator

For MSN: asksjcpl@hotmail.com. MSN Online Status Indicator

For iChat: asksjcpl. AIM Online Status Indicator

connect with staff and seek their expertise. Interestingly, libraries that offer virtual reference sometimes find that in-house patrons will use virtual methods to connect with staff members who are only several feet away.

- *Library blogs.* Blogs are a new introduction to libraries and are mainly used to announce new resources or services at the library or to give patrons another venue to communicate with staff and provide feedback. Libraries can have a single blog with general library information or various subject-oriented blogs to reach different groups in their communities (for topics such as genealogy or physics). One thing that libraries are also doing is bringing postings from other blogs into their Web sites. These groups of postings, or **feeds**, can be gathered from the blog they are posted on using a technology called **RSS** (or really simple syndication). Libraries can in turn use RSS to make their own blog feed available for individual users to read using feed reader software or to post on their own Web sites. The online diary format of blogs makes it a perfect way to keep patrons updated and help the library distribute information in a way that does not overwhelm patron e-mail inboxes.

QUESTIONS TO ANSWER

When considering current sites and planning new ones it can be useful to ask a few questions to guide this process. The areas addressed here are a starting point for discussing and then creating new Web content.

1. *Who is the audience for your site?* Having an idea of who you are trying to reach can help you plan the content of the site. One consideration is whether your in-house and remote users will see the same homepage when they arrive at the site. In-house users will likely need quick links to certain electronic resources that you tend to use with them, while remote users may have other interests in mind (renewal, etc.).

2. *How will people come to your site?* Are you publicizing your site as a direct address, or is it a destination that people will come to from a page on your primary institution's site? This can influence what reference you need to make to that home institution.

3. *What do people most want to know about your library?* Based on the types of questions that people ask through other means and your best guesses, you should try to anticipate needs and supply them on your site.

4. *What services can your library uniquely provide through the Internet?* The services listed previously (such as virtual reference) are mostly ones that can only be offered through the communication and display means of the Internet. What could your library do on the Internet that

could be done in no other way? How can you benefit your community through offering these services?

5. *What is the best way to present your information?* You should consider a style, theme, or mode of organization that you will use on your main page and all other subsequent pages. Consistency will help you as you create additional pages and will help your users navigate the site.

6. *Have you looked at your site as your audience will?* A good hard look at the site standing in the shoes of a patron can illustrate issues and questions of terminology that a library staff member might miss.

7. *Does your larger organization have any requirements about what your site should look like or any information it should contain?* Many organizations have adopted **content management systems**, which allow centralized control for many design functions in a site, or set styles that are in place for every group within it.

THE TOOLS REQUIRED FOR WEB SITE DESIGN

As sites differ, so do the specific tools that the Web site designers and maintainers choose to work with. It may also be that the library does not have a staff member who actually does the design but that someone else in a larger organization is responsible for that task. I definitely recommend that libraries either stay fully in control of their own design or at least be knowledgeable enough to pass their ideas on to a Web designer. A variety of applications can be used to program HTML (hypertext markup language) and other Web programming languages (e.g., Javascript). Typically, designers will use two pieces of software: a Web design application, such as Macromedia Dreamweaver or Microsoft FrontPage, and image manipulation software, such as Adobe Photoshop or Macromedia Fireworks.

GENERAL GUIDELINES FOR INTERFACE DESIGN

Libraries, in their sites and services, can work to improve their users' experiences through *interface design*. Interface design is the act of creating the way people will interact and navigate electronic resources, such as an OPAC or a Web site. Libraries subscribe to a large number of interfaces that we cannot alter or control, such as various public and staff-oriented electronic databases. It is therefore crucial that libraries take the opportunities they have to affect users' experiences with their services and resources. Libraries need to consider what they can do to make using their library even easier for their community.

Another way of speaking about good interface design is *usability*. Usability is the concern that libraries should have that their users are finding what they need and are able to use their sites without difficulty. This can apply as an extension of the assistive and adaptive technology of Chapter 11, but it also reaches a wider group of users. The following suggestions will all go a long way toward improving the usability of library resources.

Some tips for improving interface design include the following:

1. *Resist the desire to tell users everything.* Search screens and Web sites can easily overwhelm people with information if careful design and restraint are not used. Library staff love to share information with their patrons, but here care is needed. Keep the interface simple.
2. *Seek input from users to help improve interfaces.* The process of design involves lots of trial and error and can succeed only if users are asked to evaluate an interface along the way. It can sometimes be hard to get user feedback, but attempts must be made
3. *Look at what others have done.* There is value in being creative and inventive with interface design, but seeking existing solutions can help the process. If an interface works or appeals in some way, the principles of its design can either be applied directly to a new interface or can at least guide the new design.

A final element of interface design that bears mentioning is the need for designing Web sites for mobile devices. As the use of smartphones and other reduced screen-size devices grows, there is greater potential for individuals with the devices to connect to our Web sites. Library staff must be aware of what their pages look like on these smaller screens and learn to make adjustments accordingly. The hope is for existing pages to be able to scale downward and to really work well for users at any screen resolutions.

QUESTIONS FOR REVIEW

1. What are some questions to ask when designing a library Web site?
2. What is virtual reference and how is it conducted?
3. Which services do you think your library's patrons are most interested in?
4. What services can libraries provide through their Web sites?
5. What is usability?

SELECTED SOURCES FOR FURTHER INFORMATION

Casey, Michael E., and Laura C. Savastinuk. 2007. *Library 2.0: A Guide to Participatory Library Service*. Medford, NJ: Information Today.
> This source does a nice job of combining introductory information on Library 2.0 technologies along with the philosophy and practicalities of a new service model. The suggestions within can be applied to library Web sites and other elements of library service.

Hanson, Kathlene, and H. Frank Cervone, eds. 2007. *Using Interactive Technologies in Libraries*. New York: Neal-Schuman.
> Covers the use of RSS, blogs, wikis, and podcasting in providing instruction, information, and ongoing guidance to library patrons. Each essay in the book provides a useful case example along with how-to information to replicate the effort in your own library.

Innovative Internet Applications in Libraries. Available: www.wilton library.org/innovate.html.
> Just as the title suggests, this site links to several examples of interesting ways to "save the time of the reader" using the Internet.

King, David Lee. 2007. "An Experience to Remember: Building Positive Experiences on Library Web Sites." In *Information Tomorrow: Reflections on Technology and the Future of Academic and Public Libraries* (pp. 131–142), edited by Rachel Singer Gordon. Medford, NJ: Information Today.
> King outlines some clear approaches to considering how users will experience your Web site and offers suggestions on improving Web site design.

Lehman, Tom, and Terry Nikkel. 2008. *Making Library Web Sites Usable: A LITA Guide*. New York: Neal-Schuman.
> Addresses many methods for assessing the usability of sites and offers suggestions on implementing changes to improve them.

Library Terms That Users Understand. Available: www.jkup.net/terms .html.

A wonderful set of resources collected by John Kupersmith and aimed at focusing libraries' use of terminology on increasing user understanding. Offers research studies and best practices for naming and describing library resources and services.

Nielson, Jakob. *The Alertbox: Current Issues in Web Usability.* **Available: www.useit.com/alertbox.**

A regularly posted column by a noted Web design authority. Offers suggestions on solving Web interface design problems and gives tips on Web technologies to use and avoid when designing a site.

Wilson, A. Paula. 2004. *Library Web Sites: Creating Online Collections and Services.* **Chicago: American Library Association.**

Contains design guidance and many good ideas for Web-based services. Good suggestions on adjusting content to reach multiple audiences within your community.

Chapter 13

How Library Staff Learn and Teach: Screencasts, Distance Learning, and Course Management Systems

The educational role of the library was immortalized in the early days of the past century when the public library was pronounced the "people's university." Whether or not a given library has a formal educational program today, a key function of library staff members is to instruct groups or individuals on the use of library tools. To aid in these efforts, an examination of instructional technologies is a fitting section of this book. Technology has had a huge impact on how and where education occurs. This chapter focuses on distance learning and presentation technologies.

WHAT IS DISTANCE LEARNING AND WHAT ROLES DOES IT HOLD FOR LIBRARIES?

Distance learning can be seen as just another method for connecting learners with educational materials. While most formal education takes place in a classroom, distance learning makes it possible for individuals to participate in a learning experience even if they are geographically distant from an instructor or are unable to meet in real time with a class. The idea is that a student can learn wherever they wish, whenever they wish, in an environment that requires independent work but is structured by an instructor and perhaps involves contact with other students. Several forms of distance learning, such as correspondence courses or televised and radio courses, have been practiced for many years, and all of them have involved one or more kinds of technology in order to facilitate exchanges and discussions between an instructor and students. Two-way communication must be available so that lessons can be sent out and feedback can be gained or questions answered.

Distance learning may occur at nearly any educational level, either in support of more traditional instruction or as the primary instructional means. Its growth as a method can create increased opportunities for libraries to come into contact with it in one of the following three ways:

1. Libraries may support distance learning by providing resources for participants. This may involve making equipment available in-house or providing information sources to help students with their studies. Academic libraries may need to support classes offered by their institutions through providing access to their databases to remote students. Public libraries who offer Internet access to community users may find distance learning students using this access to download assignments or contact instructors. They may also serve as sites for community groups to participate in videoconferencing. Whether our support is direct or on an ad-hoc basis, the implications of distance learning affects many libraries of all types.

2. Libraries that instruct their communities on how to use the library or its resources may well use distance learning techniques to reach remote users or distance learning participants. This would primarily apply to academic libraries, but other libraries may have opportunities to instruct remote users on an irregular basis.

3. Library staff members may themselves participate in continuing education or professional development opportunities via distance learning technologies, perhaps taking part in graduate and associate degree programs in

library and information science. There are also a number of other courses and workshops available to staff from educational institutions or professional organizations.

Distance learning is not for everyone or for every situation. In each instance, a set of supporting resources must be available for the instruction to work out. Sometimes those resources involve your library's collections so that you can help a distance-learning student find research materials for a paper or other assignments; at other times the resources might involve equipment. Distance learning has the potential to be a liberating experience for students, freeing them from the limitations of the traditional classroom and class schedule. Since there are a number of situations in which it does fit the need, we are bound to see an increasing numbers of opportunities becoming available.

SYNCHRONOUS AND ASYNCHRONOUS DISTANCE LEARNING TECHNOLOGIES

Synchronous technologies are ones in which the instructor and students are involved in the learning process at the same time. Some possibilities for **real-time communication** and interaction include:

- An audio teleconference (like a conference call) can be used and would be relatively inexpensive since participants are likely to have access to telephones. Interaction can be accomplished over the phone if needed. With some additional equipment, video can be transmitted over the phone (a process known as audiographics).
- Television can be used to send out a seminar or a class and can reach individuals in a local area cheaply and easily. Students probably own their own televisions and so there is little equipment investment needed. Television grows more expensive if satellite or cable transmission is required to reach a wider audience. In these situations, it is more common to use television for brief (half-day) teleconferences that are sent to predetermined locations (schools, libraries, etc.) that can receive satellite or cable transmissions. Interaction is again possible through telephone or e-mail.

- Videoconferencing is an excellent way to simulate the live classroom with two-way video and interaction. Demonstrations of nearly any kind are possible. It is rather expensive, however, because it requires videoconferencing equipment on both ends. This is never likely to be used to communicate to a large group of individuals at separate locations (at home, for instance). Rather, focused connections between the instructor's location and a single remote videoconferencing classroom can be used for brief workshops or full length college classes.
- The Internet offers several possibilities for synchronous communications. A virtual classroom, instant messaging, or a virtual world can be used for students and an instructor to exchange information and questions. Virtual classrooms may be built within a course management system or may be free-standing environments. They typically allow for multiple individuals to share images, slides, video, audio, interactive chat, and shared Web browsing capabilities for meetings, **Webinars**, or credit classes. Two examples of this are Wimba (www.wimba.com) and Elluminate (www.elluminate.com). Instant messaging (IM) is another possibility for contact between an instructor and a single student. In addition to Second Life, there are a number of online virtual worlds, environments in which several individuals can interact over the Internet in a more immersive environment. The expense of IM and Second Life is typically minimal since basic access to educational virtual world space is often free and IM clients are freely downloaded. The first requires licensing of software and concurrent "seats" for participants from a vendor. Instructors and students can connect from all over the globe using their Internet accounts.

Asynchronous technologies are ones that allow delayed interaction between students and the instructor. Lessons are sent out and assignments and questions are sent back without any (or much) real-time interaction. Examples include:

- Correspondence courses, which are the longest time-tested method of distance learning, involve students reading a text or separate lessons and then taking tests to prove their knowledge. There may be a little interaction with an instructor to clarify points, but typically the student is working when and where he or she wishes in order to meet course deadlines. Much book knowledge can be communicated this way, but there is no ability to demonstrate processes or equipment in real time.

- Video-based learning involves providing videos or DVDs of lectures and demonstrations to students who watch them when they wish. It makes use of technology that students would commonly own (VCRs, DVD players, and televisions) and adds interaction by phone or e-mail. Students have the freedom to watch the instructional material multiple times to help them review the material. However, as is common to other methods of distance learning, few opportunities exist for group discussion or interaction of any kind.

- Web-based learning is somewhat similar to these other methods in that learning materials are placed on a Web site and students have the freedom to use them on their own schedule. Audio, video, and static images can be added to text and participants can interact asynchronously via e-mail or Web message boards.

COURSE MANAGEMENT SYSTEMS

Any discussion of distance learning technologies is not complete without mention of **course management systems**, which offer elements of both synchronous and asynchronous interaction. Course management systems are Web-based products that provide the technological framework for wholly distance-taught or online supplemented courses. They are often used in college and university settings as either commercial or open source products. They offer Web space to place documents and other textual course materials as well as a central place for students to find links to other online content. In addition, course management systems can host interactive chat sessions with multiple students and provide for the presentation of visuals as well as text. Testing and survey options are available. A major commercial vendor of these products is Blackboard (www.blackboard.com), and an open source example is Moodle (www.moodle.org).

As a side note, there have been some efforts in the past few years to have academic librarians interact with faculty and students in course management system classrooms. These *embedded librarians* take this step to be readily available to students at their point of need in working on class assignments and research. This is of particular import with students who are taking classes entirely online or who spend most of their time distant from the college or university offering the class. The librarian will typically post useful research links, Web-based tutorials or screencasts, and interact synchronously or asynchronously with individual students or the whole class. Some embedded librarians stay in the course for a short time and others are present during an entire semester or term.

WHAT ARE PRESENTATION TECHNOLOGIES AND HOW ARE THEY USED BY LIBRARIES?

Presentation technologies allow us to share information with an audience in a visual manner. Our presentations can be made more vivid and more informative by bringing in visual aids through the use of display equipment, media items, and presentation software. While there are many situations in which a verbal presentation will suffice, for many situations it would be nice to either demonstrate an activity, to show the resources that are being discussed, or to illustrate key points of the talk in a visible manner. The methods discussed here can accomplish these purposes.

There are three basic roles for **presentation technology** in libraries: (1) the display equipment and media items can be managed and scheduled for use within the organization that the library is a part of; (2) elements of the technology, particularly media items, may be circulated to the community at large; and (3) use of presentation technology can be incorporated into library instructional efforts. Both patron training in library resources or services and staff training can be aided by presentation technology, as can any informational presentation.

DISPLAY EQUIPMENT

Display equipment allows a user to project text, graphics, video, or live demonstrations of electronic library resources onto a screen. While historically this equipment has included such venerable items as slide projectors and film and filmstrip projectors, today the primary means of display involve **LCD (liquid crystal display) projectors**. Overhead projectors, which are still used, are able to project only either hand-drawn or mass produced transparencies. LCD equipment (often called digital projectors) can project output from computers, VCRs, television, and other items. They tend to be fairly expensive (though growing much less so) and require at least a somewhat darkened room to work well. Digital projectors can be mounted on the ceiling of room or can be mobile as part of a computer cart unit. A new technology called DLP (**digital light processing**) is currently challenging LCD. DLP provides a much brighter image in projection but is still quite expensive for wide implementation.

Another direction for display equipment is the use of interactive white boards. These items connect a large screen display with the ability to interact with presented materials by touching or "writing" on the screen. Software allows for the capture of what is drawn or written for later use (posting notes to the class, etc.). The screens resemble typical white boards but are connected to a computer, either a desktop or laptop, to enable the display of digital presentation materials or interactive Internet content.

MEDIA ITEMS

Computer presentation in all of its possibilities is overtaking traditional media items. Transparencies, typically mass-produced collections, are sometimes still found in libraries that serve an educational community, but they are rarities. Photographic slides are more effectively used in digital form now, where they can be incorporated into presentation software and included in distance learning. It is common for existing slide collections to be scanned and collected in electronic databases. Filmstrips used to be found in great numbers in many libraries, but they are very much a dead technology and have been converted to videocassette or Web delivered materials. The more common forms of media used in presentations are again those that are in wide use in society: DVDs, videocassettes, computer produced presentations, and live projections of computer software.

PRESENTATION SOFTWARE

Presentation software (e.g., PowerPoint) can bring together both old and new media to create a professional presentation. Each individual screen or segment of the presentation is known as a "**slide**." Anything that can be produced or brought into a computer can be added to that slide: text, links to Web sites, video clips, sound—you name it. The programs offer templates and preset designs for new users while leaving many creative options open for advanced users. It is not difficult to produce a professional presentation using this software.

SCREENCASTS

Libraries might also make use of software such as Captivate, Camtasia, or Articulate. With these applications, you can take presentations like those described previously and turn them into free-standing videos that can be linked from the library's Web site and available to patrons at any time. Articulate also lets you add sound to the presentation. Captivate and Camtasia add the capacity to record live action work in a Web browser or an office application to show users exactly how to move around in a resource. The resulting video tutorials, or screencasts, can prove to be powerful instructional tools. They allow users to easily review the use of a database or the process of evaluating information found on the Web. A key point with *screencasts* is to keep them short enough (or in modular format) so that patrons can quickly get to the particular piece that they need.

QUESTIONS FOR REVIEW

1. What are the three roles that libraries may assume in distance learning?

2. What is an LCD projector?
3. Explain the difference between synchronous and asynchronous technologies, and give examples of each.
4. What presentation software do you have available in your library?
5. Have you ever participated in distance learning? Would you recommend it to someone else based on what you have read in this chapter or on your own experience?

SELECTED SOURCES FOR FURTHER INFORMATION

"The Embedded Librarian." Available: http://embeddedlibrarian.word-press.com.
A blog that discusses issues related to embedding librarians more closely to researchers in all types of organizations.

Hall, Russell. 2008. "The 'Embedded' Librarian in a Freshman Speech Class." *College & Research Libraries News* **69, no. 1 (January). Available: www.acrl.org/ala/mgrps/divs/acrl/publications/crlnews/2008/jan/embeddedlibrarian.cfm.**
An example of an embedded librarian working in a course management system to assist students with research.

Heinich, Robert, et al. 1999. *Instructional Media and Technologies for Learning.* **Upper Saddle River, NJ: Merrill.**
Though a bit dated, this source remains the definitive guide to understanding and using presentation and distance learning technologies along with much more. Good explanations of teaching methods and approaches to use when using technology for instruction.

Mackey, Thomas P., and Trudi E. Jacobson, eds. 2008. *Using Technology to Teach Information Literacy.* **New York: Neal-Schuman.**
An excellent collection of chapters on different facets of teaching information literacy skills using technology, each authored by a librarian and faculty member team. Covers a wide variety of current technologies that can be used for instructional purposes.

Melling, Maxine, ed. 2005. *Supporting E-learning: A Guide for Library and Information Managers.* **New York: Neal-Schuman.**
Covers the basics of online instruction and learning as well as the training and relationships needed by the library to successfully support distance learning.

PART IV

Building and Maintaining the
Technology Environment in
Libraries

Chapter 14

Protecting Technology and Technology Users: Spam, Spyware, and Security Strips

Information technology bears few physical dangers for its users, but users can be quite dangerous to technology. Unfortunately, people can steal, damage, or even unintentionally ruin the technology we (and they) depend on. While it would be an overreaction to treat each patron like a suspect and to release guard dogs to roam among the stacks at night, we can take some steps to protect the technology we spend so much on. And, to be fair, there are ways that patrons' personal information can be put in jeopardy. This chapter will explore some of the areas of concern for security and some methods to consider.

Security measures are generally split between methods that attempt to secure equipment or media (e.g., cabling a CPU to a table) and those that attempt to secure software and electronic information resources. Security systems/**RFID (radio frequency identification**) and locks/secure locations mainly deal with the former while limiting functions and electronic security handle the latter.

SECURITY SYSTEMS/RFID

Library security systems are very common at most types of libraries and provide **physical security** for materials in the collection. While they protect more than just technology items in the library, they are an example of a technology that library staff should be aware of and familiar with. Most systems are composed of a set of sensor panels (with or without gates) at all entrances to and exits from the library. The sensors are set to detect an adhesive magnetic strip or sticker inside or on each item within the library. Items that are correctly checked out of the library at the circulation desk have either been "desensitized" (passed over a demagnetizing machine) or covered by a card and will not set off the alarm at the exit or gate. The systems are not without their flaws and failures, but they provide a sound level of protection for circulating and noncirculating books, media, periodicals, and other items in the library's collection.

RFID is a related method for libraries to protect their physical collections. RFID adds something to the security strip magnetizing/demagnetizing process mentioned. Each item in the collection has an RFID tag placed in or on it. The tag includes not only a setting that indicates if the item may or may not leave the library but also coding that identifies the item. In a sense, it combines the actions of a barcode and a magnetic strip. But wait, there's more! The tag is easily read by RFID equipment without being seen (so no need to open a book to display the tag), and multiple tags may be read at one time. The tag consists of a computer chip with an antenna attached.

From a library perspective, RFID offers the possibility of maneuvering materials around the library with great efficiency. Patrons may take tagged items to self-checkout stations and, merely by placing a pile of items on a scanner, check them all out (the alarm system is turned off for each item to go through the security gates). When the items are returned, the tags can be recognized by sorting machinery that places books (in order) on the proper book trucks to be reshelved. Once items have been shelved in the library, shelf-reading can be done with a handheld scanner that will indicate items that are misshelved by reading their tags, which include information on their call numbers. Inventories can be accomplished with a similar method.

The downsides of RFID relate to questions about privacy and start-up costs. There are ongoing questions about the signal that the tag gives off and the content stored on the tag. While vendors and others indicate that the range of the signal is quite short, between 2 and 12 inches, the fear is that individuals carrying library materials could have those items become known to other people scanning for tags from a distance. There is also a fear that patron information will become stored on the tag and thus compromise patrons' privacy if this information could be accessed, though no patron information is included in the tag. There are a number of questions yet to be fully answered about this technology, as its capabilities go beyond what libraries have typically placed on any item. The expense issue is a bit more clear-cut, as the cost of the individual tags is substantial, as is the time expense of touching every item in the collection. Despite these questions, a growing number of libraries are choosing this method of **collection control**.

A fair question to ask about security systems or RFID is whether the cost to install or replace these technologies represents a savings over the expected theft rate of materials without the equipment. A library operating with a regular replacement of stolen or missing items can do the math of these losses over the expected lifetime of the system. If, however, theft is a less regular happening at your library, you might be better off establishing a missing item replacement fund in the library's acquisition budget and save money in the long run.

LOCKS/SECURE LOCATIONS

For those technology items that need to be available to the public, a number of measures can be taken to secure them. Equipment such as computers, DVD players, televisions, etc., can be bolted or cabled to the furniture on which it sits. It may be a good idea to lock the case of a computer's CPU (central processing unit) to protect internal components from theft. If a library has any items that are meant to be moved around within the building (TV/DVD player carts, computers, film or LCD projectors, CD players, etc.), these can be locked in a storage room to prevent unexpected mobility. Media items that circulate need to be tagged the same as printed materials for the library's security system. Items held in staff areas probably do not require the same level of protection unless the overall security of the library's building is an issue. As well, items that are easily observed from a service point may not need the same security as those that are more hidden from view. Finally, a regular inventory of equipment or media can help ensure that items are present and that they are correctly secured.

Another option for securing materials and equipment is restricting the public's access to them. This can take the form of having a closed collection of media items—for instance, placing all videos behind the circulation desk or another service point, or setting time limits on the use of in-house equipment, such as a half hour time limit on Internet computers. It can also be applied in assigning shorter circulation periods to certain types of items that we might consider to be at risk. Care needs to be taken here so that undue restrictions are not placed that hinder the public's use of technology. A level of restriction should be sought that safeguards equipment but gives the public ample freedom to browse collections or use equipment. Strict time limits or closed collections should be applied only in situations where prior damage or conflict would dictate their use or where they might deter attempts to elude security measures. The danger of setting too severe restrictions in the library is that while increasing them is never hard, relaxing ingrained restrictions can be difficult.

LIMITING FUNCTIONS

This method of protection involves restricting certain uses for technology rather than controlling access to it. While many types of equipment and media can have certain functions disabled by the vendor (a key lock on the paper tray drawer of a copier, videotapes that cannot be recorded over, microfilm reader/printers that will not make multiple copies of an image), the majority of solutions offered here relate to restricting computers and software. There are a number of capabilities you would rather not let the general public have on your public computers: deleting files, installing their own software, changing the look of the operating system or software applications. Some of these limitations can be placed using restrictions available in your operating system itself. Options differ depending on whether you are using Windows XP, Mac OS X, etc. Others will require computer security software, which can lock up both individual software titles and parts of the operating system as needed. Most security applications have both preset options for shutting down a piece of software and the ability to restrict only certain functions.

The Internet has caused libraries to seek some ways to limit access to public computers. One method, mentioned in Chapter 9, is **filtering software** that can be used to eliminate access to a set list of Internet sites. Software of this sort can be set up on individual computers or at the server level to control a large number of stations. An additional method of limiting Internet access is to install a filtering proxy server to stand between library computers and the outside Internet. While it can be used to restrict sites that some people may find offensive, much use of proxy servers involves limiting the access of public computers to certain electronic resources (and not full-blown Internet access). For instance, a library may decide that of their ten computers, four should be exclusively for accessing their OPAC (online public access catalog) and periodical databases while the remaining six can be used to access the OPAC, periodical databases, and the Internet. The proxy server could be set to eliminate Web e-mail and chat sites as well. I tend to recommend against restrictions like this, but not in situations where computer use is high and keeping all ten machines open to Internet use means that no one can easily jump in and search the library's periodical indexes.

ELECTRONIC SECURITY

Electronic security measures are also primarily aimed at computers and servers in the library. The issues libraries face with electronic security of their publicly accessible servers are similar to those faced by businesses and other organizations. Anytime you make a server available to the outside world there is the chance that someone will try to break into it and either damage the server or use it for their own purposes. Library servers can contain all sorts of valuable data—OPAC records, library Web site files, personal documents—none of which library staff would like to lose and some of which they would rather no one could see, such as patron and staff ID numbers and contact information and subscription sources that are loaded on the library server. Libraries need to take steps to build a **firewall** between their server and the Internet so that only the information they would like people to access is available to the public and only those who are allowed to use secured areas of the server can do so. A variety of software options are available to accomplish this.

Wireless networks offer an extra dimension to the issue of server security. Since wireless signals by nature will travel outward from a building equipped with wireless access points, there is the potential for users outside of the library to connect to the network. While the signals can be blocked or lessened by book shelves or other metallic objects, it is inescapable that someone with a wireless laptop could sit in your parking lot and have access. By requiring users to log in to the network and by setting up a firewall that constricts their access, their usage of the network can be controlled.

Another area of electronic security is more likely to affect public and staff computers. Computer viruses are easily distributed over the Internet and by other means and can pose even an accidental threat to libraries. Part of the reason for software that limits functions on public computers is to keep individuals from either downloading a virus from the Web or bringing a virus in on disk and running it on the computer's hard drive. Viruses are not always destructive but tend to be quite annoying and time-consuming. Having had to delete the contents of a hard drive in order to rid a computer of a virus (and reload everything), I can tell you that there is only a fine line between destruction and annoyance. Viruses can cause applications to malfunction and lock up, generating effects such as a line of text that automatically inserts itself in all of your word processing documents. They can be written to reformat hard drives or to surreptitiously corrupt important data files.

The two greatest concerns with viruses are: (1) patrons either accidentally or purposely placing a virus on a public computer or (2) staff members accidentally ending up with a virus by downloading it or receiving it as an e-mail attachment. Viruses can be sent in e-mail as an attached file. If someone opens the file, the virus goes to work. E-mail attachment viruses are becoming more common and can easily be mistaken for a reputable file. Antivirus software should be installed on both staff and public computers so that the hard drive can be regularly scanned for viruses on boot-up and that downloaded files can be checked before they are run. Staff members also need to know how to react when viruses are discovered on public computers and to be aware of the dangers of viruses sent to their e-mail accounts.

Beyond viruses, the Internet is rife with opportunities for patrons to click on and download programs that hinder the speed of computers and increase the chances of identity theft. **Identity theft** is a situation where patron or staff information (e.g., Social Security numbers, other personal identification numbers, credit card or bank account information) are captured by a malicious party. **Spyware** can be loaded on a computer without the user realizing it, and this software can be used to track an individual's path online and record personal information (including passwords). Software such as Ad-Aware (www.lavasoftusa.com) or Spyware Doctor (www.pctools.com/spyware-doctor) can be used to root it out. Library staff must be sure that their antivirus software stays updated to help catch newly created spyware. As well, they can make use of the pop-up blocking capacity of various pieces of software. **Pop-ups** are Internet browser windows with advertisements that suddenly appear as a user loads a Web site. These pop-ups, annoying on their own, have been a source for spyware: if a user clicks on the ad, the spyware can start to download and install itself. Internet browsers such as Internet Explorer, Firefox, and Opera include pop-up blocking features.

Spam is one hidden consumer of **bandwidth** that can slow the Internet access of a library if staff members are not protected from it. Spam consists of junk-mail-like e-mails that are sent along to multiple users and can fill a given individual's inbox. The bandwidth-clogging aspects of hundreds of unwanted messages funneling their way toward the library's servers are bad enough. Lost productivity from sorting through the chaff for the wheat of e-mail communication is another costly problem. If a library's Internet access comes through an outside provider, it is likely that some spam filtering is already happening. But individual users will want to check their e-mail software for options to deal with junk mail, including identifying certain topics or senders as automatically ignored e-mail (sent straight to a junk folder). Larger libraries that serve as their own Internet provider will want to consider installing spam filters on their mail servers that can cut off spam before it reaches staff members. There are also services that sort through an organization's e-mail before it reaches the organization's server and holds the offending mail on the filtering service's server. This lessens the impact on the bandwidth available to the library.

SAMPLE SECURED PUBLIC COMPUTER

Here is one possible set of tools you could use and steps you could take to secure public computers. Let's say you have one or more Pentium computers running Windows XP, connected to a network, and using the following applications: Firefox, Adobe Acrobat Reader, Quicktime, a telnet application, and various other pieces of office software (Microsoft Word, etc.). You could use the following products and practices for security:

1. Set restrictions to the Windows XP registry. The Windows operating system has a list of application settings called the registry. These settings influence Windows itself and any additional applications you might install. While you should be careful about making changes directly to the registry itself, you can use a free program from Microsoft called Poledit (or Policy Editor) to stop users from changing your settings on public computers. For instance, you can stop users from changing the background image on the Windows desktop or from altering the default printer.
2. Use WINSelect software from Faronics (or a similar package). This is an example of the computer security software that can be installed to limit the functions of applications on the computer. For instance, you might wish to lock out certain functions of Firefox, such as access to an e-mail client or the ability of users to set the

default text size in the browser. FileGuard, by Intego (www.intego.com/fileGuard) is similar software for Macintosh computers.

3. Rather than a standard telnet application, which can be a security risk, you could use a product such as Secure Shell (SSH) from SSH Communications (www.ssh.com) to connect to a server.

4. Use an antivirus software package. Norton Antivirus and McAfee are two of the most trusted names available, but there are other options. Sites such as Anti-Virus Guide (www.firewallguide.com/anti-virus.htm) offer reviews and resources for protecting your computer from viruses. There are a number of free or shareware options available.

5. Set a CMOS (complementary metal-oxide semiconductor) password. The CMOS is the semiconductor or chip that runs the computer. It has a small amount of memory in it that runs on battery power. This memory holds settings for the computer that a malevolent user could access and alter during the computer's boot-up process. Setting a password for CMOS access will restrict access to basic settings on the computer that, if changed, could allow an individual to bypass other security settings.

6. The computer should be placed in an area visible to the reference or circulation desks and cabled to the furniture. The CPU case should be locked.

SAMPLE SECURED DVD/VIDEO COLLECTION AND VIEWING STATION

If you had a collection of DVDs and videos and the equipment to view them on, this is one picture of how security could look:

1. Individual DVDs and videos could be shelved behind a service desk, with the ability to search for these items in the OPAC or by browsing a print catalog of titles in a binder. Many libraries have chosen the same method that video rental stores use: display the empty cases for patrons to choose from and then have them ask for the actual DVD or video at the service desk.

2. DVDs and videos and their cases could be tagged for the library security system.
3. The DVD player and VCR and accompanying television (or VCR/DVD/TV combo) can be cabled or bolted to the furniture it sits on.
4. Patrons could be required to check out headphones in order to use the viewing station (if there was a concern about letting individuals walk in and use the equipment with their own media).
5. If there is a concern about damage to the DVDs or videos, the checkout period could be fairly short. Items could be given one or two hour loans so that they effectively could be viewed only in-house.
6. Train staff who issue media items to examine each container's contents both before checkout and after the item is returned (in the presence of the patron, if possible). The outside of the containers and/or the OPAC record should list the exact contents of each box so that missing elements may be spotted immediately.

QUESTIONS FOR REVIEW

1. Name four security issues that impact public computers in a library.
2. What is spyware and how is it used?
3. What is a filtering proxy server and what does it do?
4. How are materials secured physically in your library?
5. Are there any restrictions on what users can do with computers in your library?

SELECTED SOURCES FOR FURTHER INFORMATION

Earp, Paul W., and Adam Wright. 2009. *Securing Library Technology: A How-To-Do-It Manual.* New York: Neal-Schuman.
   The information in this book will enable a library staff to conduct a security needs assessment and to construct a comprehensive security plan for their public technologies, networks, and servers.
F-Secure Security Information Center. 2008. Available: www.f-secure.com/security_center.
   A site that identifies computer viruses and offers solutions for removing them from your computer.

Reed, Charles. 2008. "The Right Mindset." *Library and Archival Security* **21, no. 2: 59–67.**

> This article suggests taking a broader perspective on physical security in libraries beyond merely protecting the materials. A good read for thinking about what you hope your security strategy will accomplish—what are you really protecting?

"Virus Protection." 2008. Dublin, OH: WebJunction. Available: www.webjunction.org/virus-protect.

> Useful and up-to-date links from WebJunction on virus protection strategies and software (along with thoughts on dealing with spyware and malware of other kinds).

Ward, Diane Marie. 2007. *The Complete RFID Handbook: A Manual and DVD for Assessing, Implementing, and Managing Radio Frequency Identification Technologies in Libraries.* **New York: Neal-Schuman.**

> An excellent book on RFID and its practical and potential benefits in the library setting. It provides helpful advice on choosing RFID systems and implementing them in your setting.

"Workstation Protection." 2008. Dublin, OH: WebJunction. Available: www.webjunction.org/pc-protection.

> This section of the WebJunction site includes several helpful documents on technologies for public computer security. The site provides models of individual libraries' security setups, guidance on using specific products, and overviews of available options.

I would also recommend searching the archives of the **Web4Lib** electronic discussion group at **http://lists.webjunction.org/web4lib/search/index.cgi**. Many posts over the years have involved security measures of one kind or another.

Chapter 15

When Things Fall Apart: Troubleshooting Tips for Every Technology User

Unfortunately, all of the technology we have discussed in the preceding chapters is prone to stop working correctly (or at all) at some point. This can be a frustrating experience on many levels. We lose the opportunity to complete an action that is underway, as when a copier jams or our connection to a database is lost. We lose our work completely, as when word processing software locks up and our document does not save. Our first reaction is made worse in situations where we realize we are unable to fix a problem and need to wait for **technical support**.

If you spend much time using technology, you will find that many difficulties can be solved with a few basic skills. While I am by no means downplaying the importance of technical support knowledge for an organization, I would like to suggest that many "fixes" can be handled by the end user, otherwise known as "you." The goal of this chapter is equip you to troubleshoot technology. My hope is that you will learn how to solve a number of problems on your own and that you will also know when to seek the help of experts.

TROUBLESHOOTING GUIDELINES

The following is what I hope will be a useful set of suggestions for preparing to troubleshoot. Preparation is a good prescription for any activity in the library. With troubleshooting, one of the best ways to prepare is to be ready to do some creative thinking. That way, if your preparations and method fall through, you may still be able to reason your way through fixing a problem. Starting from that point, let's take a look at the preparations.

- *Gain and maintain common knowledge.* Treat each problem you encounter as a learning experience and document your solution procedures carefully. There is great value in being able to remember an earlier solution to a problem you are having. It may not be possible to keep a written record of each troubleshooting situation and the solution to each problem. However, it is crucial for two things to happen. First, if you are involved in troubleshooting a technology problem, make sure that you see the final solution applied, even if it requires an outside expert to apply it. Second, make sure that the solution is made known to all members of the library staff. This way, you can try to build up a group knowledge base and you also empower other staff members so that they can possibly fix the situation if you are not available.
- *Be safe.* When you first approach a piece of malfunctioning equipment, be sure that your goal is to do no harm to yourself or the equipment. Some elements of safe practices come from knowing something about the item you are working on (e.g., the paper can be removed from one section of the copier by lifting the green lever and turning crank number two) and others are common knowledge (e.g., do not scuff your feet on the carpet and then touch the motherboard or you might destroy or disable it with static electricity). Avoiding static electricity and always reading any warning signs on the equipment are my best advice in this area. I have burned my hand on microfilm reader/printers enough times to make me more conscious of the marked "hot" areas. Another thing: you can be safe, but I cannot guarantee that you will keep your hands clean. Any device that spews toner is bound to be messy. Get to know your equipment and do not be afraid of it. Read manuals and poke around. Having a fear of

breaking something can really hinder your troubleshooting efforts.

- *Check the obvious.* Some might reject this idea by asking, "how should I know what's obvious?" Here again, experience is our best guide. If we have a piece of equipment that breaks down on some regular basis (even months apart), we have a basis for obvious fixes: look for the problem that happened last time and try to apply the same solution. Likewise, if you know something about how a piece of equipment works, you can check a variety of parts that are essential to keeping it running (are the cables plugged in tightly, does it seem to be getting power, maybe there's a paper jam, is the projector bulb really working?). The most successful troubleshooting technique I have found is a pretty easy one. If an electronic piece of equipment is not working, turn it off and then back on. The results are sometimes quite startling, and though you really do not learn anything about the problem from this solution, it is often extremely effective. I do suggest that this technique be known by everyone in a library organization since it can be effective in so many situations. When you face a problem with a piece of technology that has never broken down before or one whose operation is a mystery to you, it is time to turn to the next steps.
- *Look for clues.* Not to overstate the obvious here, but on occasion a piece of equipment or software will give off some clues as to why it had stopped working correctly. Sometimes these are very clear, as in the case of displayed error messages, and other times they can be reached through inductive only reasoning—"the paper goes up to only this point and then jams, so there must be something making it jam back in this section." One technique I have found to be helpful is to have the patron or coworker who is having a problem with the technology explain to you how the problem began. You may be able to pick up a clue of what is really going wrong through some detail that the problem reporter provides.
- *Read the manual.* Though they are sometimes poorly written or too brief in their explanations, the manuals that

accompany technology can be helpful for finding solutions or correctly identifying a given problem. While in the heat of the moment we are probably more likely to forge ahead without reading, it can really pay to take a moment and locate any manuals or help documentation you have. We hang onto these things for some reason, right? This is the time to pull them off of the shelf. Diagrams can be helpful at times, and sometimes reading about the common problems that some manuals list can be educational. ("Well, it's not that part or that problem at least. What else could it be?") I will admit that I have been frustrated sometimes by the fact that the manual did not help at all, but I have vowed to never overlook this resource since I have had some successes.

- *Check the Web.* A natural supplement or replacement to any printed material we may have is turning to the Web for guidance from the manufacturer or from other users. Many vendors' Web sites will list troubleshooting tips or FAQs (lists of frequently asked questions) on solving problems. There may be help available here that never made it into the manual. The same goes for reading the archives of a vendor-sponsored Web forum or a public Usenet newsgroup that includes discussions of similar problems. Someone may have already located an answer and made it available to the world at large through the Internet. Some of my favorite spots to look are the following:

  1. Use the Open Directory Project's listing of library and information science chats and forums (www.dmoz .org/ Reference/Libraries/Library_and_Information_Science/ Chats_and_Forums) to ask questions of library colleagues.
  2. Check the vendor's site to see if there are troubleshooting FAQs or user forums available. The Librarian's Yellow Pages (librariansyellowpages.com) may be useful for tracking down a vendor's site, or you can use search engines such as Google (www.google.com).
  3. Google Groups (groups.google.com) is an excellent resource for searching archived discussions for specific technologies and problems.

4. WebJunction (www.webjunction.org/basic-trouble shooting/resources/wjarticles) has a section on support and troubleshooting computers and other equipment that may be helpful.

- *Ask for advice.* There are some troubleshooting situations where we find ourselves blocked from progress. Sometimes we have truly reached a dead end and are unsure of where to turn next, and other times we wisely conclude that it is too dangerous to go further. Now is the time to seek advice from any and all quarters. The previous step can be an example of this, but now it is time to try a more active approach than browsing documents or older messages. Post a message to a newsgroup, electronic discussion group, or vendor forum. Ask colleagues near and far if they have any ideas. Exhaust any technical support options that you have. I tend to try out my free options before incurring any charges, but your need for a solution may be such that you should go to the real experts right away.

- *Watch the expert at work and learn.* If you do get advice or direct assistance in person or over the phone that actually solves the problem, be sure to watch carefully and ask questions. This information can be really key to building up your experience and the general troubleshooting knowledge of the library. You may learn a new technique or discover that this really is a more difficult problem to diagnose than you thought. Be a student here and pay attention so that you can be better prepared down the road.

TIPS FOR AVOIDING PROBLEMS

The following are some thoughts that have served me well over time as general tips on solving technical problems of one kind or another. Your particular situation may not be covered here. However, one of these tips may help you in the future.

- Many problems involve paper jams or related difficulties. You should know (or learn) how paper feeds through all of the printing, copying, and faxing devices in your library.

- Printer memory errors are common when large documents are sent to older printers. Printers may lock up completely or they may print pages full of garbage characters and images. Know how to cancel print jobs and the correct steps to clear out your printer memory. It can be as easy as turning the printer off and then on. If you are in a networked printing environment, find out who has the power to cancel print jobs (if it is not you) and how to clear the entire print queue—the collection of waiting print jobs—if necessary.
- Many examples of technology equipment can get pretty dusty. Dust can collect inside CPU (central processing unit) cases and keyboards and cause them to stop working. A can of compressed air can be very helpful in these circumstances. You may wish to regularly check and clean equipment in this way. Computer mice will also pick up lint and dust and lose some sensitivity. Pop out the mouse ball every so often (look for directions on the bottom of your mouse) and shake out the foreign matter.
- If you notice even a minor problem with a piece of equipment that is used by multiple staff members or the public, be sure to note it to whoever else on staff might get a complaint about it. Forewarned can be forearmed in some cases, and in others it is good to pay attention to smaller issues before they grow into larger ones. There are times when library staff may not realize just how often a small problem or error arises because no one remarks on it. We cannot force patrons to make note of problems, but staff can try to do their best to get the word out to one another.
- Putting together a troubleshooting toolkit can be a useful exercise. This should at least be an actual toolkit, with the requisite screwdrivers, extra screws, cleaning equipment, and other items that fit your library. It can also involve organizing your printed manuals and other help documentation and having a list or set of bookmarks of where to go for more help online. I urge you to make this collection of tools available to as many staff members as are comfortable to try troubleshooting. The initial collection of items may serve as a point to educate your coworkers

(and become educated yourself) on what are some good troubleshooting strategies.

QUESTIONS FOR REVIEW

1. Make a list of common errors in or failures from technologies in your library. Be sure to ask your colleagues for input.
2. What are the steps you usually follow when technology fails? Are there one or more suggested steps in this chapter that would improve this process?
3. What common technology problem in libraries is mentioned in the chapter?
4. Which troubleshooting technique is important enough for every member of a library staff to know?
5. Identify a knowledgeable technology troubleshooter in your organization and ask them to help you create a document on troubleshooting common problems.

Chapter 16

Building the Technology Environment: Ergonomics, Infrastructure, and Gaming

Just plug it in. That's all it takes to get going with our newest technological purchase, right? Find a chair and a table, maybe, or just stick it on your desk, or maybe over there on the floor. An outlet is all it takes, right? No problem!

Well, that all depends. Each of the technologies discussed in this book have a number of characteristics: how they are used, why they might be used, and so on. What has not been covered so far are some considerations about the ability of a given library building to accommodate a given technology. Some items will indeed simply plug in to a free outlet and work right away. Others will take more thought and preparation.

Beyond talking about issues of installing technology, there are also some questions about using the technologies. How can the process of using technology be made as comfortable as possible? These questions have implications both for staff members and library patrons and will be addressed.

PHYSICAL CONSIDERATIONS

The library building needs to be considered a technological environment. A number of characteristics about a given library affect its ability to house individual technologies. Each major characteristic is discussed in this chapter. Whether a library is starting fresh with a new building, redesigning existing space, or merely adding to that space, certain general criteria should be examine. The most important characteristics will change depending on the technology involved.

Electricity

Does the library have the electrical capacity to handle an ever-growing amount of electronic equipment? Libraries can find themselves either adding new electronic equipment to a building that has never had it or trying to place additional equipment in a nearly overloaded arrangement. Many pieces of equipment, such as computers, can present a constant draw on electricity. A number of power-saving options are available, however, such as operating system settings in Windows or Mac OS that will automatically reduce processor speeds or set monitors to draw less power in periods of disuse.

Aside from overloading a library's circuitry, equipment needs to be protected from power surges by using surge protectors. It is important that surge protectors have a rating of at least UL1449. For servers or other equipment, uninterruptible power sources (UPSs) may also be needed to eliminate the effects of unexpected power losses. These will keep equipment from experiencing the jarring effects of a sudden loss of power and will keep library systems and users from losing data. Library staff members need to consult with electricians and computer support personnel to see what capabilities are available for electrical equipment and what protective measures should be undertaken.

Heating, Ventilation, and Air-conditioning

Can the ventilation and air-conditioning systems of the library keep the technology within from overheating? In the old days of library automation, it was easy to stick the computer (or computers) in a single, air-conditioned room. Now that computers and other devices are everywhere in the library, thought needs to be given to keeping the heat down. Some equipment, such as a network server, should be treated as especially sensitive to fluctuations in temperature and kept in a separate, cool area. Still, the general characteristics of a library in terms of heat, cooling, and airflow can impact all equipment. Once again, library staff members need to consult with experts in this area to determine optimum HVAC (heating, ventilation, and air-conditioning) systems and settings to keep the library comfortable for people and technology alike.

Cabling and Connections

Can the library's current network cabling support new technology devices that are purchased? Or can the library building be rewired to support a new network? These are crucial questions in this age of networked information. Chapter 5 discussed networking options and raised the issue of library buildings that are difficult or expensive to add network cabling to. In these circumstances, a library may decide to use a wireless network. Just as with the electrical capabilities of the building, libraries must assess their abilities to offer access to electronic resources through computer networks. What networking capabilities are already in place and how well are they handling the needs of the library? How will the library access the Internet (e.g., via a dedicated T-1 line or by individual modems)? How many computers will have access to a resource using the Internet or a LAN (how many computers are drawing on a limited amount of connection speed through a dedicated line)? Is it possible to connect more computers to a library's LAN, since demand for electronic resources will likely grow over time? If an unrealistic assessment is made, the library will be unable to provide the level of access that patrons and staff will demand.

Carry-in Devices

Given some of the mobile devices and mobile storage options that patrons have, it should not surprise library staff that they will bring these items into the library. Two key needs in this area are the following: (1) library staff need to be sure that their computers have easily accessible USB ports to plug flash drives and iPods and other devices into and, (2) given the surge of laptops into libraries thanks in part to libraries offering wireless network access, libraries need to have enough power outlets to accommodate these and other devices.

Computers Equipped for Many Needs

Following up on the need for USB ports, other items would make computers more helpful to patrons. Libraries should allow CD or DVD burning on their computers, much like we allow printing or copying. This is a handy form of storage that will continue to grow in use. As well, headphones should be available for patrons to listen to audio or visual content online. It is interesting to consider that a DVD drive equipped computer has the ability to act as a DVD viewing station. The profusion of content of this type, whether or not it has a research focus, means that users will be aided by this access. Many individuals like to listen to music or other audio materials while doing research in the library, and it is not much of an expense to add a pair of headphones to make this possible. As was discussed in Chapter 12, audio content in distance learning also makes headphones helpful to distance students using library computers.

Lighting

Proper lighting is crucial for any library and can have a positive impact on the use of library technology. Glare on staff or public computers or microfilm reader/printers can be distracting. While changing the lighting system of a library may not be possible, it is a factor that should be taken when deciding where to place these types of equipment. The architecture of a given library will help dictate its lighting. Generally, lighting options should be chosen to meet the functional needs of an area of the library. Just as lights should be aligned over the aisles of the book stacks so that browsing patrons can easily see the titles and call numbers, lights over the public computer area should be placed to avoid reflecting on computer monitors. Where possible, staff work areas should include adjustable lighting to give staff members control over their personal workspace. Provide adjustable lamps at each desk or computer so that light can be increased or reduced. The "Planning and Building Libraries" source in the Selected Resources for Further Information section of the chapter has some further useful information on lighting options.

Room and Layout

Technological devices are engineered to be smaller and smaller in many cases, but the technologies one might add to a library will certainly impact the space available. When assigning space in a library to new technological devices or finding areas to shelve media, be careful not to underestimate the true size that items require. Adding technology to a library may not always call for major architectural changes to the layout of the entire library. However, library staff members need to be aware that there may be a need to reposition items to ensure a comfortable working environment and to let patrons easily navigate the library. As well, when technology is placed in a library, visibility is key. It needs to be easily seen from staff service points so that it can be serviced and easily located by patrons for use. Decisions in this area, as in the others involving space, depend on the technology to be added. The general consideration to make is whether the technology is placed in such a way that it does not impede traffic patterns or obscure its function or that of another device, item, or service point and that it does allow for easy access and use by patrons and staff.

Furniture

The furniture requirements of new technology are another criterion to be considered. They can certainly have an impact on the room and layout issues. Here the emphasis is on user comfort in many cases, for example computers or media viewing stations. In others the question may simply be deciding where a new piece of technology should sit. While it would be nice to always buy new furniture to accommodate new technology, it is more realistic for libraries to assess current furniture first. The important step is to consider the technology's furniture need before the technology is purchased. Then suggestions can be sought from colleagues and vendors about the best way to fulfill the need.

Checklist of Physical Environment Issues

The following list of questions should be considered when adding any technology to a library, either whole new technological items or additional units of existing technology. They are not prescriptive recommendations, since all technologies will differ, but they are starting points for you to discuss with vendors and those responsible for the maintenance of your facility.

1. Will the new technology have an impact on the electrical demands of the library?
2. Does the new technology require any special cooling or ventilation in order to operate efficiently? Will its addition change the heating and cooling balance of the library in some way?
3. Does the library have the necessary network or communications technology on hand to accommodate a new technology, whether it is a library automation system, a CD-ROM network, or a new full-text periodical database? Will the current cabling system and Internet connection be able to handle this new item?
4. Are any lighting adjustments needed to make the use of this new technology more comfortable for users or staff? Is additional lighting needed, or should current lighting be altered to avoid glare or low-light conditions?
5. Will there be enough room in the library to accommodate the new technology? What may need to be moved in order to make it fit? Where is the most sensible place, based on its function, to put the new item(s)?
6. Will specialized furniture be needed to house the item(s) or make it available to users? Can current furniture be adapted to the purpose or will a new purchase need to be made?

GAMING IN THE LIBRARY

A great case study for these questions and issues is the desire of many libraries to support gaming activities, devices, and collections. Gaming impacts the library in a larger way than, say, adding a new collection of graphic novels. Libraries can always figure out how to shelve new collections, and even with other media types, providing equipment may not be a huge leap (for DVDs, the footprint of a television, a DVD player, and a set of headphones is relatively small). Though individual libraries may differ in their approaches, it is not uncommon for them to offer collections of video games for checkout as well as to make space and equipment available for playing the games. This makes the technological impact on the library larger in terms of adding, supporting, and maintaining the needed game equipment and designing space for its use. Here are some questions to ask when considering making gaming a service:

1. What kinds of video games do you want to add? Are we talking about games played on computers—in which case you may be able to use your regular public computers to play them—or are we talking about adding a Nintendo Wii, Sony PlayStation 3, or Microsoft Xbox 360? If it's the latter, then you will need to consider where the game consoles will be located and how they will be secured.

2. What display options do you have in mind for using the game consoles? Even with computer-based games, you might want the opportunity for players to be able to see their efforts on a larger screen than their monitor (e.g., using an LCD projector or a flat screen television for a tournament). With the game consoles, you will need to add some sort of display device, especially for group play and visibility. Flat screen televisions are popular for these uses, but in a pinch you can use any type of television or device that accepts video input.

3. How much space will be needed for game play? Part of the space question builds from the type of display you have in mind and the area you will keep the console stored (having access to needed electricity, and wall space, for example). But a big factor in space consideration is having enough of it for actual play. Dance Dance Revolution, a popular console game, requires floor space for a 34 inch square dance mat that you use to control the actions of a dancer. Playing bowling on the Wii requires a somewhat

scaled-down approximation of the space needed to actually throw a bowling ball down a lane of your choice. It is not simply a matter of sticking a television on a table with a four foot clearance between the table and a row of shelving. You may need to establish a separate room for game play or rearrange open seating and computer areas to provide enough extra room. One possibility is to establish group or collaborative work spaces in the library that can accommodate small groups playing games, watching DVDs, or working together on projects.

4. Will you host tournaments as part of your gaming experience? This is a very popular method of using your acquired games to promote the library and to offer fun opportunities to your gaming audience. Some areas to consider are: (1) do you have enough electrical outlets in a given area for patrons to bring in their own gaming systems? (2) if the tournament involves computer games, will your network security allow gamers to make modifications to public computer screen resolutions and to install gaming software? (3) do you have a space that not only accommodates the people playing at a given moment but that gives nonparticipants enough space or sight lines to watch the action?

These are just a few of the possible needs to keep in mind as you consider gaming for your library. It can be a great addition to your resources, and also establish techie-cred for your library.

ERGONOMICS: THE HUMAN FACTOR

Does technology have an impact on those who use it? It certainly does. That impact can be a positive story of efficiency and freedom. It can also be a horror tale of eyestrain, muscle spasms, and migraine headaches. The latter possibility is very real, and as such necessitates a careful look at the ergonomics of the work and public use environment with regard to technology.

Ergonomics is all about fitting an activity to a person. This primarily relates to making people's work situations as comfortable as possible for the tasks they must perform so that they can avoid injury. These injuries can be of the repetitive strain variety, also known as musculoskeletal disorders, such as carpal tunnel syndrome or tendonitis or can involve other conditions related to vision and headaches. While ergonomics are clearly a concern for library staff members, patrons and their use of computers cannot be forgotten. Not all patrons will spend extensive time working at a computer or reader/printer, but some will in the course of their research.

What steps can be taken to consider and positively impact the ergonomic effects of technologies in libraries?

1. The furniture in staff work areas should fit the person who will be using it in terms of table height and location of the computer. For furniture used by several individuals in public and staff areas, chairs and keyboard heights should be adjustable.
2. Assistive technology should be used where it might help. Anti-glare screens can be attached to computer monitors to help reduce eyestrain and headaches. Trackballs can be used in place of computer mice to reduce the strain put on an individual's hand, wrist, and arm.
3. Individuals should limit the time they spend on tasks that could cause repetitive stress injuries and take frequent breaks. Stretching exercises can help strengthen muscles that might be affected. Individuals should remember to stop doing anything that causes pain.
4. Take a look at the ergonomics resources listed in the Selected Sources for Further Information section of this chapter for specific suggestions on implementing these recommendations in libraries.

QUESTIONS FOR REVIEW

1. What questions should be asked of a new technology in terms of its impact on the physical environment?
2. Does your library offer gaming resources? Why or why not?
3. Why should libraries pay attention to ergonomics?
4. Is it possible in your library to easily see and help people who are using the technologies that you offer?

SELECTED SOURCES FOR FURTHER INFORMATION

Antonelli, Monika. "Green Libraries." Available: www.greenlibraries.org.
A collection of links to sample green building and design projects for libraries and to planning documents for environmentally aware construction.

Failla, Victor A., and Thomas A. Birk. 1999. "Planning for Power." *American School & University* 71 (Fall): 26–28.
An overview of electrical standards and issues for accommodating information technology equipment in educational facilities. Many items in the article apply to any technology environment.

Gallaway, Beth. 2007. "Game On! Meeting the Needs of Gamers in Libraries." In *Information Tomorrow: Reflections on Technology and the Future of Academic and Public Libraries* (pp. 71–85), edited by Rachel Singer Gordon. Medford, NJ: Information Today.
Gallaway offers clear justifications for the existence of gaming in libraries. She suggests important aspects that need to be present in a library for gaming to happen and provides guidance on how library staff should prepare.

"Library as Place: Rethinking Roles, Rethinking Space." 2005. *CLIR Report* 129 (February). Available: www.clir.org/pubs/abstract/pub129abst.html.
A collection of essays by six authors on how libraries are being and will be used as physical spaces now that online information is widely available.

"Library Ergonomics." 2004. Ithaca, NY: Cornell University Ergonomics Web. Available: ergo.human.cornell.edu/AHProjects/Library/librarypro-jects.html.
Details the results and recommendations from two 2004 studies of library ergonomics, one involving library signage and the other involving library computer redesign.

Lushington, Nolan. 2002. *Libraries Designed for Users: A 21st Century Guide.* New York: Neal-Schuman.
Gives excellent guidance on issues relating to technology computers in libraries. Covers ergonomics as well as technical requirements.

Mueller, Misha. 2006. "Keep Breathing: Coping with Technology." *Library Hi-Tech News* 23, no. 5: 27–30.
The author introduces paying attention to ergonomics as a method for coping with technostress. The article suggests a variety of preventative techniques to avoid injury and stress.

"Planning and Building Libraries." Available: www.slais.ubc.ca/resources/architecture.
A collection of links to vendors and projects relating to the construction and equipping of libraries.

PART V

Where Library Technology
Is Going, and How
to Get There

Chapter 17

Writing a Technology Plan

How can you offer enhanced services in your library? How can you prepare to afford forthcoming technologies? How can you be sure you will have staff members with the skills needed to implement them? Without at least some advanced planning, you simply cannot. Planning is sometimes looked at as a waste of time, or just a chance to dream a bit, put some ideas on paper, and then file them away. A **technology plan**, in my view, is not a static document. It is an attempt by a library to take inventory of their current technology, survey the needs of their users and themselves, and make a plan to acquire technologies to meet these needs.

Your technology plan needs to be a flexible document. It can be a very specific, short-term list of equipment that needs to be purchased to meet current service needs. It can be an inventory of current equipment that serves to create a long-term replacement schedule. It can be a mixture of current and future needs, including both easily attainable and wish list goals to acquire new technology. Again, the plan is not set in stone; it is more of an ongoing process to assess and meet needs. Brainstorming is required.

There are many fine technology plans and planning processes to use as models when creating your own plan, but do not feel so tied to one that you ignore specific needs or characteristics of your organization. No two technology plans are alike, nor should they be. On occasion, you may find that a particular funding agency will require a certain type of technology plan.

TECHNOLOGY PLANNING STEPS

How does a technology plan come together? The following list of seven steps provides an overview of the process and the key tasks to complete. There are a number of books and Web sites that offer more detailed processes, and these are listed in the Selected Sources for Further Information.

Step 1: Inventory Your Current Technology

Start by seeing what technology you already have. It may be a count of equipment, or of media types, or both. This serves a number of purposes. First, you can get an idea of how up-to-date and functional your current technology is. You may realize from your inventory that you have a number of items that should be upgraded or replaced in the near future. Second, you may discover technologies that you did not realize you had—software, older media types, peripherals, etc. Realizing that these items exist may lead you to new uses for them. Third, you can refer to the inventory to check for gaps in your technology holdings that you had not recognized before. You may generally know what you have and what items are needed (at least approximately) in your library. However, in instances when you decide to add new technology, you may overlook the cost-saving fact that you already own a part of the items you need. Replacement, reallocation, and recognition of gaps are all crucial benefits of an inventory.

Step 2: Conduct a Needs Assessment

Next, think about what needs you have that technology could meet. There are times when simply adding more of existing items (videotapes, computer **workstations**, etc.) will do the trick, and other situations in which entirely new approaches to technology must be taken. Fund, or at least encourage, staff members to attend technology exhibitions, new product expositions, and conference seminars on cutting-edge technologies. Then take a hard look at your current situation. Be sure to ask your patrons. Those who are using your library can give you some insight on what items you may still need to add or alter.

I mentioned the need to brainstorm earlier in this chapter. This is where brainstorming should happen in earnest. Consider needs you may not have thought of before. As you assess your needs, keep an open mind. There will be a later stage where you will need to prioritize your needs and provide justifications for them. Your assessment at this stage can be based on both hard facts and on perceptions.

Step 3: Investigate Your Options and Opportunities

Once you have some new technology uses or whole new services in mind you can turn to technology information sources to research your options. Chapter 2 outlines a number of resources to use when searching for advice, comparing similar products, or investigating a given technology. This process should be focused on the ideas you form in the previous step, but should still be one where new ideas and concepts are allowed into the mix. You may encounter a completely new solution to a need only when you start investigating the options available. Likewise, you may determine that you could follow another library's example and implement a new service you had not imagined.

Step 4: Set Priorities and Make Justifications

Now comes the time to hash out the importance of each change or addition you have established. Take the facts you have discovered during the previous step and make the best case you can for each idea you have had. Be sure to also note the negative points of each change. Then decide which ones have the most merit in terms of the immediacy of the need they will fill and in terms of the ability you have to bring them into being (both fiscally and operationally). This is also the point at which you can clearly articulate the benefits of the changes you are planning. Justifying the changes will help you decide priorities. With a clear list of changes organized by priority, you now have a sense of the timeline in which you can implement the technologies.

Step 5: Create a Budget

With so many technology changes, the deciding factor for when or whether something happens is money. Having organized your list of options by priority of need, now price them out. Consider all of the equipment or media costs involved as well as the needed staff time to install the technology, train and be trained on it, and to handle any other incidental costs. You can also think about what funding you can expect in the near future and whether there are additional funding sources to pursue. You may be in a situation where the only way to provide for your high priority items is to seek grant funding. On the other hand, you may not have additional options and so you can use the budget process to help finalize your timeline.

It is crucial to allow some room in the budget for innovation, or, said more honestly, for trial and failure. If at all possible, having some funding for projects or technology implementations that carry some risk should be built in. This gives you some freedom to experiment or to take on a newly developing technology and see what you and your patrons can do with it. You do not want to be so structured that you miss out on the opportunity to bring something into being of great value and use to your library community.

Step 6: Develop a Timeline

Once you have worked out the details you should be ready to move ahead with your plan as funding and other resources allow. This is the time to establish a timeline for the projects you would like to undertake. This can be rather straightforward if your technology planning process involves a single or a couple of short-term projects. It can be harder to juggle a large number of projects over, say, a ten-year period. Bring together your best guesses and estimates of when you can afford your changes and realistically implement them. Create a document that is specific enough to get started on immediate goals and projects (or ones that require a long lead time) and gives some guidance regarding all of your prioritized items. Keep in mind that you are writing a plan that can be altered as circumstances require and solidified as target dates near.

Step 7: Plan to Evaluate

One step that is needed before you actually purchase new technologies is making a plan to evaluate them. I already discussed evaluating technology for purchase, but next you must evaluate how successful the technology is once it is implemented. Is it accomplishing the goal you have set for it? Are your users actually using the technology? The idea here is to come up with some way of assessing the technology that will guide you in making adjustments to your current situation and in making future plans.

QUESTIONS FOR REVIEW

1. Does your library already have a technology plan?
2. How well is your current technology meeting patrons' needs?
3. What would you like to see added to your library over the near future?

SELECTED SOURCES FOR FURTHER INFORMATION

The following list of resources should be of help when putting together a technology plan. All of the sources offer examples of technology plans that others have produced. The Cohn and colleagues (2000) source has examples of plans from every type of library. The MaintainIT Project (2008) publication compiles suggestions on public library technology planning and implementation from over 100 librarians (and it's free). The WebJunction (2008) link has documents on various aspects of the planning process and links to the TechAtlas planning tool. TechAtlas provides technology inventories and staff surveys and assessments along with a budget worksheet.

Cohn, John M., Ann L. Kelsey, and Keith Michael Fiels. 2000. *Writing and Updating Technology Plans: A Guidebook with Sample Policies on CD-ROM.* New York: Neal-Schuman.

"Joy of Computing—Planning for Success." MaintainIT Project (November 2008). Available: www.maintainitproject.org/cookbooks/planning-for-success (accessed November 23, 2008).

Matthews, Joseph R. 2004. *Technology Planning: Preparing and Updating a Library Technology Plan*. Westport, CT: Libraries Unlimited.
Mayo, Diane. 2005. *Technology for Results: Developing Service-Based Plans*. Chicago: American Library Association.
"Technology Planning." Dublin, OH: WebJunction (2008). Available: www.webjunction.org/techplan (accessed November 23, 2008).

Chapter 18

Our Technological Future: Ranganathan Meets Googlezon

The future of libraries, much like their history, is impossible to consider without talking about technology. Chapter 1 clearly shows that the history of libraries is a story of technology. When we think about the future of libraries, we need to approach the question much as we might approach the future of information technology. What technological developments in the world at large may impact libraries? What are libraries doing on their own that may affect their services and improve how they do business? Here are a few issues, trends, and predictions to provide a sense of what the future may hold.

NEW CHALLENGES

Some have suggested that as the Internet rises as an information source and communications mechanism it eventually may replace libraries. It can easily be argued that the Internet lacks many of the information sources found in libraries and has no one to provide the services of libraries. However, as information on the Internet continues to grow in volume and quality and reaches a wider audience, how much longer will those objections be accurate? Four movements in our current society have started us down a road where it is less clear what libraries do that is distinct: (1) bona fide information resources start to appear on the Internet as free services—*The Christian Science Monitor*

(www.csmonitor.com) and the *Information Please Almanac* (www
.infoplease.com) are but two examples; (2) reference question
answering services keep popping up, both nonlibrary services
such as Yahoo! Answers or AllExperts.com and free Ask-a-
Librarian services such as the one available through the Library
of Congress (and just about every public and academic library
around); (3) Internet organizations or groups of individuals
could even take on the library's role of organizing information,
and some would argue this is already happening with search
tools, Wikipedia, and elsewhere; and (4) Google and Amazon
are providing the ability to search free collections of full-text
books that are either free of copyright restrictions or that have
been licensed to the companies.

One interesting look into the future that suggests where
search engines and other online sources may take us involves
two of the Internet services covered in Chapter 9: Google and
Amazon. A mock newscast set in the future (available at www
.albinoblacksheep.com/flash/epic) shows the events leading
up to the formation of "Googlezon," a corporate conglomeration
of information services that takes over the world in 2015 with
a personalized news and information service called EPIC
(Evolving Personalized Information Construct). All information
content is produced by individuals, not the press or media corporations, and then rewritten to fit the interests and specifications
of each individual in the world. As the media disappears and
information is so individualized, will there be a place for
libraries to even archive some subsection of the information?

I am not saying that the Internet will replace libraries or that
it is already starting to, but I do find it difficult to ignore these
trends (and some potential futures that they point toward). We
may well see libraries change into virtual, rather than physical,
locations much more quickly than I would have imagined.

PREDICTING THE FUTURE

Predictions are a lot of fun. We start with something we know
well and then try to take logical steps to leap ahead into the
future. What we end up with is at once magical and unrealistic
and wonderful and perhaps horrible. As examples of this

process, I offer two interesting predictions involving technology and libraries that were made over a century apart. One has already been proved while the other has between six months and nearly two decades to go before we can evaluate it.

The estimable Charles Ammi Cutter made a speech at the 1883 American Library Association Conference in Buffalo, NY (Cutter, 1883). The entire address recounted his imagined visit to the Buffalo Public Library one hundred years in the future, in 1983. In it, Cutter predicted devices similar to fax machines, a huge library collection, thermostats to control heat and ventilation, and a method for sharing print catalog information among worldwide libraries, all of which existed in 1983. Not so successfully, he imagined a library that employed a huge staff (including uniformed pages), had drastically cut the circulation of fiction titles (an evil of the day), and offered public readings of books via a "reading machine."

A modern prophet, Ray Kurzweil, inventor of the Kurzweil Reader and many other bits of technology, offered the following predictions in one of his books (Kurzweil, 1999). By 2009, Kurzweil sees wearable computers as common and inexpensive and most text being created by voice-recognition software (how close are we to this?). In another ten years, 2019, he states that paper books and documents will rarely be used and that by 2029, visual and aural implants allow humans to connect directly to a worldwide computer network that would put the Internet to shame. Sound crazy?

Here we see two different predictions at either end of their life span. Cutter's vision of a future library shows that it is possible to predict general developments and even be dead on about some things that would have seemed outrageous at the time. However, his visions that seem more fitting of his time show that it is difficult to entirely leave behind our present day understandings. The predictions we make can be trapped by our understandings of technology or processes and can keep us from making the right jumps to imagine completely new technology. Cutter wrote his speech after the invention of the telephone and he was able to project that the telephone could carry data as well as voices. However, he had no context for imagining computers. Likewise, it is hard for us to imagine new processes that might be invented and implemented in the future, and so it is hard to even come close to predicting the changes that will take place.

Kurzweil's view of the near future needs to be treated with the same caution. His leaps are similar to those of Cutter in that they follow known technologies. Wireless computers and cell phones are here now and growing more widespread, wearable computers are being played with already—many cell phones even have computer applications, we can use voice recognition software, documents are produced in only electronic formats, and a worldwide computer network exists. Kurzweil is taking the known and making it more common and also letting some technology jump ahead much in the same way technology as a whole has jumped around and ahead during the twentieth century. Cutter's vision is familiar today, but we will have to wait and see if Kurzweil's will become so. As someone who plans to be gainfully employed in libraries beyond 2029, I am interested to see how close he comes.

TRENDS AND TECHNOLOGIES TO WATCH

Looking toward the future allows us to see what is happening right now and project what the future may hold. The following list of trends and issues involving technologies is not complete, but it is designed to be suggestive of what is happening now in libraries and where libraries are going. Some of the items on the list have been influenced by the Library and Information Technology Association's list of technology trends (Library and Information Technology Association, 2008), which are available from their Web site.

1. Libraries' move to add electronic sources has caused a tremendous reliance on them. The ability of libraries to continue to afford electronic sources could seriously decrease their purchases of print, microformat, and physical media resources, absent significant budget increases.
2. The influx of many more electronic sources has made well-designed, aesthetically pleasing library Web sites crucial for accessing them. If we cannot get our users to the resources we offer, we are wasting our money and their time.

3. Patrons still desire interaction with the human face of the library: its staff. Library staff members need to continue to find ways to aid individuals in-house and remotely that maintain the high level of service our patrons expect and provide relationship-building moments.

4. E-books and digital reference resources are growing more available. It will be interesting to see what impact this has on print publishing as a whole and whether libraries will continue purchasing these sources. The continuing growth of handheld devices (cell phones, PDAs, MP3 players) and the ability to download e-books and audio e-books to them means that libraries will need to pay attention to developments among these devices. Doing so will ensure that we can provide materials in the formats that these devices can handle.

5. Blogging is continuing to have an impact in the creation of news and opinion sources by individual "citizen journalists." Will this phenomenon grow into the creation of source materials that libraries will feel called on to locate for patrons and perhaps archive? How can libraries improve the organization and searching of blog posts? There are great opportunities here.

6. Folksonomies will continue to develop in various forms online. Libraries will need to decide if user-supplied descriptive terms can be added to our controlled vocabulary systems (OPACs [online public access catalogs], periodical databases, etc.) and study whether this addition aids patrons in finding information. OCLC (Online Computer Library Center) has taken steps in this direction with WorldCat.org, in that registered users may tag individual catalog records. My own institution has a faceted version of our catalog (beta.lib.muohio.edu/drupal) that allows tagging by Miami University students, faculty, and staff.

7. Full-text periodical indexes and electronic reference sources are growing in number and scope. What impact will this have on the collection development decisions at libraries that now sometimes duplicate their holdings between print and electronic versions? Can any library continue to afford this? Will patrons be so drawn to

electronic full text that they abandon printed periodicals? The answer to the second question is already "yes" at many libraries.

8. Computer hardware appears to be getting relatively cheaper while software is holding place or getting more expensive. This trend, if it holds, could allow more individuals to purchase computers and gain access to the Internet (for which the software and accounts are relatively inexpensive). Meanwhile, libraries may find the services of their automation system and database vendors growing more expensive. Will this lead more libraries to open source solutions?

9. Increasing bandwidth is allowing more data to be moved along the Internet and into individuals' homes. Related to this are the growing availability of wireless networks and the ever-enhancing capabilities of cell phones and other mobile devices. These changes will encourage even more individuals to access information from beyond the library, making remote patron authentication and the provision of digital reference services an even greater priority for libraries.

10. Libraries are forming and joining consortiums and co-ops. This leads to increased access to informational resources for library patrons at a lower cost to their libraries. It can also lead to decreasingly-unique collections of electronic resources, as libraries can offer only what is decided by the consortium.

11. Libraries and library staff need to stress their abilities to help patrons evaluate the information they find on the Internet and elsewhere. Patrons often have too many choices of information sources and need help comparing them.

12. Full-text sources of all kinds are affected both by copyright issues and the unwillingness of some publishers to make their sources available at reasonable prices (or at all). Solving the copyright questions that these sources raise could mean that e-books and other electronic resources would become more widely available, so long as the issue of digital rights management for digital

audio is solved alongside copyright concerns. Also, the current fluid nature of full-text periodical and reference sources could be controlled. Libraries would not have to fear titles being pulled from a database by publishers.

13. As costs decrease, libraries are likely to install RFID (radio frequency identification) in greater numbers and make use of its related services (automated sorting, inventory control, self-checkout). Staff may benefit from fewer repetitive motion injuries due to decreased handling of materials during checkout. The jury remains out on whether patrons will use self-checkout in large numbers or will demand attention from staff members. Expect privacy concerns to be discussed more widely (and hopefully addressed) as the technology gains wider use.

14. Equipment and software vendor mergers are resulting in fewer distinct products. The downside of this development is that lack of competition may drive up prices for these products. The upside to the situation is that interface navigation and equipment operation will become more standardized.

15. While library staff members are used to assuming technology management, installation, and troubleshooting tasks in addition to their regular duties, the need for dedicated technology staff members will grow. This is perhaps more of a wish than a trend, but the dependence of libraries on information technology is going to make the lack of such personnel harder to justify. Even in smaller settings, a technology-predominant position will become common. In larger libraries, existing technology units will grow in staff members as well as importance. These units are crucial not only for the skills they house and the tasks they undertake but also as a crucible for new technology investigation.

THE COMPLEX LIBRARY

Today and for the near future, we will likely have what might be called a complex library: an amalgamation of various types of media and information sources. Traditional print sources and electronic sources will continue to be added to libraries. The need to integrate the use of these sources will also continue. As long as libraries can offer value-added services unlike those of other organizations or individuals, there will always be a place for our work. Libraries need to stay rooted in their essential functions and societal expectations (books and access to information) while reaching toward amazing changes (such as truly virtual libraries that provide a wealth of resources over the Internet). The potential advancements and adaptations are rather exciting. With this combination of tradition and ongoing experimentation and development we fulfill the intent of S. R. Ranganathan's Five Laws of Library Science:

1. Books are for use.
2. Every reader his book.
3. Every book, its reader.
4. Save the time of the reader.
5. A library is a growing organism. (Ranganathan, 1963)

QUESTIONS FOR REVIEW

1. What changes do you see in the immediate future for libraries? How about further down the road?
2. Watch the EPIC 2015 video. What strikes you as possible about this forecast of the future, and what seems improbable? Is any element of it already present?
3. Look at the list of trends and note if any of these are already impacting your library or libraries around you.
4. Build the future. (I wish you the best!)

SELECTED SOURCES FOR FURTHER INFORMATION

Cleyle, Susan E., and Louise M. McGillis. 2005. *Last One Out Turn Off the Lights: Is This the Future of American and Canadian Libraries?* Lanham, MD: Scarecrow Press.

A collection of essays that examine various elements of the future of libraries: the Web, the library as place, pushing to the desktop, certification, and the future of associations.

Cutter, Charles Ammi. 1883. "The Buffalo Public Library in 1983." *Library Journal* 8 (September/October): 211–217.

A famous, forward-looking article that describes the author's imagined tour of a future library.

Kurzweil, Ray. 1999. *The Age of Spiritual Machines: When Computers Exceed Human Intelligence.* **New York: Viking.**
Offers predictions about changes in humans' lives due to the development of affordable computing devices and artificial intelligence.

Library and Information Technology Association. 2008. "LITA Top Technology Trends." Chicago: Library and Information Technology Association. Available: www.lita.org/ala/lita/litaresources/toptechtrends/toptechnology .htm.
LITA experts identify the trends to watch in the fields of library and information technology.

Ranganathan, Shiyali Ramamrita. 1963. *The Five Laws of Library Science.* **Bombay: Asia Publishing House.**
The classic statement of Ranganathan's philosophy of library science. For an interesting update of his rules, see Cloonan, Michele V., and John G. Dove. 2005. "Ranganathan Online." *Library Journal* 130, no. 6 (April 1): 58–60.

Sapp, Greg. 2002. *A Brief History of the Future of Libraries: An Annotated Bibliography.* **Lanham, MD: Scarecrow Press.**
A catalog of library-related futuristic predictions made between 1978 and 1999.

Glossary

56Kbps line: A leased telephone line used to connect to the Internet. Can transmit data at 56 kilobits per second (Kbps).

56Kbps modem: The current top transmission speed for modems: 56 kilobits per second (Kbps).

abstract: A brief summary of a periodical article. Often found in electronic periodical databases along with article citations and sometimes the full text of an article.

adaptive technology: Technology used to adapt other technological equipment for use by people with disabilities. Somewhat synonymous with the term "assistive technology."

ADSL: *See* ASYMMETRIC DIGITAL SUBSCRIBER LINE.

API (Application Programming Interface): The rules and code needed to create mashups by hand.

application: A general term for a piece of software or a program that can be used on a computer (e.g., word processing applications or Internet applications).

assistive technology: Any technology that can be used to help people with disabilities find and use the information they need. Somewhat synonymous with the term "adaptive technology."

Asymmetric Digital Subscriber Line (ADSL): A method for connecting to the Internet over standard telephone lines that allows for transmission speeds between 1.5 and 9 megabits per second (Mbps).

asynchronous: Refers to technologies used for communication or instruction that do not work in real time (e.g., electronic mail or correspondence courses). Users of these items send out a message and then must wait for a response.

audiocassette: An audiovisual or media format for recording sound for playback. Consists of magnetic tape that advances between two reels in a plastic case.

audiovisual items (or audiovisuals): Items in a library collection that utilize sound or visual images or both. Examples include compact discs, videocassettes, and audiocassettes.

authentication: The process of ensuring that an individual has the right to use a database or other electronic resource.

avatar: A virtual character who serves as the symbol of a person using a virtual worlds environment.

bandwidth: A term referring to the capacity of a data transmission mechanism, such as a telephone line or a coaxial cable, to transmit data. The less bandwidth a mechanism has, the slower it will transmit data.

bar code technology: A commonly used feature of library circulation services that involves placing an adhesive bar code on circulating items. These bar codes are then scanned into the library's circulation system (using a bar code reader) when a patron checks out the item.

bibliographic utility: A company that makes a database of cataloging records in MARC format available to libraries at a subscription fee (e.g., OCLC).

bit: Simplest level of computer information. A bit can have the value of 0 or 1.

bits per second (Bps): Common measurement of data transmission through modems or computer networks.

blog (or Web log): An online diary or journal in which an individual or a group can post entries about topics of interest. The postings are typically arranged in reverse chronological order.

boot-up: The starting process of a computer, in which the computer determines whether its components are in working order and starts its operating system running.

broadband internet access: Using DSL or a cable modem to access the Internet. Much faster than using dial-up Internet access using a standard modem.

browser software: An Internet application that allows users to view Web sites (e.g., Internet Explorer and Netscape).

bulletin board: A method for communicating online in which messages are posted on a Web page to be read and replied to by others.

byte: Eight bits, which is enough memory to represent a single alphanumeric character.

cable modem: A device that uses the coaxial cable laid for cable television to provide users with Internet access speeds up to 2 megabits per second (Mbps).

card: A device that can be plugged into the central processing unit (CPU) of a computer to accomplish a particular function (e.g., a soundcard allows sounds to be played on the computer and heard through speakers). Other examples include video cards and modems.

card catalog: A paper-based method for organizing the materials owned by a library, invented in 1791 in France. Individual cards are filed for each item, and the cards are typically arranged by author, title, and subjects. Also known as print catalogs, these are now being replaced by online catalogs.

CD: *See* COMPACT DISC.

CD-ROM: *See* COMPACT DISC: READ ONLY MEMORY.

CD-ROM drive: A device used to read the information or run an application stored on a CD-ROM disc.

CDRW drive: Compact disk read/write; a device that allows a user to place computer files on a blank CD-ROM disc.

central processing unit (CPU): The part of a computer that contains the main working components of the system, including the random access memory (RAM), the motherboard, and the computer's processor.

chat: A method for online communication in which individuals type messages back and forth to one another in a text-based, real-time exchange.

classification system: A method for organizing a library collection so that it can be browsed by subject. Examples include

252   NEAL-SCHUMAN LIBRARY TECHNOLOGY COMPANION

the Dewey Decimal Classification and the Library of Congress Classification System.

client/server: A computing concept in which a user's computer (the client) can make use of an application or resource based on another computer (the server). This concept underlies the workings of the Internet.

clock speed: A measurement of how quickly a computer processor works, measured in megahertz (MHz).

coaxial cable: A type of cable used to connect workstations and other devices in computer networks. Particularly good for transmitting large amounts of audio and video (as in cable television networks, which use coaxial cable).

collection control: The maintenance, organization, and growth of library collections using technological devices (in the context of this book).

collection development profile: A picture of the collection development needs of a given library (or part of a library) that can be configured in an electronic acquisitions system to shape the selection of materials through that system.

compact disc (CD): A disc that is 4.75 inches in diameter that is used to hold up to 74 minutes of audio recordings.

compact disc: read only memory (CD-ROM): A disc that is 4.75 inches in diameter that can be laser-pitted to hold up to 600MB of electronic information.

consortium: A number of libraries that agree to work together to seek group pricing for electronic resources and may also participate in sharing their resources among other members of the group. Just one term for this sort of cooperative arrangement among libraries.

content management systems: Software that is used to manage large Web sites by providing a consistent interface to pages and assisting in the organization and searching of documents.

copy cataloging: The process of creating a catalog record for a new item in the collection by taking an already produced MARC record for the item and modifying it as needed for local use. Unlike original cataloging, which involves creating a new record from scratch.

course management systems: Web-based products that provide a framework for Web-based distance learning or Web-supplemented teaching. The software allows instructors to post course materials, provide grades, and interact with students.

CPU: *See* CENTRAL PROCESSING UNIT.

custom search engine: A search engine populated with source material and Web sites of the creator's choosing. A refinement of a general purpose search engine.

data: A descriptive term for information held in electronic format. Data may be a text document, an image file, a file written in a computer programming language, or an audio file (among other possibilities).

database: A method for electronically organizing information in a way that it can be easily searched and retrieved. Databases consist of a collection of records, which are made up of a number of fields, each of which contains a piece of information.

database software: An application that allows you to create your own databases for a variety of purposes (e.g., Microsoft Access).

desktop: The interface for the Windows operating system in which one can interact with applications using the mouse and keyboard; also a standard personal computer (CPU and monitor) that are typified by fitting on a desktop.

dial-up connection: The method used to connect to an online catalog or the Internet using a modem to dial a phone number and connect to a modem at a library or an Internet service provider.

digital light processing (DLP): A technology for producing digital projectors that results in much brighter images than is possible using LCD projection.

digital rights management (DRM): Technological means used by content providers to protect their material from copying or alternative use beyond what they specify in license agreements.

discovery layer: An interface to library resources that allows for combined searching and display of library catalog searches alongside periodical database results and those from other electronic resources.

distance learning: A method of teaching and learning that makes it possible for individuals to participate in a learning experience even if they are geographically distant from an instructor or are unable to meet in real time with a class.

domain name: The alphabetic name given to an Internet site in place of its numerical Internet protocol address (e.g., www.yahoo.com rather than 129.137.146.1).

DOS (Disk Operating System): One of the first text-based computer operating systems.

DSL: *See* Asymmetric Digital Subscriber Line.

dumb terminal: *See* Terminal.

DVD: A disc that is 4.75 inches in diameter that can be used in hold audio recordings (up to 50 hours per disc) and video (DVD-Video can hold between 2 and 8 hours of high quality video). DVDs have much larger capacities than CDs or CD-ROMs and run much faster.

DVD-ROM: A disc that is 4.75 inches in diameter that can be laser pitted to hold between 4.7 and 17 gigabytes (GB) of computer data.

DVD-ROM drive: A device that when installed in a computer workstation can play either DVD-ROMs or CD-ROMs.

DVDRW drive: A device that when installed in a computer workstation can be used to "burn" data onto a DVD or CD for later use.

e-book (electronic book): An electronic version of a book that may be read via the Web on a computer workstation or using a handheld device (e.g., a special reader or a PalmPilot). There are also audio e-books that can be listened to on a computer workstation or using a handheld MP3 player.

e-mail (electronic mail): A form of communication that uses the Internet to send messages to other users. It requires an e-mail account and electronic mail software.

electronic discussion group: An e-mail based method for holding discussions with many other individuals on a topic of interest. Each message in the discussion is sent out as an e-mail message to each person who subscribes to the group.

electronic mail software: A software application that allows users to send electronic mail messages.

electronic reference source: A source of information in electronic format (Web-based periodical databases, CD-ROM encyclopedias, etc.) that can be used to meet users' reference information needs.

electronic resource: Any information source that is found in electronic format. Can include electronic reference sources, Internet sites, e-books, and e-journals, among others.

electronic resource management system: A module for a library system that assists the library in keeping track of its electronic subscriptions to periodicals and other online resources.

electronic security: Using software-based means for securing library workstations and servers to protect against viruses, hackers, and inadvertent errors.

ergonomics: The science of fitting an activity or work space to a person's needs to ensure his or her comfort and productivity.

ethernet: A local area network architecture that supports data transfer rates of 10 Mbps.

external storage device: A method for storing computer data in a medium that can be removed from the computer itself. Examples include flash drives and CD-R drives.

faceted browsing: The ability, in a library catalog, to limit a search by clicking on various facets or aspects of items included in the search results (item type, location, subject headings, etc.).

FAQs: A document containing answers to frequently asked questions. Very common on the Internet as help guides to using a site or resource or as a source of detailed information on a topic.

feeds: The delivery of postings from a blog using RSS (Really Simple Syndication).

fiber-optic: A type of cable used in computer networks. Tends to be more expensive than other cabling options but provides clear and quick transmission of data between workstations and servers. Used extensively in telephone networks.

field: A section of a record in a database that holds a specific piece of information. For instance, a MARC record for a book contains a field for the author's name.

file: A container of computer information that can be read or displayed by software applications (e.g., a word processing file, an HTML file, or a file that makes up part of an application).

file server: *See* NETWORK SERVER.

filtering software: An application that is designed to restrict Internet users from viewing material that might be considered offensive.

firewall: A combination of software measures that restricts who can access information on a Web server or network server. Protects the server from being used or ruined by individuals who should not have access.

flash drives (also known as pen drives or key drives): Extremely small hard drives that can be used to move files, software, and even whole operating systems from computer to computer.

floppy disk: A 3.5-inch square disk that can be used to externally store computer data. The disk can be removed from the computer and stored elsewhere or used to transport data from place to place. It has a capacity of 1.44 megabytes (MB).

floppy drive: A device that is used to store data on a floppy disk.

folksonomy: A collection of information that has been classified by individual users' choices of terminology rather than by following a set classification system.

full text: A term used to describe the provision of the entire text of a periodical article or other source. An item that is described as "full text" should contain everything in it that appeared in a printed version (or other original format).

full-text reference source: Electronic reference sources such as encyclopedias, handbooks, and biographical sources that may be Web-based or available on CD-ROM. The electronic reference source repeats the text information of the original printed source.

gateways: Devices used in wide area networking situations to help translate between local area networks that use different communication protocols.

gigabyte (GB): one billion bytes; common measurement of hard drive and storage space.

gopher sites: Internet sites that are accessed using gopher protocol, an older method for arranging and displaying information online. Now superseded by the World Wide Web.

graphical user interface (GUI): A computer interface that allows you to interact with applications, Internet sites, and other items using a computer mouse to select graphical icons on your computer monitor.

hard drive: An internal storage device for a computer workstation. Has the capacity to hold many different software programs and files. Current hard drive sizes are typically measured in gigabytes.

hardware: The physical devices that make up or can be used with a computer workstation (e.g., CPU, monitor, keyboard, printer, and scanner).

high-speed Internet access: Using DSL or a cable modem to access the Internet. Much faster that using dial-up Internet access using a standard modem.

host computer: Another way to describe a network server, which holds and serves—or hosts—a database or application of some kind. For instance, in order to run a library system, the library will need a server to host the system so that users can access it.

hyperlink: The ability to construct a word or image on a Web page that a user can click on to be linked to another Web site or document.

hypertext document: A Web document created using hypertext markup language (HTML).

hypertext markup language (HTML): A series of tagged commands that can be used to construct a Web document. HTML controls the formatting and interactivity of Web pages with other files on the Web (e.g., audio, video, images, etc.).

icon: Small graphical images that are used in computer operating systems and on the Web as links to applications or documents.

identity theft: The capture of personal information and identification numbers from online databases by malicious parties.

image tag: In HTML documents, an element that controls how an image is displayed.

information appliance: A computing device, perhaps a smartphone, netbook, or other mobile device that offers the user quick access to online information resources.

information technology: Any items or methods for containing, transmitting, and storing information.

input device: Used to enter information into a computer (e.g., a keyboard or mouse).

instant messaging (IM) software: Software that allows two individuals to send messages and files back and forth to each other using the Internet.

integrated library system (ILS): *See* LIBRARY SYSTEM.

interface: The place in which we interact with a computer operating system, a library database, or anything else created or accessed using a computer. The interface is what displays on the screen as we use an application and controls how we can influence the application through keyboard or mouse commands.

internal storage device: A device that stores computer data that are located within the computer's central processing unit.

Internet: The "network of all networks"; a worldwide computer network (developed in 1969) that has revolutionized communications and information exchange.

Internet access: The means by which an individual connects to the Internet to use its services.

Internet protocol (IP): A system for naming Internet servers to make it easy for individuals to connect to other network servers located anywhere in the world. Each server on the

Internet has its own Internet protocol (IP) number, or address (e.g., 209.34.122.4).

Internet service provider (ISP): A company that provides Internet access to individuals or organizations for a fee.

Internet-based resource: An information source or reference database that sits on the Internet and requires Internet access to use it.

intranet: A network that has limited its access to the members of a particular company or organization.

intranet-based resource: An information source or database that sits on an internal network that controls its access.

IP address: *See* INTERNET PROTOCOL.

iPod: An MP3 player produced by Apple.

ISBN: International Standard Book Number. Assigned to each book as an identifier. Often a searchable field in library systems and acquisitions systems.

ISDN: Integrated services digital network. A method for connecting to the Internet that uses standard telephone lines to provide access speeds up to 128Kbps.

ISP: *See* INTERNET SERVICE PROVIDER.

ISSN: International Standard Serial Number. Assigned to each periodical as an identifier. Often a searchable field in library systems and bibliographic databases.

ITN: Intention to negotiate. A call for bidders to respond with bids for a needed product. Similar to an RFP, but often less restrictive in terms of bidding rules.

keyword: A term that can be used to search a database or Internet search engine.

keyword searching: Gives users the flexibility to search all of the information in a bibliographic record or a full-text periodical article to retrieve items that hold the keyword.

kilobyte (K): One thousand bytes; equivalent to a short note on a single sheet of paper.

LAN: *See* LOCAL AREA NETWORK.

LCD: Liquid crystal display. A technology that enables the creation of thin (flat panel) computer monitors and data projection.

LCD projector: Display equipment that allows a user to project text, graphics, video, or live demonstrations of electronic library resources onto a screen.

library system: A product that computerizes a variety of library functions including the public catalog, circulation, cataloging, acquisitions, and serials.

Linux: An open source computer operating system developed with networking in mind.

local area network (LAN): A network that extends over a relatively small geographical area. Can involve anywhere from two to several dozen workstations connected to a network server.

login ID: The username and password required to allow an individual access to a network.

Lynx: A text-based browser commonly used by individuals with visual disabilities.

machine readable cataloging (MARC) record: An electronic record that contains a number of fields full of information about an item in an online catalog (e.g., books, videos, Internet resources, and so on).

Macintosh: A computer developed in the early 1980s by the Apple Corporation. The first computer to popularize a graphical user interface (GUI) and the use of a computer mouse.

Mac OS: The operating system for Macintosh computers.

magnetic media: Storage devices created by using electrical impulses to inscribe information in a certain pattern on magnetic material. Examples include hard drives, floppy disks, zip disks, magnetic tape, videocassettes, and audiocassettes.

magnetic tape: A form of magnetic media primarily used for the archival storage of computer data. Looks a lot like an audiocassette.

mainframe: A powerful computer that has been used in the past to host library systems and other applications. Now superseded by smaller network servers.

management software: Applications that assist with the operation of libraries. Examples include a variety of office software tools that provide word processing, spreadsheet, and database capabilities.

MARC: *See* MACHINE READABLE CATALOGING RECORD.

mashups: Any combination of multiple sets of data that results in a new online service.

media items: *See* AUDIOVISUAL ITEMS.

megabyte (MB): One million bytes; equivalent to 200–300 pages of text.

megahertz (MHz): Common measurement of the internal speed of a computer's processor.

metasearch software: A type of application that can be installed on a computer with Internet access or a network server that allows a user to search a variety of information sources at the same time. For instance, a library may wish to offer combined searches of their online catalog and their periodical databases from a single search blank.

microfiche: A medium used to store miniaturized images of pages of text or diagrams on a small sheet of photographic film. A standard microfiche sheet can hold between 60 to 98 pages.

microfilm: A medium used to store miniaturized images of pages of text or diagrams on a roll of photographic film. Microfilm can accommodate between 1,000 and 1,500 pages per 100 foot roll of 32mm film.

microformat: A term used to speak about microfiche and microfilm together.

mirror site: A Web site that serves as a backup to another Web site in case of a system failure on the primary site.

modem: A device that translates the data a computer is sending into a format, or protocol, that can be sent through standard telephone lines at speeds up to 56 kilobits per second (Kbps).

Allows anyone with a computer, a modem, and a telephone line gain access to the resources on a network.

module: A software program that handles a specific function within a library system (e.g., a circulation module).

monitor: A device that provides visual display of computer applications. Monitors may be flat panel devices (which are narrower and use LCD technology) or CRTs (cathode ray tubes, which are bulkier).

motherboard: A piece of circuitry that serves as the foundation for the workings of a computer.

mouse: A computer input device that controls applications through the movement of an arrow in a graphical user interface.

MP3: A digital format for audio files. Much online audio and audio e-books are stored in this format. PDAs and other handheld devices have the ability to serve as MP3 players. There are also MP3 players that play only digital audio.

multifunction system: A library system that offers more than one module in the same package.

multiple user access: The ability for more than one user to access an electronic library resource at one time.

multitasking: The ability of a computer operating system to have multiple applications running at the same time and to allow users to switch back and forth between them.

multiuser dimension, object-oriented (MOO): Software used to create an environment in which several individuals can interact over the Internet.

netbooks: A class of smaller-screen-size laptops with a focus on Internet access and network applications.

network: A method for sharing applications or information between two or more workstations. Very common in the library world for sharing information resources.

network cabling: The cables that are used to connect the components of a network. Common cable types include unshielded twisted pair, coaxial, and fiber-optic.

network interface card: A card that plugs into the motherboard of a computer so that it can communicate with other computers through a network.

network operating system: Software used to manage access and operations in a network.

network server: A computer that is configured to offer applications, files, or other resources to the workstations connected to a network.

network topology: The arrangement of servers, workstations, and other devices in a network. Common network topologies include bus, ring, and star.

Novell Netware: A common network operating system.

OC-3 line: A leased telephone line that can transmit data at 155 megabits per second (Mbps). These lines form the backbone of the Internet, quickly transmitting e-mail messages, files, and requests to view Web pages from a individual's computer to another computer or server.

online catalog (OPAC): *See* ONLINE PUBLIC ACCESS CATALOG.

online pathfinder: A Web document that contains lists of electronic and print resources that are useful for research in a particular topic area. The electronic resources can be directly linked to from the pathfinder.

online public access catalog (OPAC): The computer version of the card catalog. Allows an individual to search the holdings of a library through an electronic interface.

online searching: The ability to search electronic versions of periodical indexes and other reference resources through a dial-up connection or the Internet.

on-screen keyboard: A keyboard interface that displays on the computer screen and can be used by clicking on its keys with a mouse in order to enter text. Helpful for those individuals with physical disabilities that constrain their abilities to type with a standard keyboard.

OPAC: *See* ONLINE PUBLIC ACCESS CATALOG.

open source software (OSS): Software that is created by a collaborative group of individuals and then has its source code distributed to other programmers for them to alter. Open source software is often free (at no cost) but it is always freely available (to anyone who wishes to use or improve on it).

OpenURL: A protocol that makes connections between databases that index periodicals and collections of full-text sources. An OpenURL server helps patrons see that an article citation in Database A is available in full text in Journal Collection B.

operating system: The environment in which all other software operates in a computer (e.g., Microsoft Windows and MacOS).

optical character recognition (OCR): A process of using software to scan typewritten or printed copies of text and turn them into word processing documents that can be manipulated.

original cataloging: A process in which a skilled cataloger examines an item and enters author, title, and publication information as well as meaningful subject headings into a cataloging system to create a MARC record for display in the online catalog.

parallel: One method for connecting scanners and other devices to a computer workstation, in this case using a parallel port on the central processing unit.

periodical: A publication that appears on some regular basis (e.g., magazines, journals, and newspapers).

periodical database: An electronic version of a periodical index. Can contain article citations, abstracts, and full-text articles.

periodical index: Began as a printed reference source that allows a user to search for periodical article citations alphabetically by subject (or perhaps by author or title as well). Now available in electronic format as periodical databases with added searching features and, in some cases, the full text of an article linked to its citation.

peripheral: A variety of computer hardware items that have specific functions or capabilities (e.g., printers and scanners).

personal computer (PC): A computer workstation that includes a central processing unit, a monitor, and a keyboard and mouse.

personal digital assistant (PDA): A handheld computing device that can be used to keep a calendar, contain an address book, take notes, and access files created by various types of software.

physical security: Security measures put in place for the purpose of keeping library technology materials from being removed from the library (e.g., cabling or bolting equipment to work area furniture and utilizing a library security system to tag media items).

plasma display: A technology that allows for the creation of extremely thin flat panel computer monitors and televisions that have extremely high resolution and sharp images.

podcasting: The process of creating and sharing audio content with interested recipients, either through downloading MP3 files from the producer's site or by receiving updated content through an RSS feed.

pop-ups: Internet browser windows with advertisements that suddenly appear as a user loads a Web site. Pop-ups can simply be annoying, or they may contain links to download spyware.

presentation software: Computer software that allows a presenter to organize a collection of information and media into a professional presentation.

presentation technology: Allows information to be shared with an audience in a visual manner using display equipment, media items, and presentation software.

print catalog: *See* CARD CATALOG.

printer: A computer peripheral that is used to produce paper copies of information displayed in a computer application.

processor: A device that powers the calculations a computer must make to run software and process information. Located inside the central processing unit attached to the motherboard. Common processors include the Pentium line for PCs and PowerPCs for Macs.

program: *See* SOFTWARE.

protocol: A format for communicating data through a network or between different networks (e.g. Internet protocol).

proxy server: A device that stands between public workstations and the Internet. It can be used to allow those workstations to seamlessly connect to subscription databases or to restrict the workstations to access only preselected Internet sites.

radio frequency identification (RFID): A method used by libraries to protect their physical collections by placing a small tag on items. The tag consists of a computer chip with an antenna attached. Security gates or self-checkout systems can then read the tag to complete their functions.

RAM: *See* RANDOM ACCESS MEMORY.

random access memory (RAM): Memory cards that plug into a computer motherboard to give software temporary space to use while it is running. Generally, the more RAM a computer has, the faster it can operate.

real-time communication: Communication that happens on a synchronous basis, as in an in-person conversation (i.e., one person speaks and is heard by another person at the same time, then the two switch roles; there is no gap or loss of time in their interchange as there can be in Internet communications).

recon: The process of converting catalog cards to MARC records for each item in a library's collection when it moves to an online catalog.

record: A segment of a computer database that represents all of the information on, say, one book or one article. The information within a record is broken down into individual fields, which are typically searchable in online catalogs or periodical databases.

remote access: The ability for users to connect to library resources (e.g., Web sites, online catalogs, and periodical databases) from locations other than within the library.

remote information services: A corporate term for remotely accessed information sources such as Internet-based resources and those reached through the process of online searching.

removable storage: Devices that allow for the storing of computer data on media that can be removed from the central processing unit (e.g., floppy drives and disks, zip drives and disks, CD-R drives and CD-ROMs).

request for proposal (RFP): A process in which vendors respond to a written-out set of criteria for a needed product or service with detailed proposals of how they will meet the criteria. Typically used with technology purchases that involve large amounts of money.

RFID: *See* RADIO FREQUENCY IDENTIFICATION.

routers: Devices that help exchange information between separate networks that are combined in a wide area network (e.g., the Internet).

RSS: Really simple syndication—a way of sending new postings to blogs out to RSS feed reader software or to individual Web sites.

scanner: A computer peripheral device that copies physical items (e.g., periodical articles and photographs) into digital form. The process requires that the device be connected to a computer and that the computer has scanning software installed on it.

screen reading software: Software that will read aloud whatever text appears on a workstation screen when it is installed and run on a workstation. It extends the accessibility of any material one can display on a workstation screen to those with no or extremely low vision.

screencasting: The process of offering short video tutorials to library users to teach or review database searching or information literacy skills.

SCSI: One method for connecting scanners and other devices to a computer workstation, in this case using a SCSI connector on the central processing unit. SCSI stands for Small Computer System Interface and is pronounced "scuzzy."

search engine: Internet search tools that allow for keyword searches of huge, robot-built databases of Web sites and documents.

search directory: Internet search tools that allow for keyword searching or topical browsing of human built collections of Web sites and documents.

server: General term for a computer that makes files, applications, or Web sites available to users of a network or the World Wide Web. *See* NETWORK SERVER and WEB SERVER.

slide: (1) An individual screen or segment of a presentation created using presentation software. (2) An audiovisual format that uses small pieces of photographic film that can be projected on a screen (decreasing in number as an item found in library collections).

smartphones: Cell phones with computer functionality built in, including e-mail, Web browsing, and other capacities.

software: Programs or applications that makes the computer do what we want it to do. Examples include operating systems, word processors, and Internet browsers.

soundcard: A device that enables a computer to play sounds through speakers or record them through a microphone. It plugs into the motherboard of the computer inside the central processing unit.

source aggregator: A term describing electronic library resource vendors that provide access to a large number of different information sources (e.g., periodical databases and full-text reference sources).

spam: Unwanted e-mail, often sent by advertisers.

spreadsheet software: A computer application used to compile budget and other statistical information in spreadsheet form.

spyware: Software that can be loaded on a workstation to track an individual's path online and record personal information.

stand-alone system: A library system that uses only a single module or a combination of nonintegrated modules that do not share data (i.e., a system that has just a cataloging module, or that has a circulation module that does not automatically update the OPAC module when a book is checked out).

stylus: A penlike device that can transmit commands and other inputs into the screen of a tablet PC or a handheld device.

synchronous: Refers to technologies used for communication or instruction that work in real time (e.g., chat or video-conferencing). Users of these items are able to hold conversations as if they were talking in person.

T-1: A leased telephone line that can transmit data at 1.544 megabits per second (Mbps). Used by organizations that require high-speed connections to the Internet.

tablet PC: A mobile computer (similar to a laptop) that allows direct input on its screen using a stylus. A tablet PC can capture a user's handwriting on the screen and store it as an image file or convert it into text.

tagging: The practice of adding user-supplied descriptive terms to blog posts and other resources to create user-specific access points to content. Tagging can also provide the larger community with additional terms beyond those in the Library of Congress Subject Headings to help in searching for information.

tape drive: Device used to save computer files on magnetic tape cassettes for archival storage.

technical support: The help provided by vendors for their products. Technical support may be available at no charge for those who have purchased a product or it may be fee-based. It is usually only available by telephone.

technology: A practical or industrial art that involves both products and processes invented by people.

technology plan: An attempt by a library to take inventory of their current technology, survey the needs of their users and themselves, and make a plan to acquire technologies to meet these needs.

teletypewriter (TTY): A device that users who have difficulty hearing can use to type messages back and forth with a library staff member in order to access library information.

terminal: A device resembling a computer monitor with a keyboard that was used to access applications placed on a mainframe computer.

text based: Refers to an application (e.g., database or library system) that does not make use of a graphical user interface (GUI) but rather relies on text commands that are typed in.

touchpad: A computer input device that fulfills the functions of a mouse by having the user touch a flat pad to move an arrow on the screen.

trackball controller: A computer input device that fulfills the functions of a mouse by having the user move a ball with his or her palm to move an arrow on the screen.

troubleshooting: The act of investigating and solving technical problems with computer equipment, software applications, and other devices.

TTY: *See* TELETYPEWRITER.

turnkey: A product (e.g., a local area network or a library system) provided by a vendor that includes all of the necessary components so that all a library needs to do to start using it is to "turn the key" (i.e., press the power button). In this situation the product is also typically assembled on site by the vendor.

ubiquitous computing: The concept of computing and network resources being close at hand for individuals at all times. Often this state is brought about by the use of mobile devices.

uniform resource locator (URL): The address of a Web site (or other Internet resource) that for the Web takes the form http:// followed by the domain name and specific location of the site's files.

universal design: Making products and services usable by people with a wide range of skills and abilities.

UNIX: A computer operating system initially used only on mainframes that is widely used for large scale networking purposes and on the Internet. Tends to appear only on network servers and not on individual workstations.

unshielded twisted pair (UTP): A type of cable used in computer networks. Used extensively for data transmission in libraries and educational institutions.

URL: *See* UNIFORM RESOURCE LOCATOR.

USB: A method for connecting peripheral computer devices to a central processing unit. It stands for Universal Serial Bus and is now widely used because it provides high speed communications between devices and the CPU and because it is easy to add many devices to the same USB port on the CPU.

Usenet: An asynchronous method of communications on the Internet that consists of posting questions, announcements, or replies to messages in a topical newsgroup. Thousands of newsgroups are accessible using a Web browser or a separate newsreader application.

vendor: A producer or seller of a product.

vendor-based resource: An electronic resource that is accessed directly from a vendor's server. This requires subscribing libraries to use whatever method of authentication the vendor requires in order to allow access to their patrons.

video card: A device that enables a computer to display images on its monitor that are generated by applications. It plugs into the motherboard of the computer inside the central processing unit.

videocassette: An audiovisual or media format for recording video and sound for playback. Consists of a reeled, linear tape in a rectangular plastic case. It is currently the most popular means for sharing and viewing video and is widely available in libraries.

videodisc: An audiovisual or media format for recording video and sound for playback. Consists of a large disc (like an oversized CD or DVD) that can contain up to 2 hours of high quality audio or video. Videodiscs are on their way out as a technology with the steady popularity of videocassettes and the emergence of DVD. Also known as laserdiscs.

virus: Maliciously written computer applications. Once downloaded and run on an individual's computer, they can cause applications to malfunction and lock up. In extreme cases they can be designed to reformat hard drives or to surreptitiously corrupt important data files.

voice-over Internet protocol (VoIP): The ability to transmit speech and video communications from computer to computer using Internet communications.

WAN: *See* WIDE AREA NETWORK.

Web server: A network server that hosts a Web site.

Webinars: Informational or training presentations that are conducted entirely online, often through virtual classroom software.

Webmail: The process of accessing e-mail online using a Web browser rather than locally applied software.

wide area network (WAN): A network that connects multiple local area networks (e.g., a network at a branch library with a network at the main library).

widgets: Software applications that provide database searching, IM, and other services when run from within social networking software or on standard Web pages.

wiki: A Web site that can be edited and updated by anyone. Often used for group editing of documents.

Windows: The computer operating system used for most PC workstations.

wireless network: A network in which radio signal and infrared transmission technologies allow computers to communicate with other workstations and network servers. Makes use of devices called wireless access points to spread the wireless network within a building or throughout a broader area.

word processing software: Applications that are used for preparing memos, handouts, and other documents.

workstation: *See* PERSONAL COMPUTER.

Z39.50: An international standard for electronic information resources that allows compatible resources to be searched from a single interface.

zip disk: A square disk (just slightly larger than a floppy disk) that can be used to externally store computer data. The disk can be removed from the computer and stored elsewhere or used to transport data from place to place. It has a capacity of 100 or 750 megabytes (MB).

zip drive: A device that is used to store data on a zip disk.

Index

Page numbers followed by the letter "f" indicate figures; those followed by "t" indicate tables.

About the Author

John J. Burke is the director of the Gardner-Harvey Library on the Middletown regional campus of Miami University (Ohio). In addition to his responsibilities within the library, he serves on the leadership collaborative of the campus's Center for Teaching and Learning. John is a member of the Library Council executive committee for the Southwest Ohio Council on Higher Education, a two-year college libraries representative to the OHIOLINK Library Advisory Council, and a past president of the Academic Library Association of Ohio. He holds an master's degree in library science from the University of Tennessee and a bachelor's degree in history from Michigan State University.

John's past work experience includes service as both systems/public services librarian and program director for a Web-based associate degree in library technology at the University of Cincinnati–Raymond Walters College and also as a reference and electronic resources librarian at Fairmont State College (West Virginia). He is the author of two earlier editions of the *Neal-Schuman Library Technology Companion: A Basic Guide for Library Staff* (Neal-Schuman, 2001 and 2006), *IntroNet: A Beginner's Guide to Searching the Internet* (Neal-Schuman, 1999), and *Learning the Internet: A Workbook for Beginners* (Neal-Schuman, 1996). He has presented on technology topics at the Association of College and Research Libraries, the American Library Association, the Library Information and Technology Association National Forum, and various regional and state conferences. John may be reached at techcompanion@gmail.com.